D1602893

The Foundations of American Constitutional Government

Compiled by Robert D. Gorgoglione

The Foundation for Economic Education, Inc.
Irvington-on-Hudson, New York

The Foundations of American Constitutional Government

Copyright © 1996 by the Foundation for Economic Education, Inc.

The Foundation for Economic Education, Inc.
30 South Broadway
Irvington-on-Hudson, NY 10533
(914) 591-7230

Publishers Cataloging in Publication
(Prepared by Quality Books Inc.)

The Foundations of American constitutional government / compiled
   by Robert D. Gorgoglione. — Irvington, N.Y.: Foundation for
   Economic Education, 1995.
      p. cm.
   Includes index.
   ISBN: 1-57246-018-0
   1. United States—Politics and government—1783–1789.
   2. United States—Constitutional history. I. Gorgoglione, Robert D.,
   comp.

E303.F68   1995   973.3'18
                               QBI95-20333

Library of Congress Catalog Card Number: 95-61369

First edition, October 1995

Cover design by Beth Bowlby
Manufactured in the United States of America

Table of Contents

Acknowledgments

The Foundation for Economic Education owes special thanks to Robert D. Gorgoglione of Willimantic, Connecticut, for urging us to print an anthology of essays on the principles of the U.S. Constitution. Mr. Gorgoglione's compilation of *Freeman* articles and historical documents forms the basis of this present collection. We appreciate his care and diligence in organizing *The Foundations of American Constitutional Government*.

Introduction

The Constitution of 1787—otherwise known as the United States Constitution—was, and is, a remarkable document. It became even more so when the first ten amendments—the Bill of Rights—was added to it in 1791. Viewed in the context of the 1770s and 1780s, however, the Constitution of 1787 may retain its rank as a notable achievement but it was hardly a singular event. Americans had just been going through a season of constitution making. After the Declaration of Independence, most of the former colonies were without constitutions of their own. Most of them were royal colonies and traced their authority from the king of England. All the states, except Rhode Island and Connecticut, which had been charter colonies, drew up new constitutions soon after independence had been declared. And there was considerable tinkering with these in the ensuing years. Moreover, the first United States constitution, the Articles of Confederation, went into effect in 1781. So, Americans had considerable experience at constitution making before they produced the Constitution of 1787.

These earlier ventures, however, were but preludes to the document which was known ever afterward as *the* Constitution of the United States. The Articles of Confederation receded into the background of the document which replaced it. Over the years, state constitutions came more and more to resemble that of the United States. In the course of the nineteenth century, more and more peoples around the world came to admire and to imitate features of our Constitution. Above all, for Americans it had become *the* Constitution, its provisions hallowed, and its language revered.

What was so distinctive about this document? What made it stand out above the numerous constitutions of the nineteenth and twentieth centuries? As a document, there are some rather obvious things to be said about the Constitution. It is brief, concise, felicitously worded, yet surprisingly comprehensive in its description of and provisions for a government. Amendments were rare in the nineteenth century; there were only three between 1804 and 1913. Thus, it provided an example of stability as counterpoint to the argument that republics were unstable.

But, above all, the United States Constitution is informed by a few guiding principles. It established a republican form of government, which means that those who govern represent the electorate and are

1

chosen directly or indirectly by them. The people do not govern directly but rather indirectly by those chosen to represent them or appointed by those so elected. Thus, while the majority rule holds sway, its impact is limited by a filtering process in a republic.

Second, the Constitution brought into being a federal system of government for the United States. What this means, essentially, is that the powers of government are divided between the general government, on the one hand, and the states on the other. Each has a jurisdiction over the people within its bounds; each can act directly upon those in its jurisdiction, though what matters fall within the jurisdiction of the United States and of the states are usually different. This kind of federal structure was an American invention, invented in the course of the making of the Constitution.

There are other principles informing the Constitution, for example, the separation of powers, but there is one overarching principle which guides, makes necessary, and gives cogency to all the rest. That principle is limited government. Americans generally, and the Founders particularly, believed that if men are to be tolerably free governments must be limited. Now it was undoubtedly the case that the Constitutional Convention which met in 1787 assembled to provide for a more effective general government, one that would at least be adequate "to the exigencies of the Union," as was said. If they were bent on empowering and strengthening the general government, how did this square with the principle of limited government? The most direct answer is that those who wanted a stronger and more effective government came to see that any plan to achieve that would only meet with general acceptance if it were more rigorously limited than those that preceded it.

To put it another way, Americans held counterbalancing views about government. In the first place, most men of the time who wrote or spoke on the matter professed a love and devotion to liberty. George Washington may have described the matter best in his Farewell Address. He wrote, "Interwoven as is the love of liberty with every ligament of your hearts, no recommendation of mine is necessary to fortify or confirm the attachment." They also believed that government is necessary, as Thomas Jefferson put it in the Declaration of Independence, to secure the rights to "Life, Liberty and the pursuit of Happiness." But governments are a great danger to life and liberty, as well as to property. This was especially the case, many of them thought, where the government is remote from the people governed, as they understood any government of the United States would be. Government must be limited to forstall tyranny. It must be limited so that it not trample on the rights of the people and usurp the powers of the states. The limitation of government was the counterbalance to the dangers of necessary government.

The idea of using a constitution to limit the powers of rulers was not new in 1787, nor did it originate in America. It went back at least to 1215 and the issuance of Magna Carta in England. The germ of the idea at least is hoary with age. No more was the idea of written constitutions new to America. Aristotle compiled a large number of them from countries and city-states on or around the Mediterranean. But constitutions have usually been much more adept at empowering governments than limiting them. The famed British constitution never did get around to limiting the House of Commons. Despite Magna Carta, and its reissuances, it took the British more than half a millennium to effectively limit the monarch.

The distinctive thing about the United States Constitution is that it did about as thorough a job as could be done in limiting those who governed. The powers to be exercised were enumerated in the Constitution, and who was to exercise them listed. Not only are the branches of government separate from each other but they are independent of one another in their powers to negate government acts. For example, either house of the Congress can negate a bill and thus deny its passage. The President can independently veto a bill and prevent it becoming a law, though it can be passed into law by unusual majorities in both houses. The courts can refuse to apply a law to particular cases and it may become a nullity. Congress may pass a law and the courts may apply it, but in criminal cases, the President may nullify it by pardoning those convicted and sentenced under it. On the other hand, most positive action requires the cooperation of two or more branches, thus limiting what government can do to agreement by more than one branch about what is to be done.

The Constitution contains lists of specific limitations on both the general government and upon the states. For example, Congress is prohibited to pass a "Bill of Attainder or ex post facto Law," "No Tax or Duty shall be laid on Articles exported from any State," "No Money shall be drawn from the Treasury, but in Consequences of Appropriations made by Law. . . ." And so on and on the limitations go. The first ten amendments are all precise limitations on government. The crowning one is the tenth which makes about as clear as can be that the United States government has only such powers as have been granted to it in the Constitution. It says, "The powers not delegated to the United States by the Constitution, nor prohibited by it to the States, are reserved to the States respectively, or the people." There is a list of things which the states are prohibited to do in Article 1, Section 10 of the Constitution, such as, "coin Money, emit Bills of Credit, make any Thing but gold and silver Coin a Tender in Payment of Debts," and the like.

In sum, the great and overarching principle informing the Constitution is that of limited government. These limitations are there not only in specific restrictions but also in the separation and independence of the branches. The assumption is that they will be jealous of their powers and guard against the encroachment of others upon them, thus limiting government. The same was supposed to be the case for the basically independent state governments. They had come into the union by their own decision, had formed their own governments, had their own constitutions and were expected to restrain the general government by the jealous assertion of their own powers. Politically, the people were limited by the Constitution, which was difficult to amend, and those who governed were not only limited by the Constitution but also by the electorate who could deny them reelection.

However well the Constitution might be drawn and however carefully the government might be limited, the Founders doubted that liberty could prevail if the generality of governers and electorate became corrupt. And today, we must regretfully note that our Constitution no longer works as it was intended to do. It has been bent out of shape, particularly in the twentieth century, by those who would concentrate all power in the general government and use that power to seduce and subdue the populace. Even so, the great principles are still there in the written Constitution, awaiting a sustained effort to limit government and free the people.

—CLARENCE B. CARSON

I. PROLOGUE

A New Message on the Constitution

by Jackson Pemberton

There are those among you who heap fault upon your heads, and declare you derelict for your shallow knowledge of the basis and workings of your government. While it is true that you evidence a dangerous lack of understanding of those most significant principles of your own prosperity and political security, yet I shall not judge you, for I know not but that I myself might have had the same fault had I been born in your day. Had we enjoyed the peace and wealth you have now even in all your troubles, we may have slumbered as well as you. Then too, our condition was such that our choices were painfully clear; when we received the report that King George had said, "The die is cast, the colonies must submit or triumph," we recognized that as a clear declaration of war.

In your day, those who would draw honor and power to themselves have confused your minds with conflicting reports, inconsistent principles, and deliberate deception; all of which imbues you with a feeling of hopelessness and indifference. Nay, while I must admit your apathy, yet there is cause for it; which makes a declaration of guilt an uncertain pronouncement.

One matter is clear however: should you remain in your present condition; filled with discontent and disdain for your government, yet surrounded by the information and facilities needed to reform and restore it; and then go on about your lives with a halfhearted hope that things will somehow improve; then another time will reveal your guilt, and it will be said that you, with a little work could have discovered the technique of restoring a good, old government to its former brilliance, but you were too lazy to have the honor.

You have much reason to be discouraged, even frightened; but you have more to be confident. You are surrounded by troubles and problems, but your most crucial illness is the easiest to cure, and while it is virtually hidden from you, I see it before I recognize any other. You are ignorant!

In this essay the author draws upon the extensive collection of the thoughts of the Founding Fathers and lets them speak to us relative to the problems we face in the United States today. "On the Constitution," originally published in the July 1976 *Freeman*, was part of a Bicentennial *Freeman* series by Mr. Pemberton.

7

You know neither the source nor the substance of your rights, but you know they are being violated. You do not know the proper bounds of your government's operation, but you know it has gone beyond them. You do not know the foundation of a stable currency, but you know yours is floating out of your hands. You do not know the rules of free enterprise, but you know your businesses are being crippled. You do not know the correct principles of foreign trade and alliances, but you know you have been made the fool in your foreign affairs. You do not know the Constitution, but you know that when it was followed diligently, it rewarded you abundantly with peace and prosperity.

Yes, you are ignorant, and while it is understandable, yet the day of reasonable excuse is gone, for you are aware of your danger. It is the nature and extent of your trouble and the way out of it that still escapes you; but you will find to your delight, that only a little effort is required to rid yourselves of the ill effects of that deficiency which now dampens your spirits and clouds your minds. Only a little effort for such wonderful rewards! How a tiny lamp dispels a great darkness!

There is a feeling generally among you that the workings of government are extremely complicated and the guidance of it must be left to those who would like you to worship their political wisdom, for they love to impress you with their vast intelligence, yet if they were but half so wise as they pretend, you would have no need to hear from me. The full truth of the matter is that the basic principles of liberty and free enterprise are simple; but these political pretenders have manipulated them so much, that they, more than anything else, have confused the issues, bewildered themselves, and entangled all of you in their shortsighted expediency programs.

We knew, even as you do today, what it was that we did not want in our government. We had had our fill and more of oppression on the one hand and anarchy on the other. The Almighty had thus trained us in the evils of both extremes through our experience with the tyranny of the Crown and the turmoil of the Articles of Confederation.

Oh, those were dark days! The colonies had struggled as partners and a real sense of unity had emerged from our common effort to secure our liberty, but in a few short years we were writing to one another in the discouraged tones of forlorn patriots who had discovered to their dismay and alarm that the nation was not at all prepared for its new freedom and that too little government was as despairing an evil as too much.

In those dismal days between the routing of the British and the launching of the Constitution, amidst a disastrous inflation and frightening civil turmoil, some of us assembled in Philadelphia in convention. As we were only getting under way, one of the delegates said that measures to alleviate existing conditions and repairs to current laws would be more acceptable to the people than any thoroughgoing actions. At that, the President of the Convention, Mr. Washington, arose and declared earnestly, "If, to please the people, we offer what we ourselves disapprove, how can we afterward defend our work? Let us raise a standard to which the wise and the honest can repair; the event is in the hand of God." Thus he crystallized our desire to build a new government upon liberty and strength, and sent us on the long, toilsome task of creating a new national charter.

We determined to form a government which would at once be able to discharge its necessary functions, but which, even under the hands of ambitious and self-seeking men, would be virtually unable to encroach upon the native rights of the citizens. That we were successful is evidenced by the fact that it has required nearly a century for men of precisely that stamp to twist and violate that Constitution to bring you to your present condition of rising alarm. But I find still deeper satisfaction in the knowledge that in spite of the awesome control now wielded by your government, yet you have in the Constitution all the tools you require to bring it carefully down to its proper size and function, for that was one of our goals. We sought for a golden mean between anarchy and oppression, for contrivances which would give government its requisite authority, yet place fixed and enduring bounds upon the activities that men would seek to have it perform for their own selfish benefit.

It was toward that objective we strove in the miserable heat of the summer of 1787. For more than a month we expounded upon one principle after another with some contention and seeming little progress. Then, near the end of June, in the midst of a hotly contended issue, our eldest statesman made a speech which both shamed and inspired us.

Mr. Franklin said, "The small progress we have made after four or five weeks is, methinks a melancholy proof of the imperfections of Human understanding. We indeed seem to feel our own want of political wisdom, since we have been running about in search of it in this situation, groping as it were in the dark to find political truth. How has it happened sir, that we have not hitherto once thought of humbly applying to the Father of Light to illuminate our understanding? I have lived, sir, a long time and the longer I live, the more convincing proofs I see of this truth, that God governs in the affairs of men. And if a sparrow cannot fall to the ground without His notice, is it probable that an empire can rise without His aid?"

Mr. Franklin proposed that a clergyman be retained as chaplain for the Convention, but his motion could not pass as we had no funds. Nevertheless, the occasion served to bring us up short, and to cause us to recognize and to remember our dependence upon the Almighty. Had He not guided and inspired our generals? Was it not He who answered our prayers with the hurricane which demolished the British fleet in Boston harbor before the war had even begun? Had not every step by which we had advanced been distinguished by some token of providential agency? How soon we forget!

From the day of Mr. Franklin's observation forward, we were led to an understanding of the mechanisms necessary to the preservation of liberty under the effective but limited federal plan. In order to thwart the designs of self-seeking men, we set up three branches of government, each equal in power but separate in authority and function, and each with certain limited but effective sanctions upon the other two.

We reserved most of the powers of government to the states, thus dividing those powers and placing them as close as possible to the inspection and control of the people, for history had abundantly shown that centralization of power and tyranny were but different titles of the same monster. There was no question but that the plan was somewhat inefficient. We desired that, for we were well aware that the most efficient government is despotism. The deficiencies of decentralized government (which are not so extensive as your Tories would have you believe) is but a small price for the people to pay for control of their government.

It has been reported among you that we founded your government upon the emergencies of our day, and that our work was the conclusion of manifold compromises. While it is true that each of us brought our personal objectives and opinions to the Convention, we found that we agreed that most of those goals were not only worthy but necessary to the security of the nation.

There was great unity in our purpose; our compromise was between too much and too little government. The lengthy deliberations were not the result of disunity, but a meticulous searching for correct principles among governments from the most ancient to our own time. When we had finished our work a wonderful feeling of harmony and peace came over us; we knew we had been instruments in bringing a miracle into being.

The story that "the Constitution was designed for an eighteenth-century agrarian society," also deserves attention. That is a myth I now take pleasure to debunk!

The Constitution is based on three timeless truths. First, it is founded on the fact that it is necessary in a society, that the citizen must either control himself by his own moral self-discipline, or he must be restrained so that he cannot abuse his liberty. Second, it is the nature of man to seek recognition, then influence, and then power in his relationships to his fellows. Third, it is the nature of man to work untiringly for himself when he is confident in the usefulness of his effort. Those are the footings of the Constitution and there is nothing there that is either eighteenth century or agrarian! To say that we designed the national charter for an agricultural economy is to display a palpable desire to deceive (or a profound ignorance, for you will notice that those who promulgate that fable would replace constitutional principles with laws which would give them great authority over you. Thus do their words reveal their motives.

Nay, we founded the Constitution upon an exquisite recognition of one great decisive reality; human nature: a recognition of the dual disposition of man: his propensity for good and his capacity of evil. Our first and foremost consideration was to place the forces of human nature in a framework which would cause those forces to lift man, to protect and release his conscience, his will, his talents, and his noble desires, and at the same time would discourage and punish him in his vices. That this mechanism was successful is written in the glories of your history. I do not claim perfection for it, but I will justly assert that it is the most nearly perfect system for the elevation of man that has ever existed among governments.[1]

But let me explain those three footings of the Constitution a little more, for we are at the very basis of a good government.

First, it was abundantly clear to us that if the time should come when the citizens would turn from morality and good religion, they would also turn from liberty; for if man is to be free, he must control himself lest his society circumscribe his liberty to protect itself from his abuse. It was therefore our desire that religion should be thoroughly protected and even encouraged. That does not mean that we wanted any particular religious philosophy to have the advantage over another, but that the citizens' rights to complete liberty of private and public belief and practice should in no way be infringed; for if those rights be trammeled by government then it establishes the state philosophy of irreligion, which must signal the beginning of the demoralization of the people and the accompanying loss of liberty. I shall discuss this matter in greater detail when we examine the Bill of

Rights. It will suffice to say here that we intended, through careful protection of religion, to secure the only enduring basis for liberty: individual morality and self-control. Secondly, we set up the plan of government so that its powers were restricted, separated, and dispersed throughout the states in order to defeat the tendency of men to consolidate power and ordain themselves rulers over the people. Then we applied the checks and balances to set each branch of government as a watchman over the other two, and gave each certain prerogatives so as to place the ambition of self-aggrandizing men in opposition to the ambition of other similar men. Thus we placed human nature in control of human nature, and gave the states and the people the final determination, by ballot, of which men would be allowed to bring their natures into the government.

Finally, we recognized that man is most inclined to produce an abundance when his property rights are held inviolate. Man, by nature, will strive with great energy and innovation to improve himself, his circumstances, and his relationship to his neighbors, so long as he has confidence that he will be allowed to enjoy the fruits of his labors. But as soon as he loses that assurance, so soon will he begin to do as little as may scarcely suffice him. Our study of history testified that excessive taxation and regulation, an infringement of property rights, was ever the cause of slackening productivity, while the freest economies were the greatest source of plenty.

There you have founding principles of the most successful government on the records of civilizations, and they, in turn, are based upon that most crucial reality: human nature. That is the groundwork of the Republic; but in spite of all our careful effort, we knew that it was not sufficient to merely launch the ship of state correctly, it needed to be tended by an alert, informed, and jealous citizenry. But history, like nature, travels in cycles; both liberty and oppression contain the seeds of their own destruction. Our success has brought the security which put you to sleep.

Now, basking in the dimming brilliance of the lights of liberty, you have been neither vigilant nor informed, and only recently have you begun to realize the correctness of your rising jealousy for your rights. Let those feelings of jealousy well up within you and cause you to alert yourselves to your true condition.

Your executives have taken upon themselves to form foreign alliances and make domestic regulations without proper authority. They have violated your most fundamental law. Your judiciary has ignored the amending process and altered the meaning and intent of the Constitution they were sworn to defend. They have betrayed your most fundamental law. Your congress has been watchful, yet not of the encroachments of the other two branches, but for opportunity to gain influence by purchasing your favor with your own money. They have ignored your most fundamental law. And you—you—seek for a remedy while it stares you in the face! You have lost the vision of your most fundamental law. Let me show you. You call the national charter "the Constitution of the United States," and that simple phrase contains both the totality of your plight and the seeds of your salvation; for in those six words you reveal your feeling that both you and your law are subject to your government. You are not the slave of government at all, but because you think so, you may as well be! Nay! The Constitution is *your* servant and the master of your government. It is not the Constitution of the United States, it is the Constitution *of the people,* and *for* the United States! It is not only the law by which you are governed, it is the law by which you may govern your government! It is not the law by which high-handed politicians may impose their collective will upon you, it is for you to impose it upon them! It does not belong to the government, it belongs to you! It is yours! It is yours to enforce upon your government! It is yours to read to those self-wise do-gooders; and if you will hold it high in your hand, they will quail and flee before it like the cowardly knaves they are, while those who are your true friends will rejoice in your new commitment. And so may you divide the government goats from the statesmen sheep; but beware of the cunning deceit of those who pretend to serve you while they betray your trust. Civil government has always suffered the intrusions of self-seeking men, and while they may not always be detected, they may at least be controlled. And that is part of the miracle of the Constitution. Yes, you bear a multiplicity of problems: usurpations, alterations, violations, centralizations, plundering of the rich, corruption of the poor, inequities in the courts, irresponsible economic policies, disastrous foreign stratagems, and on and on. It is overwhelming, bewildering, and discouraging; a disease seeming beyond remedy. It is clear that the individual citizen has no hope of discovering all the errors, to say nothing of forming and applying corrections. What can one man do? Ah! There are miracles in the Constitution! There is wisdom in the Republic! It is not necessary that you understand all the intricacies of your regulatory agencies, your welfare bureaucracies, and all the legal vagaries. Only four things are required of you, and although each of them demands deliberate effort, they are easily within your reach and crucial to your political salvation:

    1. See that you are a blessing to your society; furnish your own

livelihood; associate only with that which is noble and uplifting; obey the law; give your government no excuse to make new laws or to infringe your rights.

2. Study the Constitution until you know its fundamentals in the spirit we intended; we were careful to an extreme, you will not be disappointed.

3. Seek out and elect wise, successful, honest, and most of all, humble men for officers; your system fails you because your politicians seek office, but the offices are yours to fill; therefore, you must seek out the men you desire to serve you.

4. Watch your public servants, encourage them, counsel them, see that they understand the Constitution and keep the oath of their offices; when they show themselves approved, honor and trust them; above all, be charitable with them especially now while their burden is heavy. Only a part of them deserve your disdain.

You have every reason to take heart. The basics of good government are not difficult at all. We managed to acquire them in our day, and although we were the most educated men of our time, our knowledge was vastly inferior to yours (we only looked on the moon). Once you have gotten a comprehension of the fundamentals of free government, you will have a standard to which you may hold any of the proposals of your day and ascertain whether you ought to support or oppose them.

So simple it is! Have faith; act; and you will soon behold the miracle! Can you see that the Constitution we formed by the light of the divine lamps of liberty can save both you and itself? Is that not a miracle? It is a magnificent thing, our ship of state; but you must tend the rudder and mend the sails.

There are voices in the land even now which expand upon the vices of your government in order to defame the Constitution. The words go forth from those who fancy themselves worthy to rule you that you must drastically change it or even replace it if you are to survive the crises of your time. With what will you replace it? Our nation is still far and away the freest under heaven. Have you forgotten the source of so great a liberty? To whom will you turn for an improvement upon the inspiration of Almighty God? Do you know your own history?

When the government was held within its proper bounds by the chains of the Constitution our nation was the fulfillment of the vision of liberty that dwelt in the hearts of freedom-loving people in every quarter of the globe. Will you now continue your course from such freedom back to oppression? Will you cast aside that instrument which has given greater liberty to the hearts and hands of more of the children of God than any combination of times and governments you may please to conceive? A supreme act of folly at best; and a fall into the pits of despotism at worst! Nay! Away with that! The nation has already come from under the hands of a tyrannical aristocracy into the light of liberty, and now drifts again into the clouds of oppression. Then listen together! Let the cry go up! Restore the Constitution! Restore the free exercise of the rights of the people! Reverse the drift! Put down again the anchor of liberty and fasten to it the ship of state by the chains of the Constitution! Let every man learn his duty and perform it with diligence!

Is there a cause more just, a goal more worthy, a need more dear, or a pastime more sweet than this; to bind up the wounds of the national charter, to reassert the natural rights of man, and to secure the blessings of liberty to yourselves and your posterity? You—my Sons of Liberty; ponder it in your hearts, speak of it in your gatherings, and pray for it in your secret chambers! Let the cry go forth throughout the land and echo across a world groaning and starving under the crush of tyrants: restore the rights of man!

Oh hear the voice of your Father! Rise up my people and lift up your heads! Come out of darkness into the rightful day of your glory. Secure and cherish the liberty wherewith we made you free! You are free; for we declared you free and bought your liberty with our blood!

---

1. This mechanism is rather like a ratchet and pawl wherein upward movement is completely free and downward movement is stopped by the pawl. The Constitution has thus resulted in the citizens lifting their society to unprecedented heights. Your upward progress has lately been seriously impeded, however, by the stifling effects of too much government (which discourages personal initiative in the citizens), and by the "liberation" of the baseness of man which even now is disengaging the pawl and allowing your civilization to slide, nearly unhindered, back down to the meanness of anarchy which resembles the uncultured, uneducated, and undisciplined tribes of primitive societies.

II. THE BLESSINGS OF LIBERTY

The Essence of Americanism

by Leonard Read

Someone once said: It isn't that Christianity has been tried and found wanting; it has been tried and found difficult—and abandoned. Perhaps the same thing might be said about freedom. The American people are becoming more and more afraid of, and are running away from, their own revolution. I think that statement takes a bit of documentation.

I would like to go back, a little over three centuries in our history, to the year 1620, which was the occasion of the landing of our Pilgrim Fathers at Plymouth Rock. That little colony began its career in a condition of pure and unadulterated communism. For it made no difference how much or how little any member of that colony produced; all the produce went into a warehouse under authority, and the proceeds of the warehouse were doled out in accordance with the authority's idea of need. In short, the Pilgrims began the practice of a principle held up by Karl Marx two centuries later as the ideal of the Communist Party: From each according to ability, to each according to need—and by force!

Now, there was a good reason why these communalistic or communistic practices were discontinued. It was because the members of the Pilgrim colony were starving and dying. As a rule, that type of experience causes people to stop and think about it!

Anyway, they did stop and think about it. During the third winter Governor Bradford got together with the remaining members of the colony and said to them, in effect: "This coming spring we are going to try a new idea. We are going to drop the practice of 'from each according to ability, to each according to need.' We are going to try the idea of 'to each according to merit.'" And when Governor Bradford said that, he enunciated the private property principle as clearly and succinctly as any economist ever had. That principle is nothing more nor less than each individual having a right to the fruits of his own labor. Next spring came, and it was observed that not only

Leonard Read (1898–1983) was the founder of The Foundation for Economic Education and the author of many books and articles. This article was delivered as a speech in December 1961 and was subsequently published in the November 1983 issue of *The Freeman*.

19

was father in the field but mother and the children were there, also. Governor Bradford records that "Any generall wante or famine hath not been amongst them since to this day."

It was by reason of the practice of this private property principle that there began in this country an era of growth and development which sooner or later had to lead to revolutionary political ideas. And it did lead to what I refer to as the real American revolution.

Now, I do not think of the real American revolution as the armed conflict we had with King George III. That was a reasonably minor fracas as such fracases go! The real American revolution was a novel concept or idea which broke with the whole political history of the world.

Up until 1776 men had been contesting with each other, killing each other by the millions, over the age-old question of which of the numerous forms of authoritarianism—that is, man-made authority—should preside as sovereign over man. And then, in 1776, in the fraction of one sentence written into the Declaration of Independence was stated the real American Revolution, the new idea, and it was this: "that all men are created equal; that they are endowed by their Creator with certain unalienable Rights; that among these are Life, Liberty and the pursuit of Happiness." That was it. This is the essence of Americanism. This is the rock upon which the whole "American miracle" was founded.

This revolutionary concept was at once a spiritual, a political, and an economic concept. It was spiritual in that the writers of the Declaration recognized and publicly proclaimed that the Creator was the endower of man's rights, and thus the Creator is sovereign.

It was political in implicitly denying that the state is the endower of man's rights, thus declaring that the state is not sovereign. It was economic in the sense that if an individual has a right to his life, it follows that he has a right to sustain his life—the sustenance of life being nothing more nor less than the fruits of one's own labor.

It is one thing to state such a revolutionary concept as this; it's quite another thing to implement it—to put it into practice. To accomplish this, our Founding Fathers added two political instruments—the Constitution and the Bill of Rights. These two instruments were essentially a set of prohibitions; prohibitions not against the people but against the thing the people, from their Old World experience, had learned to fear, namely, over-extended government.

Benefits of Limited Government

The Constitution and the Bill of Rights more severely limited government than government had ever before been limited in the history of the world. And there were benefits that flowed from this severe limitation of the state.

Number One, there wasn't a single person who turned to the government for security, welfare, or prosperity because government was so limited that it had nothing on hand to dispense, nor did it then have the power to take from some that it might give to others. To what or to whom do people turn if they cannot turn to government for security, welfare, or prosperity? They turn where they should turn—to themselves.

As a result of this discipline founded on the concept that the Creator, not the state, is the endower of man's rights, we developed in this country on an unprecedented scale a quality of character that Emerson referred to as "self-reliance" All over the world the American people gained the reputation of being self-reliant.

There was another benefit that flowed from this severe limitation of government. When government is limited to the inhibition of the destructive actions of men—that is when it is limited to inhibiting fraud and depredation, violence and misrepresentation, when it is limited to invoking a common justice—then there is no organized force standing against the productive or creative actions of citizens. As a consequence of this limitation on government there occurred a freeing, a releasing, of creative human energy, on an unprecedented scale.

This was the combination mainly responsible for the "American miracle," founded on the belief that the Creator, not the state, is the endower of man's rights.This manifested itself among the people as individual freedom of choice. People had freedom of choice as to how they employed themselves. They had freedom of choice as to what they did with the fruits of their own labor.

But something happened to this remarkable idea of ours, this revolutionary concept. It seems that the people we placed in government office as our agents made a discovery. Having acquisitive instincts for influence and power over others—as indeed some of us do—they discovered that the force which inheres in government, which the people had delegated to them in order to inhibit the destructive actions of man, this monopoly of force could be used to invade the productive and creative areas in society—one of which is the business sector. And they also found that if they incurred any deficits by their interventions, the same government force could be used to collect the wherewithal to pay the bills. I would like to suggest to you that the extent to which government in America has departed from the original design of inhibiting the destructive actions of man and invoking a common justice; the extent to which government has invaded the productive and creative areas; the extent to which the government in this country has assumed the responsibility for the security, welfare, and prosperity of our people is a measure of the extent to which socialism and communism have developed here in this land of ours.

The Lengthening Shadow

Now then, can we measure this development? Not precisely, but we can get a fair idea of it by referring to something I said a moment ago about one of our early characteristics as a nation—individual freedom of choice as to the use of the fruits of one's own labor. If you will measure the loss in freedom of choice in this matter, you will get an idea of what is going on.

There was a time, about 120 years ago, when the average citizen had somewhere between 95 and 98 percent freedom of choice with each of his income dollars. That was because the tax take of the government—federal, state, and local—was between 2 and 5 percent of the earned income of the people. But, as the emphasis shifted from this earlier design, as government began to move in to invade the productive and creative areas and to assume the responsibility for the security, welfare, and prosperity of the people, the percentage of the take of the people's earned income increased. The percentage of the take kept going up and up and up until today it's not 2 to 5 percent. It is now over 35 percent.

Many of my friends say to me, "Oh, Read, why get so excited about that? We still have, on the average, 65 percent freedom of choice with our income dollars."

I would like to interpolate here a moment and say that we ought to be careful how we use that term, "on the average." Take a person who works 40 hours a week, who goes to work at 8:00 o'clock in the morning, takes an hour off for lunch, works Monday through Friday. That's 40 hours. The average person in this country has to work all Monday and until 2:15 on Tuesday for the government before he can start earning for himself!

But, if the individual has been extraordinarily successful, he finds that he has to work all day Monday, Tuesday, Wednesday, Thursday, and until noon on Friday for the government before he can start earning for himself.

Nonetheless, on the average, we do have 65 percent freedom of choice with our earned income. But, please take no solace from this fact for it has been discovered, as research work has been done on the fiscal behavior of nations covering a period of many centuries—this is a very important point—that whenever the take of the people's earned income by government reaches a certain level—20 or 25 percent—it is no longer politically expedient to pay for the costs of government by direct tax levies. Governments then resort to inflation as a means of financing their ventures. This is happening to us now! By "inflation" I mean increasing the volume of money by the national government's fiscal policy. Governments resort to inflation with popular support because the people apparently are naive enough to believe that they can have their cake and eat it, too. Many people do not realize that they cannot continue to enjoy so-called "benefits" from government without having to pay for them. They do not appreciate the fact that inflation is probably the most unjust and cruelest tax of all.

Methods of Inflation

There are numerous ways governments have inflated. You may recall reading in your history books about coin clipping. That was where the sovereign called in the coin of the realm and clipped off the edges. He kept the edges and returned the smaller pieces to the owners. That was a good stunt until the pieces got too small to be returned.

During the French revolutionary period, the government got itself into dire financial straits and began to issue an irredeemable paper money known as "assignats" secured not by gold but by confiscated church properties. Well, of course, France went bankrupt under that.

In Argentina, a situation with which I am reasonably familiar, the policy of the national government has been to spend about 100 billion pesos a year. But all they can collect by direct tax levies are 50 billion pesos a year. How do they handle that? Very simple. They just print 50 billion pesos a year. You don't have to be a great economist to realize that when you increase the volume of money, everything else being equal, the value of money goes down. And when the value of money goes down, all things being equal, prices tend to rise.

You can imagine what has happened to bank accounts, insurance, social security, and to all forms of fixed income in Argentina. They are practically worthless.

Now in this country, we have a method of inflation which has one distinguishing merit. It is so complicated that hardly anyone can understand it.

What we do here is monetize debt. The more we go in debt the more money we have. Since we started our program of monetizing debt and deficit financing, we have enormously increased the quantity of our money. You have observed that our dollar isn't worth quite as much as it used to be. Perhaps you have also observed that prices are tending to increase.

The Russians, in my judgment, have the most honest system of dishonesty. There the government compels the people to buy government bonds. And then, after the people have bought the government bonds, the government cancels them. There are quite a number of Russians who are aware that some sort of chicanery is going on.

Frankly, I wish we were using this system, because then more people would understand the significance of inflation. If we were inflating this crudely, our people wouldn't be fooled as they are now.

What I am trying to say is this: Inflation is the fiscal concomitant of socialism or the welfare state or state interventionism—call it what you will. Inflation is a political weapon. There are no other means of financing the welfare state except by inflation.

So, if you don't like inflation, there is only one thing you can do: assist in returning our government to its original principles.

One of my hobbies is cooking and, therefore, I am familiar with the gadgets around the kitchen. One of the things with which I am familiar is a sponge. A sponge in some respects resembles a good economy. A sponge will sop up an awful lot of mess; but when the sponge is saturated, the sponge itself is a mess, and the only way you can make it useful again is to wring the mess out of it. I hope my analogy is clear.

I want to say a few more things about inflation because it is particularly relevant to this country. To do this I want to take a look at somebody else because it's always difficult to look at ourselves. Let's take a look at France, which in numerous respects has resembled the United States economically.

French Experience

France began this thing I am talking about—that is, government invasion of productive and creative areas, government assuming the responsibility for the security, welfare, and prosperity of the French people—just 47 years ago, in 1914.

If my previous contentions are correct, the French franc should have lost some of its purchasing power in these 47 years for, I have argued, state intervention can be financed only by increasing the volume of the money and such increases result in a decline of the circulating medium's value. Thus, the franc should have declined in value. How much?

The French franc has less than one-half of one percent of the purchasing value it had 47 years ago, or to put it another way, the franc has lost more than 99½ percent of its value in these few years, and by reason of inflation brought about by government intervention.

In Paris, during World War I, I bought a dinner for 5 francs, then the equivalent of the 1918 dollar. I didn't get to Paris again until 1947. I took a friend to lunch, admittedly at a better restaurant than the one I went to as a soldier boy. But I didn't pay 20 or 30 or 50 francs for the two luncheons. I paid 3,400 francs! I was there two years later with Mrs. Read, same restaurant, same food, because I wished to compare prices. It wasn't 3,400 but 4,100! Recently, when I was in Paris, the price for the same two luncheons was about 6,000 francs.

Visualize with me, if you can, a Frenchman back in the year 1914. Let's say he was in his late teens. A forethoughtful lad, he was looking forward to the year of 1961 when he would reach the age of retirement. So, at that time he bought a paid-up annuity, one which would return him 1,000 francs a month beginning January 1961. Well, back then he could have eaten as well on 1,000 francs as Grace Kelly's husband. But my doctor friends are of the opinion that no one can exist on only one meal every 30 days. That is all 1,000 francs will buy today, and that would be a meal about one-third the quality that any of us would buy were we in France at this time.

"Creeping" or "Galloping"?

Inflation, in popular terms, is divided into two types. There is what is called "creeping inflation," and what is called "galloping inflation." "Creeping inflation" is supposed to be the type that we are now experiencing.

I don't think the term is quite lusty enough to describe a dollar that has lost somewhere between 53 and 62 per cent of its value since 1939.

"Galloping inflation" is the type that went on in Germany during the years after World War I, in France after the revolutionary period, in China recently, and in the Latin American countries today. Here is an example of what I mean.

I hold in my hand the currency of Bolivia. This little piece is 10,000 Bolivianos. In 1935 this piece of paper was worth 4,600 present-day dollars. Do you know what it's worth now? Eighty cents! That's what you call "galloping inflation." It was all brought about—they didn't have any wars—by government interventionism.

Now then, what I want to suggest is that inflation in this country has ever so many more catastrophic potentials than has ever been the case in any other country in history. We here are the most advanced division-of-labor society that has ever existed. That is, we are more specialized than any other people has ever been; we are further removed from self-subsistence.

Indeed, we are so specialized today that every one of us—everybody in this room, in the nation, even the farmer—is absolutely dependent upon a free, uninhibited exchange of our numerous specialties. That is a self-evident fact.

Destroying the Circulatory System

In any highly specialized economy you do not effect specialized exchanges by barter. You never observe a man going into a gasoline station saying, "Here is a goose; give me a gallon of gas." That's not the way to do it in a specialized economy. You use an economic circulatory system, which is money, the medium of exchange.

This economic circulatory system, in some respects, can be likened to the circulatory system of the body, which is the blood stream.

The circulatory system of the body picks up oxygen in the lungs and ingested food in the mid-section and distributes these specialties to the 30 trillion cells of the body. At those points it picks up carbon dioxide and waste matter and carries them off. I could put a hypodermic needle into one of your veins and thin your blood stream to the point where it would no longer make these exchanges, and when I reached that point, we could refer to you quite accurately in the past tense.

By the same token, you can thin your economic circulatory system, your medium of exchange, to the point where it will no longer circularize the products and services of economic specialization. When this happens, the economy of our nation will be "discombobulated."

Let me show you how it works. Right after the Armistice my squadron was sent to Coblenz with the Army of Occupation. The German inflation was underway. I didn't know any more then about inflation than most Americans do now. I liked what I experienced—as do most Americans now—because I got more marks every payday than the previous payday—and not because of a raise in pay. I had security. The government was giving me food, shelter, clothing, and so forth. I used the marks to shoot craps and play poker, and the more marks, the more fun.

German inflation continued with mounting intensity and by 1923 it got to the point where 30 million marks would not buy a single loaf of bread.

About the time I arrived, an old man died and left his fortune to his two sons, 500,000 marks each. One boy was a frugal lad who never spent a pfennig of it. The other one was a playboy and spent it all on champagne parties. When the day came in 1923 that 30 million marks wouldn't buy a loaf of bread, the boy who had saved everything had nothing, but the one who spent his inheritance on champagne parties was able to exchange the empty bottles for a dinner. The economy had reverted to barter.

Those of you who are interested in doing something about this, have a right to ask yourselves a perfectly logical question: Has there ever been an instance, historically, when a country has been on this toboggan and succeeded in reversing itself? There have been some minor instances. I will not attempt to enumerate them. The only significant one took place in England after the Napoleonic Wars.

How England Did It

England's debt, in relation to her resources, was larger than ours is now; her taxation was confiscatory; restrictions on the exchanges of goods and services were numerous, and there were strong controls on production and prices. Had it not been for the smugglers, many people would have starved!

Now, something happened in that situation, and we ought to take cognizance of it. What happened there might be emulated here even though our problem is on a much larger scale There were in England such men as John Bright and Richard Cobden, men who understood the principle of freedom of exchange. Over in France, there was a politician by the name of Chevalier, and an economist named Frederic Bastiat.

Incidentally, if any of you have not read the little book by Bastiat entitled *The Law*, I commend it as the finest thing that I have ever read on the principles one ought to keep in mind when trying to judge for oneself what the scope of government should be.

Bastiat was feeding his brilliant ideas to Cobden and Bright, and these men were preaching the merits of freedom of exchange. Members of Parliament listened and, as a consequence, there began the greatest reform movement in British history.

Parliament repealed the Corn Laws, which here would be like repealing subsidies to farmers. They repealed the Poor Laws, which here would be like repealing Social Security. And fortunately for them they had a monarch—her name was Victoria—who relaxed the authority that the English people themselves believed to be implicit in her office. She gave them freedom in the sense that a prisoner on parole has freedom, a permissive kind of freedom but with lots of latitude. Englishmen, as a result, roamed all over the world achieving unparalleled prosperity and building an enlightened empire.

This development continued until just before World War I. Then the same old political disease set in again. What precisely is this disease that causes inflation and all these other troubles? It has many popular names, some of which I have mentioned, such as socialism, communism, state interventionism, and welfare statism. It has other names such as fascism and Nazism. It has some local names like New Deal, Fair Deal, New Republicanism, New Frontier, and the like.

A Dwindling Faith in Freedom

But, if you will take a careful look at these so-called "progressive ideologies," you will discover that each of them has a characteristic common to all the rest. This common characteristic is a cell in the body politic which has a cancer-like capacity for inordinate growth. This characteristic takes the form of a belief. It is a rapidly growing belief in the use of organized force—government—not to carry out its original function of inhibiting the destructive actions of men and invoking a common justice, but to control the productive and creative activity of citizens in society. That is all it is. Check any one of these ideologies and see if this is not its essential characteristic.

Here is an example of what I mean: I can remember the time when, if we wanted a house or housing, we relied on private enterprise. First, we relied on the person who wanted a house. Second, we relied on the persons who wanted to compete in the building. And third, we relied on those who thought they saw some advantage to themselves in loaning the money for the tools, material, and labor. Under that system of free enterprise, Americans built more square feet of housing per person than any other country on the face of the earth. Despite that remarkable accomplishment, more and more people are coming to believe that the only way we can have adequate housing is to use government to take the earnings from some and give these earnings, in the form of housing, to others. In other words, we are right back where the Pilgrim Fathers were in 1620–23 and Karl Marx was in 1847—from each according to ability, to each according to need, and by the use of force.

As this belief in the use of force as a means of creative accomplishment increases, the belief in free men—that is, man acting freely, competitively, cooperatively, voluntarily—correspondingly diminishes. Increase compulsion and freedom declines. Therefore, the solution to this problem, if there be one, must take a positive form, namely, the restoration of a faith in what free men can accomplish.

Let me give you an example of how faith in free men is lost. If I were to go out today and ask the people I meet, "Should government deliver mail?" almost everybody would say, "Yes." Why would they say yes? One reason is that the government has preempted that activity, has had a monopoly for so many decades that entrepreneurs today would not know how to go about delivering mail if it were a private enterprise opportunity. You know, you businessmen have a very odd characteristic. You don't spend any time working on something you will never get a chance to try out!

Anyway, I did a little research job a while ago and found that we deliver more pounds of milk in this country than we do pounds of mail. I next made a more startling discovery. Milk is more perishable than a love-letter, a catalogue, or things of that sort. And third, I found out that we deliver milk more efficiently and more cheaply. I asked myself what appeared to be a logical question: Why should not private enterprise deliver mail? We deliver freight, and that's heavier. But many people have lost faith in themselves to deliver as simple a thing as a letter!

Who are these people who have lost faith in themselves to deliver a letter? I am going to stick just to the subject of delivery and to recent times.

Less than a hundred years ago the human voice could be delivered the distance that one champion hog-caller could effectively communicate with another champion hog-caller, which I have estimated at about 44 yards. Since that time man, acting freely, privately, competitively, voluntarily, has discovered how to deliver the human voice around the earth in 1/7 of a second—one million times as far in about the same time that the voice of one hog-caller reached the ear of the other. When men were free to try, they found out how to deliver an event like the Rose Bowl game in motion and in color into your living room while it is going on. When men were free to try, they found out how to deliver 115 individuals from Los Angeles to Baltimore in three hours and nineteen minutes. When men are free to try, they deliver gas from a hole in the ground in Texas to my range at Irvington, New York, without subsidy and at low prices. Men who are free to try have discovered how to deliver 64 ounces of oil from the Persian Gulf to our eastern seaboard, more than half the way around the world for less money than government will deliver a one-ounce letter across the street in your home town. And the people who accomplish these miracles have lost faith in their capacity to deliver a letter, which is a Boy Scout job. You may get the idea that when it comes to productive and creative work, I have more faith in free men than in government.

Now then, why is this happening to us? I don't know all the reasons. I am not sure that anyone does. If pressed, however, for the best reason I could give, the most profound one, it would be this: the American people, by and large, have lost track of the spiritual antecedent of the American miracle. You are given a choice: either you accept the idea of the Creator as the endower of man's rights, or you submit to the idea that the state is the endower of man's rights. I double-dare any of you to offer a third alternative. We have forgotten the real source of our rights and are suffering the consequences.

Millions of people, aware that something is wrong, look around for someone to blame. They dislike socialism and communism and give lip service to their dislike. They sputter about the New Frontier and Modern Republicanism. But, among the millions who say they don't like these ideologies, you cannot find one in ten thousand whom you yourself will designate as a skilled, accomplished expositor of socialism's opposite—the free market, private property, limited government philosophy with its moral and spiritual antecedents. How many people do you know who are knowledgeable in this matter? Very few, I dare say.

Developing Leadership

No wonder we are losing the battle! The problem then—the real problem—is developing a leadership for this philosophy, persons from different walks of life who understand and can explain this philosophy.

This leadership functions at three levels. The first level requires that an individual achieve that degree of understanding which makes it utterly impossible for him to have any hand in supporting or giving any encouragement to any socialistic activities. Leadership at this level doesn't demand any creative writing, thinking, and talking, but it does require an understanding of what things are really socialistic, however disguised. People reject socialism in name, but once any socialistic activity has been Americanized, nearly everybody thinks it's all right. So you have to take the definition of socialism—state ownership and control of the means of production—and check our current practices against this definition.

As a matter of fact, you should read the ten points of the *Communist Manifesto* and see how close we have come to achieving them right here in America. It's amazing.

The second level of leadership is reached when you achieve that degree of understanding and exposition which makes it possible to expose the fallacies of socialism and set forth some of the principles of freedom to those who come within your own personal orbit. Now, this takes a lot more doing.

One of the things you have to do to achieve this second level of leadership is some studying. Most people have to, at any rate, and one of the reasons The Foundation for Economic Education exists is to help such people. At The Foundation we are trying to understand the freedom philosophy better ourselves, and we seek ways of explaining it with greater clarity. The results appear in single page releases, in a monthly journal, in books and pamphlets, in lectures, seminars, and the like. Our journal, *The Freeman,* for instance, is available to schools and libraries on request. We impose no other condition.

The third level of leadership is to achieve that excellence in understanding and exposition which will cause other persons to seek you out as a tutor. That is the highest you can go, but there is no limit as to how far you can go in becoming a good tutor.

When you operate at this highest level of leadership, you must rely only on the power of attraction. Let me explain what I mean by this.

On April 22 we had St. Andrew's Day at my golf club. About 150 of us were present, including yours truly. When I arrived at the club, the other 149 did not say, "Leonard, won't you please play with me? Won't you please show me the proper stance, the proper grip, the proper swing?" They didn't do it. You know why? Because by now those fellows are aware of my incompetence as a golfer. But if you were to wave a magic wand and make of me, all of a sudden, a Sam Snead, a Ben Hogan, an Arnold Palmer, or the like, watch the picture change! Every member of that club would sit at my feet hoping to learn from me how to improve his own game. This is the power of attraction. You cannot do well at any subject without an audience automatically forming around you. Trust me on that.

If you want to be helpful to the cause of freedom in this country, seek to become a skilled expositor. If you have worked at the philosophy of freedom and an audience isn't forming, don't write and ask what the matter is. Just go back and do more of your homework.

Actually, when you get into this third level of leadership, you have to use methods that are consonant with your objective. Suppose, for instance, that my objective were your demise. I could use some fairly low-grade methods, couldn't I? But now, suppose my objective to be the making of a great poet out of you. What could I do about that? Not a thing—unless by some miracle I first learned to distinguish good poetry from bad, and then learned to impart this knowledge to you.

The philosophy of freedom is at the very pinnacle of the hierarchy of values; and if you wish to further the cause of freedom, you must use methods that are consonant with your objective. This means relying on the power of attraction.

Let me conclude with a final thought. The business of freedom is an ore that lies much deeper than most of us realize. Too many of us are prospecting wastefully on the surface. Freedom isn't something to be bought cheaply. A great effort is required to dig up this ore that will save America. And where are we to find the miners?

Well, I think maybe we will find them among those who are reasonably intelligent. I think we will find these miners of the freedom-ore among those who love this country. I think we will probably find them in this room. And if you were to ask me who, in my opinion, has the greatest responsibility as a miner, I would suggest that it is the attractive individual occupying the seat you are sitting in.

Natural Rights

by Ronald Cooney

The concept of natural rights no doubt has its origin in the Roman Stoic idea of a "law above the law," of an unwritten law which precedes and is superior to man made law. Christian philosophy, in the persons of St. Augustine and St. Thomas Aquinas, developed and refined the natural law idea, and it was a significant tenet of the eighteenth century Enlightenment. The doctrine has come down through the centuries as one of the major arguments against arbitrary and unrestrained governmental power.

In much the same way is the belief in the natural rights of man a belief in "rights above rights." Likewise, natural rights have been used in the resistance to unjust authority. Natural rights were partial justification for the Glorious Revolution of 1688, for the American Revolution (the Declaration of Independence cited man's "unalienable rights"), and for the French Revolution and the Declaration of the Rights of Man. All of the revolutions since the eighteenth century have drawn at least some of their power from appeals to natural rights.

The connection between natural rights and natural law is instantly recognizable. Both exist prior to the State, and both transcend it. Natural law, like the law of the State, provides protection for the individual's rights from violation by another individual, or—and this the State does not do—by the State itself. Natural rights and natural law are the final arbiters of liberty. Finally, natural rights and natural law are both denied by those who exalt the State over the individual citizen, those who make the State all and the individual nothing. It is to this, as it is to all forms of Statism, that natural rights make a direct and implacable challenge.

Dictatorial Delusion

The common delusion of the defenders of unlimited governmental dominion is that the State confers upon the individual whatever political and economic rights he may enjoy. This was certainly the view of

Mr. Cooney, a free-lance writer, wrote this article for the October 1972 issue of *The Freeman*.

Thomas Hobbes, the defender of absolute monarchy and the author of the *Leviathan*. Hobbes, in 1651, argued for the complete sovereignty of the king as ruler and lawmaker. Hobbes sought to repudiate natural law by placing it on equal terms with the civil law. He states in the *Leviathan*, "The law of nature and the civil law contain each other, and are of equal extent." In other words, natural law (and by extension, natural rights) is as high as, *but* no *higher than*, civil law. The sovereign makes civil law, and in Hobbes' kingdom there can be no law higher than the decrees of the sovereign. He, in effect, is the law.

Whatever the political repercussions of a system like that which Hobbes postulates, there are certain moral and ethical questions which it poses. Hobbes felt that morals and ethics had no place in determining whether or not a system of government was good or evil. Such a judgment, according to Hobbes, could not be made, or if made, could not be proved. The correlation between Hobbes' disavowal of natural law/natural rights and objective morality is palpable and direct. Hobbes realized that the acceptance of unalienable rights of life, liberty, and property would compel one to make a moral judgment of a political system which violated those rights. Having given the sovereign absolute authority to make laws, Hobbes goes on to say that no ethical determination can be made about the sovereign's action, about its goodness or evilness. Ethics, to Hobbes, are purely subjective and inapplicable in political affairs. The sovereign, it would seem, is above both law and morality; or, like Nietzsche's superman, "beyond good and evil."

Hobbes wrote in defense of authoritarian rule by one man, the monarch. Monarchy was, in Hobbes' day, the most widespread form of government. With the gradual decay of the monarchical form, and the general democratization of governments, came the belief that it was not the leader of the nation who was sovereign, but the people themselves. The divine right of kings had become, as Herbert Spencer observed, the "divine right of majorities." But whether they represented the interests of monarchy or democracy, the enemies of natural rights had the same intention—to deny the individual any rights but those granted by the State.

Bentham's Faith in Democracy

Of the type of thinker who spoke for democracy and against natural rights was the great utilitarian Jeremy Bentham. No statist in economic concerns, Bentham was curiously inconsistent when it came to limiting, or not limiting, the State's sphere of influence. Government's function, as Bentham saw it, was "creating rights." He considered natural law and natural rights "fictions," and in his first work, the *Fragment on Government*, he castigated Blackstone for a contrary belief. Bentham's antipathy to natural rights sprang from the conviction that natural rights were obstacles to reform, and he was against checks and balances and a system of separation of powers for the same reason.

Bentham thought, with the faith of the statist in the ability of government to solve all human problems, that by making the act of legislating as easy as possible, the State could deal more readily with society's dilemmas. Bentham did not see what others, most notably the Framers of the Constitution, saw so penetratingly: that the power of the State to achieve good was equaled by its power to achieve enormous harm, that in seeking the former one necessarily braved the latter. Bentham did not perceive the difficulty inherent in placing all right-giving power in the State's hands. He failed to understand that the capacity for bestowing rights could become the capacity for withdrawing rights. Finally, Bentham, like Hobbes before him, was incorrect in assuming that the State could create rights out of nothing. The State is a delegated authority, and what power it has derives from the individuals who comprise it. Such being the case, it is absurd to assume that the State can bestow rights on its own creators. The State may give order to rights, define them more clearly, and protect them with laws; but it can no more grant rights to the members of society than a child can grant rights to his parents.

The Ethical Case

The ethical arguments in favor of natural rights are perhaps even more telling. If it is true that men have only the rights the State has seen fit to give them, what is to stop the State, at any time and for any reason, from taking back those rights? Furthermore, how can we say that the State acts wrongly if it chooses to take that action? By the logic of the opponents of natural rights, the Nazi regime had a perfect justification for recalling the rights, including the right to life of 6,000,000 human beings, and should not be condemned or thought of as evil for simply exercising the prerogative to which, as a state, it was clearly entitled. Thus, the denial of natural rights quickly resolves itself into a rejection of the ethical differences between governments, making a slave-state the moral equal of a republic.

We now arrive at the final question, "What are the natural rights?" Although it cannot be answered precisely, that does not mean it is unanswerable. As has been said before, natural rights precede the

State and hence are *a priori* in character. Natural rights are every man's at birth and are not State-granted. If each man has an equal claim to liberty, that is, the use of his rights, he can be limited in his freedom only by the claims of other men to an equal share of liberty. The circle of rights around every man extends as far as it may without intruding on the rights of other men. For this reason are the "rights" granted by the State bogus rights. A right to receive welfare, for example, is invalid since it requires the abridgment, however partial, of the rights of the citizen who is compelled to pay for the welfare benefits given to someone else. Natural rights, by contrast, require no abridgment of another individual's rights to exist, but are limited only by the same natural rights of another person.

Natural Law and the American Tradition

by Davis E. Keeler

Legal and political philosophy came to America with the first New England colonists. These Puritans were not concerned with politics itself but treated upon it as it was involved with their religious problems. Outside of New England, though the colonists were also taken up in the problems of establishing governments and framing laws, there was virtually no writing dealing with the philosophy of politics or laws.

In those first years, the Puritan conception of law was quite clear: the only true law was that of God's making. It was only when the rules of man were based squarely on the revealed will of God that they attained the dignity of law. The concept of natural law was completely absorbed in divine law. An English lawyer in Boston wrote in 1642 that the colonial tribunals ignored English Common law and sought to administer Mosaic law.

Although the colonies did not produce legal philosophy, they avidly consumed the two monumental writers of English law: Coke and Blackstone.

Lord Coke was a product of the seventeenth century, which saw not only the ascendancy of the doctrine of natural law as a restriction on the sovereign's relations to his subjects, but in England saw it established that there were certain fundamental common law rights which the courts would enforce even against the king. To Lord Coke, the common law limitations on royal authority became natural limitations on all authority; the common law rights of Englishmen became the natural rights of man.

Because of the inexact manner in which the common law was developed and handed down, in his expositions of the content of these natural rights of Englishmen Coke seldom rested solely upon the Magna Carta or other authority but would invariably invoke "common right and reason" to justify his position.

Yet however these rights might be discovered, it is clear that they transcended both parliament and king. In Bonham's Case (1610), Coke said: "And it appears in our books, that in many cases, the common

---

Mr. Keeler wrote this article for the May 1981 issue of *The Freeman*.

law will control the acts of Parliament, and sometimes adjudge them utterly void; for when an act of Parliament is against common right and reason, or repugnant, or impossible to be performed, the common law will control it and adjudge such an action to be void."

In 1765, William Blackstone published his *Commentaries on the Law* and within a short time he became as well read in America as in England. These quotations are from an American edition published in Philadelphia in 1771: "When the Supreme Being formed the universe and created matter out of nothing, he impressed certain principles upon that matter from which it can never depart and without which it would cease to be. . . . This then is the general significance of law. . . . But laws in their more confined sense, and in which it is our present business to consider them, denote rules not of action in general, but of human action . . . that is the precepts by which man . . . endowed with both reason and free will, is commanded to make use of those faculties in the general regulation of his behavior . . . . So when He created man . . . He laid down certain immutable laws of human nature . . . and gave him also the faculty of reason to discover the purport of those laws. The Creator . . . has been pleased so to contrive the constitution and form of humanity that we should want no other prompter to inquire after and pursue the rule of right but our own self-love, that universal principle of action. . . . God has not perplexed the law of nature with a multitude of abstract principles . . . but has graciously reduced the rule of obedience to this one paternal precept that man shall pursue his own true and substantial happiness."

Though Blackstone speaks of the natural liberties and absolute rights of man, he adds a reservation: "I know it is more generally laid down more largely, that acts of Parliament contrary to reason are void. But if parliament will positively enact a thing to be done which is unreasonable, I know of no power in the ordinary forms of the Constitution that is vested with the authority to control it."

In that he was right, for in England the Revolution of 1688 had established the supremacy of Parliament and in the Mother Country Lord Coke's fundamental rights of Englishmen could no longer prevail over the will of the legislature.

Whatever reservations Blackstone may have had about the ultimate supremacy of natural rights, they were not shared by the colonists who eagerly consumed Blackstone on the rights of Englishmen and ignored Blackstone on the supremacy of Parliament.

And this was what the Revolution was about. The Declaration of Independence was a statement of these principles. Far from being an extravagant rallying cry for a difficult cause, it was a simple statement of the general political and legal consensus of the colonists. When the infuriated colonists denounced the Stamp Tax and demanded the rights of Englishmen, they were not demanding those rights which Parliament had from time to time granted its subjects but rather those immemorial rights of Englishmen granted by God and manifest in nature which no parliament however representative may take away or alter.

The Spirit of Freedom

by Robert Bearce

On July 3, 1776, the events of the previous day were fresh on John Adams' mind when he wrote to his wife Abigail: "The second day of July, 1776, will be the most memorable epocha in the history of America. I am apt to believe that it will be celebrated by succeeding generations as the great anniversary festival. It ought to be commemorated as the day of deliverance, by solemn acts of devotion to God Almighty. It ought to be solemnized with pomp and parade, with shows, games, sports, guns, bells, bonfires, and illuminations, from one end of this continent to the other, from this time forward forevermore."

John Adams was enthusiastic about the historic action taken by the Continental Congress on July 2. A resolution favoring independence from Great Britain had been carried by the affirmative vote of twelve Colonies. Not until the fourth of July, though, was the actual Declaration of Independence formally adopted. Although Adams missed foretelling the exact day of future celebrations, he accurately described the manner in which America's Independence Day would be remembered by later generations.

Each Fourth of July, Americans commemorate the adoption of the Declaration of Independence. "Old Glory" comes out of the closet and appears on front porches across the nation. Bands play "The Stars and Stripes Forever." Thoughtful citizens give thanks for the blessings of liberty.

Such patriotic enthusiasm appears as a yearly ritual across the United States. The outward display of loyalty is there, but does this allegiance reflect an in-depth understanding of the Declaration of Independence—a real commitment to personal freedom?

Although John Adams wrote triumphantly to Abigail about the vote for independence, he added a critical observation: "You will think me transported with enthusiasm, but I am not. I am well aware of the toil and blood and treasure that it will cost us to maintain this Declaration and support and defend these states."

Mr. Bearce is a free-lance writer living in Houston, Texas. This article originally appeared in the June 1985 issue of *The Freeman*.

The Critical Challenge

We are now facing that same critical challenge. The Declaration of Independence may be extolled, but just praising it as a relevant, thoughtful document of freedom will not preserve it. Enshrining it will not strengthen freedom. Instead, we must re-examine and reassert the principles outlined in the Declaration of Independence.

Consider the second inspiring sentence of the document: "We hold these truths to be self-evident: That all men are created equal; that they are endowed by their Creator with certain unalienable rights; that among these are life, liberty, and the pursuit of happiness...." The colonists had enjoyed these God-given rights and others since the first settling of America. With varying degrees of freedom, they could own property, bear firearms, and worship as they pleased. They had the right of trial by jury, and they practiced representative government. Most important, they had been free to live their own lives as they—not the government—best saw fit.

When these freedoms were threatened by Parliament and King George III, the colonists became indignant. Receiving no just response to their grievances, they chose to separate themselves from the mother country. The Declaration of Independence was the formal statement of their decision to be totally independent and self-governing.

The real importance of the Declaration, however, is its fundamental assertion of *individual freedom*. Even if the demand for political independence had not been made, the document would still be a profound statement in defense of human dignity. When the Thirteen Colonies proclaimed their independence as the United States, they were reaffirming personal freedom and rejecting authoritarian rule by government over the individual.

Several years after the United States had won independence from Great Britain, a veteran of the Lexington-Concord fight in 1775 was asked why he had fought against the British. "We had always governed ourselves," replied the rugged old minuteman, "and we always meant to. They didn't mean we should."

His forthright answer reveals the main issue of the American War of Independence—*freedom*. The minuteman understood that if he was to have freedom, he would have to enjoy the right of self-government. He reasoned that he could govern himself only to the extent that he exercised personal judgment and choice over his own affairs. For almost 150 years, the colonists had done just that—accepted individual freedom, responsibility, and accountability for their own lives. Government regulations and controls threatened that freedom.

Oppressive Government

The Declaration of Independence clearly states the objection to oppressive governmental authority. The central portion of the document shows that the colonists were protesting abuse of power, usurpation of their rights, obstruction of justice, and governmental interference. Speaking of the King of England, they pointed to this abuse of government authority: "He has erected a multitude of new offices, and sent hither swarms of officers to harass our people and eat out their substance."

Although he was eventually characterized as such, King George III was not a tyrant. He and Parliament had shown a rather benevolent, paternalistic attitude toward the Thirteen Colonies—an attitude similar to the "compassion" and "concern for the disadvantaged" supposedly shown by our modern-day politicians. Like young immature children, the Colonies were to benefit from the fatherly hand of the British Crown. But they were not very impressed by this paternal hand of regulation, decrees, taxes, and other bureaucratic interventions.

"Tyranny!" shouted the colonists. They saw unlimited government power for what it was—the seed of repression and subjugation. Patriots like Thomas Jefferson fought for the principles of limited government and individual freedom. They knew that the main role of government was twofold: (1) apprehending and punishing domestic evildoers—those people who would violate other people's right to "life, liberty, and the pursuit of happiness" and (2) organizing the defense of law-abiding citizens against foreign aggression. Government was *not* to be the source of a people's material welfare.

The Declaration of Independence speaks eloquently of "life, liberty, and the pursuit of happiness" for the individual. These rights could be secured only when government itself was held within strict boundaries of power and authority. The colonists realized they could improve their own personal lives if they were free of government interference. They did not want the government trying to do for them what they could and should do for themselves. They asked only for the freedom to enjoy the just fruits of their daily labors.

Even as the Crown continued to infringe upon their "unalienable rights," the colonists followed legal channels of protest, expressing loyalty to the King. There was the firm intention of retaining the traditional political relationship with England. The preservation of freedom—not revolution—was on the colonists' minds.

Eventually, patience ran out, prompting Patrick Henry to declare: "We have done everything that could be done to avert the storm which is now coming on. We have petitioned, we have remonstrated, we have supplicated, we have prostrated ourselves before the throne, and have implored its interposition to arrest the tyrannical hands of the ministry and Parliament. Our petitions have been slighted; our remonstrances have produced additional violence and insult; our supplications have been disregarded; and we have been spurned with contempt from the foot of the throne."

Individual Dignity

The American War of Independence was fought to preserve a truly "revolutionary" truth—each of us is a unique individual, able to accept self-responsibility and thus to enjoy personal dignity. For the most part, the governments, systems, revolutions, societies, and ideologies of the world have tried to suppress that truth. People have been enslaved, tortured, and killed by those who reject man's God-given right to "life, liberty, and the pursuit of happiness."

The American colonists had seen the approach of slavery. In the Declaration of Independence, they accused King George III of seeking the "establishment of an absolute tyranny over these States." Similar language was used by the revolutionary Jacobins during the French Revolution when they assailed the monarchy under Louis XVI. The French radicals shouted lofty slogans about liberty, but their bloody revolution against the monarchy hardly parallels the spirit of the American Revolution—the true spirit of freedom.

"Liberty! Equality! Fraternity!" clamored the revolutionaries of France. Louis XVI lost his head on the guillotine. So did thousands of other Frenchmen.

The leaders of the French Revolution of 1789 had read the Declaration of Independence. They admired America's document of freedom. Unfortunately, they lauded it but rejected its principles. They failed to comprehend what Jefferson and Adams meant when they said "all men are created equal." Equality as it is outlined in the Declaration says that individuals are equal in their right to be free and independent—to be free and independent as long as they respect the rights of others to be free and independent, with everyone respecting property and other individual rights.

Each person should have the right to rise to the height of self-realization consistent with that person's individual talents, ambition, and willingness to accept personal accountability. In seeking this self-fulfillment, each person must respect the equal rights of other individuals.

When a government respects true equality—the equal right to enjoy personal freedom—the result will be that many differences will exist among the citizenry. This natural condition of *inequality* is consistent with freedom, justice, and human nature. Individuals are unique. Each person has varying talents, aspirations, and weaknesses. If individuals are free to arrange their own lives, they create a diverse society where men and women attain different social, intellectual, and economic status.

Equal Treatment Results in Many Differences

Individuals are equal in their right to "life, liberty, and the pursuit of happiness"—so long as they accept responsibility for their own lives and recognize their personal accountability for their failures, shortcomings, and misdeeds. Regrettably for mankind, modern-day politicians and "social architects" like the French revolutionaries reject this truth.

Robespierre, Danton, and other leaders of the French Revolution believed they could bring about the regeneration of humanity through the power of the State (government power and authority). Although they spoke much about freedom, they actually denied self-determination and the free will of the individual. They insisted that man was the product of his environment. Crime, poverty, greed—these were supposedly inflicted upon humanity by corrupt political, social, and economic conditions/institutions. By the use of government authority and power, the revolutionaries believed they could erect a near perfect if not perfect society.

The visionaries of Revolutionary France had a distorted view of human nature—a distorted view still held by many people today in the media, in politics, in our universities, and even in our religious institutions. The theory-minded leaders of the French Revolution believed that the individual was inherently virtuous. If a person committed murder, he should not be harshly condemned for a criminal act. Rather, he should be regarded as the victim of adverse social or economic conditions which drove him to the act of taking another individual's life.

Thus, the French revolutionaries focused their efforts to build the virtuous society by removing what they mistakenly thought caused people to act in "antisocial" ways. By reconstructing society through the power of the State, they were convinced that people would return to their basic goodness, virtue, and righteousness.

The government leaders of the French Revolution said that they

loved humanity. They said that they were for the "poor and home-
less," "the helpless and abused," and "the needy," but in reality, they
rejected the true meaning of human dignity contained in the Declaration of Independence. They placed society and the State above the
individual and individual freedom, whereas the 56 signers of the Declaration of Independence in America placed the individual above the
State.

The patriots of the American Revolution had faith in individual
freedom. Freedom—not government power—was the foundation for
true progress, self-improvement, and happiness. Absolute equality
and perfection brought about by government authority were illusions.
Only free individuals in a truly free nation could achieve material
welfare, human dignity, and personal fulfillment. Only when the individual has both the freedom to make choices and the corresponding
obligation to abide by the just consequences of those choices, can he
achieve self-respect.

By adhering to the principles of the Declaration of Independence,
Americans have attained material abundance and personal dignity.
The blessings of liberty have been enjoyed because free individuals
have been allowed in the past to labor freely in a free society. Yet, we
have also been abandoning the basic truths upon which America was
founded.

"Omnipotent" Government

From the halls of Congress to the academic forum, we hear that
government has the answer to all of our society's ills. We are assured
that government can and should solve every problem from hunger to
faulty automobile bumpers. Commissions . . . regulations . . . controls
. . . rules . . . coercion . . . Congressional committees . . . subcommittees
. . . regimentation . . . and more regimentation—all should remind us
of the grievances listed in the Declaration of Independence.

Coercion, paternalism, restrictive legislation, and unconstitutional
government intervention will gain ground to the extent that we are
different to the cause of true freedom. When we remain silent, we will
be responsible for our own destruction—moral degeneracy, material/
economic stagnation, and eventual physical slavery.

The principles of freedom will continue to be eroded as long as
free individuals relax in their complacency. "Is this the part of wise
men," asked Patrick Henry in March 1775, "engaged in a great and
arduous struggle for liberty? Are we disposed to be of the number of

those who, having eyes, see not, and having ears, hear not, the things which so nearly concern their temporal salvation?"

Freedom is threatened today just as it was threatened at the time of the Declaration of Independence. The colonists wanted less government—not more of it in their daily lives. They wanted to be free to release their own creativity and energies. The "pursuit of happiness" was their own responsibility. They stated in the Declaration "that, to secure these rights, governments are instituted among men, deriving their just powers from the consent of the governed." The early patriots of America believed that government should protect their "unalienable rights." It had no right to interfere with "life, liberty, and the pursuit of happiness" other than that of prosecuting law-breakers and maintaining self-defense from foreign aggression. The colonists were free people struggling to remain free.

Living in freedom had strengthened the character of the colonists. They recognized the existence of moral absolutes. Right was right. Wrong was wrong. They were individuals who valued honesty, hard work, thrift, and an equal respect for the rights of others. They knew what they believed and *why* they believed it. They said what they meant and *meant* what they said.

Humble Before God

Although the colonists were self-reliant and independent, they were humble before God. True liberty was found in a genuine reverence for Almighty God and obedience to His commandments—not worship of government authority. Their spiritual faith gave them a clear understanding of their personal roles in life. They accepted the rugged challenges of life, knowing that in worldly affairs the Lord, indeed, helped those who helped themselves.

The farmers and shopkeepers who took up arms against the Redcoats heeded Ben Franklin's admonition: "They that can give up essential liberty to obtain a little temporary safety deserve neither liberty nor safety."

The patriots of 1776 chose both liberty and the responsibility of defending that freedom. The Continental soldier fought at Trenton and Germantown ... suffered at Valley Forge ... and finally won independence. The "Spirit of '76" is the faith and spirit of freedom. If Patrick Henry and other patriots were willing to die for freedom, certainly we should *live* for freedom. We face the continued struggle for liberty. Battles lie ahead. We are in continual warfare. These are facts that we must accept honestly as we consider Patrick Henry's words back in 1775:

"The battle, sir, is not to the strong alone; it is to the vigilant, the active, the brave. Besides, sir, we have no election. If we were base enough to desire it, it is not too late to retire from the contest. There is no retreat but in submission and slavery!"

A State of War

Today, free people are in a state of warfare—a continued battle prompted by those who oppose freedom. We need to acknowledge our current challenge to keep alive the spirit of freedom and to strengthen freedom.

First, we need an honest, sincere, and broad understanding of the basics of freedom. We cannot very well defend that which we cannot adequately explain and present to other people. We should ask ourselves how well we truly understand such principles of freedom as the free-market exchange of goods and services ... personal freedom/accountability ... no coercion against law-abiding citizens ... voluntary cooperation ... limited, strictly defined government power.

Do we understand these principles? Are we doing what we can to understand them better?

Second, in order to rejuvenate the spirit of freedom, we must practice the freedom faith continually, consistently, and earnestly in *our own personal lives.* Some warriors for the cause of freedom know the ABCs on the subject, and they are on the battlefronts, such as actively campaigning for pro-freedom candidates for Congress.

Such "activism" is to be cheered and encouraged, but woe! Some of those hard-charging freedom warriors will (1) on Monday, demand the total elimination of the federally funded Legal Services Corporation, but (2) on Tuesday lobby the federal government for an increase in federal subsidies and low interest loans for farmers. The wayward, backsliding freedom troopers in this case are an association of farmers who are more interested in their "special interest" than in individual freedom and responsibility.

No, we cannot have that type of inconsistency if the spirit of freedom is to be enhanced and strengthened.

Third, we must diligently protect freedom. Patrick Henry advised that those who would defend liberty must be strong, active, brave, and vigilant. "Vigilance is the price of liberty," and today we should be vigilant—seeing where and how freedom is being undermined.

For example, we ought to see that many reporters, commentators, editors, publishers, and news anchosr are not the fair, objective, accurate, and honest people they would like us to believe. Instead, they are prejudiced against freedom. They show a clear bias in favor of more government—a support for more government intervention that daily translates into a corruption of the truth.

A good portion of the major news media people have a personal belief that the government should be spending more—not less—for education, the arts, welfare, health, and the like. They personally believe that government regulations and programs—not free people working freely in a free society—are the best way to make sure individuals are sufficiently housed, clothed, fed, and given proper medical care.

Even though we may have a very sound grasp of the basics of freedom, we must be vigilant to the distortions, half-truths, and slanted reporting we receive from media sources around us.

Fourth, we should be earnest spokesmen for freedom, actively taking a part in the current battles affecting our daily lives. It isn't enough to appreciate the writings of Bastiat, Jefferson, Burke, Tocqueville, and Ludwig von Mises. Nor do we accomplish much by railing at the supper table about Congress's latest repudiation of the oath of office to defend the Constitution of the United States. Rather, we should practice what we preach by becoming intelligently, firmly, and consistently involved defending freedom, explaining it, and strengthening it.

Words of Wisdom

Two men who signed the Declaration of Independence back in 1776 still speak to us as we seek to learn more about freedom. "A wise and frugal government," advises Thomas Jefferson, "which shall restrain men from injuring one another, shall leave them otherwise free to regulate their own pursuits of industry and improvement, and shall not take from the mouth of labor the bread it has earned. This is the sum of good government. . . ."

Dr. John Witherspoon, the only active clergyman to sign the Declaration, gives us a final insight into the spirit of freedom:

"A good form of government may hold the rotten materials together for some time, but beyond a certain pitch even the best constitution will be ineffectual, and slavery will ensue. On the other hand, when the manners of a nation are pure, when true religion and internal principles maintain their vigor, the attempts of the most powerful enemies to oppress them are commonly baffled and disappointed."

Individual Rights: The Crumbling Foundation of American Government

by Robert Higgs

Almost everyone recognizes that government can perpetrate great evils. One has only to think of the regimes of Stalin, Hitler, and Pol Pot, three of the most hideous examples. But government is also widely regarded as a potential source of great good. Even Ludwig von Mises, an archenemy of statism, declared that government is "the most necessary and beneficial institution, as without it no lasting social cooperation and no civilization could be developed and preserved."[1] How can people enjoy the benefits of government while avoiding the dangers? Upon what principles must a tolerable government be built?

The Nature of Government

When we say the word "government," we may mean various things. Sometimes we refer to certain institutions, the established rules and proceedings by which the body politic is ordered and incorporated into the making and maintaining of collective arrangements for social life. At other times we refer to the particular persons who wield established authority over the citizenry. The two meanings are connected. Government as rulers operates according to government as institutions, which people often call "the system." This connection holds whether the type of government be dictatorship, oligarchy, monarchy, or representative democracy.

Governments have existed for thousands of years. Philosophers have argued that they are either natural—it would be inconceivable that humankind not have them—or that people without a government would be, in Thomas Hobbes' words, so "few, fierce, short-lived, poor, nasty, and deprived of all that pleasure and beauty of life, which peace and society are wont to bring with them," that no one would want to be without a government.[2] In Hobbes' estimation, it would be a good bargain for individuals to surrender all their freedom of action to a ruler in exchange for a modicum of peace and social order.

Dr. Higgs is Research Director for the Independent Institute. This article was first published in the October 1991 issue of *The Freeman*.

49

A government, by definition, claims a monopoly of legitimate coercion within its jurisdiction. Every government, ultimately if not immediately, relies on physical violence to enforce its rule. If it cannot do so effectively, it probably will be replaced by another government that can. Hence it is entirely natural that governments maintain police, prisons, and armed forces, whereas General Motors, Exxon, and IBM do not. People sometimes talk about "economic power" as if it were comparable with governmental power. It isn't.

Every government recognizes that people will obey orders more readily if they believe the orders are proper and, in some sense, in the best interests of the ruled as well as the rulers. Historically, a close linkage of the warrior class and the priesthood has characterized most societies. The blessing of religion has given many governments a more effective claim to obedience. Whether by appeal to religion or by appeal to secular principles of right or virtue, governments always try to legitimate their actions. This striving after legitimation is the principal difference between governments and mere criminal gangs.

Whether government really is necessary (and a few of us still consider the question open to debate), once a society has a government, the potential exists for rulers to abuse their power by pursuing their own ends rather than those cherished by the people they rule. Unchecked government can give rise to tyranny. Accordingly, many lovers of liberty have called government a necessary evil: necessary because they see no alternative institution to maintain peace and domestic order, and evil because the rulers, by virtue of their exclusive control of legitimate coercion, may overextend their powers at the expense of the well-being and liberties of the ruled.

Revolutionary Ideals

The men who founded the United States were, in the eyes of the established British government, outlaws—traitors, thieves, and murderers. Americans nowadays so venerate the memory of Jefferson, Madison, Washington, Hamilton, Adams, Franklin, and the other Founding Fathers that we easily forget the raw reality of what they undertook to do between 1775 and 1783. They armed themselves, laid claim to authority denied them by established law, and set out to overthrow the established government by killing the men who defended it.

They were not murderers by profession. Indeed, they probably were the most thoughtful, best educated, and most articulate band of outlaws in history. When they decided to take up arms to overthrow the government, they debated their cause at length, and they wrote down in various places their reasons for resorting to killing other human beings, their justification for actions they ordinarily would have strongly condemned. How did they justify their actions?

They claimed that they, in common with all men, had rights, and that in the existing circumstances they could effectively defend their rights only by violence. In 1774 the First Continental Congress made a declaration of what its members called "their indubitable rights and liberties; which cannot be legally taken from them, altered or abridged by any power whatever, without their own consent. . . ." They claimed that they were "entitled to life, liberty, and property. . . ."

Where did the asserted rights come from? They said that they held the rights "by the immutable laws of nature, the principles of the English constitution, and the several charters or compacts" establishing the British colonies in North America.[3] Again and again the rebels justified their cause by claiming a right to liberty. They insisted that the legitimacy of government required the consent of the governed.

The Continental Congress's "Declaration of the Causes and Necessity of Taking Up Arms," issued July 6, 1775, declared that "a reverence for our great Creator, principles of humanity, and the dictates of common sense, must convince all those who reflect upon the subject, that government was instituted to promote the welfare of mankind, and ought to be administered for the attainment of that end. . . . Honour, justice, and humanity, forbid us tamely to surrender that freedom which we received from our gallant ancestors. . . . The arms we have been compelled by our enemies to assume, we will . . . employ for the preservation of our liberties; being with one mind resolved to die freemen rather than to live slaves. [And finally] in defence of the freedom that is our birth-right, and . . . for the protection of our property, . . . we have taken up arms."[4]

Then, in 1776, the Continental Congress issued a Declaration of Independence. Here is the justification the rebels gave for their actions:

> We hold these truths to be self-evident, that all men are created equal, that they are endowed by their Creator with certain unalienable Rights, that among these are Life, Liberty and the pursuit of Happiness. That to secure these rights, Governments are instituted among Men, deriving their just powers from the consent of the governed, That whenever any Form of Government becomes destructive of these ends, it is the Right of the People to alter or to abolish it, and to institute new Government, laying its foundation on such principles and or-

ganizing its powers in such form, as to them shall seem most likely to effect their Safety and Happiness.

The Declaration continued by explaining that the rebels had not rashly taken up arms against the established government:

> Governments long established should not be changed for light and transient causes; and accordingly all experience hath shown that mankind are more disposed to suffer, while evils are sufferable, than to right themselves by abolishing the forms to which they are accustomed. But when a long train of abuses and usurpations, pursuing invariably the same Object evinces a design to reduce them under absolute Despotism, it is their right, it is their duty, to throw off such Government, and to provide new Guards for their future security.

The Declaration went on to present a lengthy list of grievances against the King, including the complaint that he had "erected a multitude of New Offices, and sent hither swarms of Officers to harass our People, and eat out their substance."

During the Revolutionary era, individual states enacted bills of rights. The Virginia Bill (1776), almost entirely drafted by George Mason, began, "all men are by nature equally free and independent, and have certain inherent rights. . . .[5]

The Massachusetts Bill (1778), written almost entirely by John Adams, began, "all men are born free and equal, and have certain natural, essential, and unalienable rights; among which may he reckoned the right of enjoying and defending their lives and liberties; that of acquiring, possessing, and protecting property; in fine, that of seeking and obtaining their safety and happiness." Article seven of the Massachusetts Bill of Rights declared: "Government is instituted for the common good . . . and not for the profit, honor or private interest of any one man, family, or class of men. . . ." And Article 10 read: "Each individual of the society has a right to be protected by it in the enjoyment of his life, liberty, and property. . . . No part of the property of any individual can, with justice, be taken from him, or applied to public uses, without his own consent, or that of the representative body of the people. . . . And whenever the public exigencies require that the property of any individual should be appropriated to public uses, he shall receive a reasonable compensation therefor."[6]

Later, in the national Bill of Rights, the ten amendments to the United States Constitution ratified in 1791, many of the rights proclaimed by the individual states in the 1770s became part of the entire country's supreme law. Later still, in the 14th Amendment, added to the Constitution in 1868, each state was forbidden to "deprive any person of life, liberty, or property, without due process of law; nor deny to any person within its jurisdiction the equal protection of the laws."

Clearly, government in the United States was founded on an explicit recognition of rights—natural, inalienable rights of each individual—and governments were understood to be legitimate only insofar as they acted to protect those rights. Individuals and their rights were regarded as morally prior to government and its mandates; governments were to serve the people, not the people the government. Government was justifiable only as an instrument of the governed. When governments proved abusive of their powers, when they destroyed rather than protected the natural rights of individuals, the people had a right to defend their rights and to overturn the government that threatened them.

Current Suppression of Rights

Comparing the ideology of the Founders with the currently dominant ideology, we encounter a stark contrast: on the one hand, the deep regard that the Revolutionary ideals expressed for individual rights; on the other hand, the rampant disregard for individual rights with which the present governments of the United States—federal, state, and local—conduct themselves and justify their actions. To make matters worse, not only do most Americans not recognize that their governments massively invade rather than protect their rights; most Americans actually talk as if they live in a free society.

Many people remain unaware of the extent to which government controls a vast range of human conduct in our society because they are not themselves on the receiving end of many of the particular forms of control. If you are not an automobile designer, you may not be aware that the government prescribes many requirements that all automobiles must meet. If you are not a real estate developer, you may not be aware of the multitude of government permits that must be acquired before you may commence building, and of the plethora of regulations that constrain how you may build. If you are not a pharmaceutical manufacturer, you may not be aware of the long process of testing and certification that must be endured before the government will permit you to sell your product. If you are not an importer or exporter, you may not be aware of the many controls and paperwork requirements that impede your business. If you are not a personnel or payroll officer, you may not be aware of the huge number of requirements you must meet with respect to collecting taxes and providing benefits to employees, and with respect to the makeup of your work force as regards race, sex, and other criteria. If you are not a dealer in stocks and bonds, you may not be aware that acting on the basis of certain information, which the government considers "inside information," may land you in jail. If you do not have complicated business or financial dealings, you may not be aware of how extensively you must give an account of your affairs to the tax authorities. If you are not a business person, you may not be aware that any number of seemingly proper and mutually beneficial business arrangements may cause you to be charged with violating the antitrust laws. And so on and so on, endlessly.

Everyday Controls

But even an ordinary person unavoidably runs up against government controls every day. Perhaps you wake up when your clock radio comes on, bringing you signals transmitted by a radio station permitted to operate only after being granted a license by the Federal Communications Commission. You get dressed, putting on clothing and shoes that cost you more than they would have if the United States government had not restricted the importation of clothing, textiles, and footwear. You drive to work in a car constructed in accordance with a variety of government regulations; or you ride the bus, paying a fare established by a government regulatory commission. You work or go to school with people who have been selected in part on the basis of governmentally prescribed rules and quotas regarding race, sex, ethnicity, handicap, or veteran status. You eat lunch at a cafe that is allowed to operate only after acquiring various permits. You make telephone calls and pay for them at a rate set by a public utility commission. You go home to sit down to an entree of meat sold only after mandatory inspection by the Department of Agriculture. What you paid for the food reflects the price supports on farm products and the restrictions on the importation of farm products into the United States. In the evening you turn on the television, watching a program broadcast by a station licensed by the Federal Communications Commission. Just before turning in for the night, you may take some medicine that you could legally purchase only by prescription and which can be sold to you only because it has been approved by the Food and

Drug Administration. Yours has been an uneventful day, yet you have moved at every moment within a web woven by government.

How the United States evolved from a nation that held individual rights in high esteem (at least as ideals, if never consistently in practice) into a collectivist regime in which individual rights are subjugated in countless distinct ways every hour of every day is a long and complicated story—in many respects, it is the whole story of American society during the past 200 years. Not that liberty diminished at every place and time. The emancipation of the slaves, for example, was a triumph of liberty against which anything else in our history pales. But that was an anomaly, just as the existence of slavery had been an anomaly in the early days of the Republic. In most respects the trend, sometimes quicker, sometimes slower, was relentlessly toward a less and less free society. The pace of the movement accelerated during the past 75 years; it shows no sign of slowing now. Each day Americans become a little less free.

The tragedy is that most neither know nor care. Like George Orwell's character in *1984*, who inhabited a world in which the official language held that war was peace and slavery was freedom, most Americans have actually learned to love Big Brother. Indeed, they spend much of their time actively seeking, or supporting the efforts of those who seek, to extend the grip of government over the whole of human affairs. Nothing is too intimate or too personal or too important to be left for free individuals to decide: not the education of young people, not the care of children or the sick, not even vital decisions involving life and death—nothing escapes the tentacles of government.

Lovers of liberty watch in horror as their fellow citizens stitch new and unnatural organs onto the Frankenstein monster. One marvels that they can take these actions in the name of "doing good," "being fair," "promoting prosperity," "maintaining national security," and a variety of other noble-sounding purposes. Perhaps in some cases they know what they are doing and have simply decided that the loss of liberty entailed by the new government power they support is an acceptable price to pay for the prospective benefit they anticipate—especially when they expect only other people's liberty to be diminished. In many cases, though, they surely act with no awareness that the new government program entails a further throttling of human liberty, an overriding of individual rights.

In 1991, according to official sources, federal bureaus alone—not to mention the 50 states, more than 3,000 counties, and scores of thousands of cities, townships, and other government units, all imposing restraints on individual action—will propose or make final the issuance of 4,675 new rules. Those are *new* rules.[7] When added to all the existing rules, laws, ordinances, regulations, decrees, injunctions, orders, requirements, prohibitions and other official directives, they make up a heap of coercive measures so enormous that not even an army of lawyers can hope to grasp them all, and tax accountants throw up their hands in exasperation.

Budgetary Tyranny

To carry out their thousands of projects, the governments of the United States take at gunpoint—remember, payment of taxes is *not* a voluntary contribution—a sum of money beyond human comprehension, currently about $2 trillion. Question: How far would total government revenues, put into the form of a string of two trillion dollar bills, reach? Answer: It would stretch from the earth to the sun and back, leaving enough of the string to wrap around the earth about 167 times. And this illustrates just this year's government revenues. Watch out for next year!

Remember the American colonists' complaints about taxation without representation? Well, they paid at most a few percent, probably no more than 3 percent, of their annual incomes in taxes. Americans now pay about 36 percent of their vastly larger incomes to their governments. Much of this huge revenue amounts to taking from Peter to pay Paul, then taking from Paul to pay Peter—in order to be fair. Along the way, government officials and bureaucrats take a hefty broker's commission on each transaction. Fully one worker in seven is on the government payroll. Vast numbers of others, supposedly in the "private sector," also work for the government, because they do what they do only because of government spending, taxing, and, regulating.

So utterly devoid of principle is the current activity of U.S. governments that no project whatsoever is too silly to exclude from the trough. Recall the scandal involving the hundreds of thousands of dollars recently appropriated to fix up the boyhood home of Lawrence Welk somewhere in the lost reaches of the Dakotas. (The appropriation was repealed when the news media publicized it heavily, but rarely does anyone take much notice of the equally outrageous appropriations that lard the budget.) You probably haven't heard of the $566 million appropriated to fly cows to Europe, supposedly to promote exports. Or the $107,000 to study the mating habits of the Japanese quail. Remember, every dollar is taken from you or someone else at gunpoint. Would *you* put a gun to someone's head to get money for studying the Japanese quail?

There's much more, including the $2.8 million for a fish farm in Stuttgart, Arkansas; the $1.3 million for repairs to a privately owned dam in South Carolina; the $500,000 for the 1992 American Flora Exposition; and the $49 million for a rock-and-roll museum. Consider next the $500,000 to revitalize downtown Ada, Oklahoma—not a place many Americans are likely to visit—and the $772,000 to construct a skeet shooting club at Tinker Air Force Base. After all, one never knows when the Russians will attack with clay pigeons. There is also $375,000 to renovate the House of Representatives beauty parlor; plus $98 million for Congressional mail no one wants to receive, hyping the virtues of your local member of Congress; and $1.5 million to spruce up a military golf course. (Is this what the framers of the Constitution had in mind by the phrase "provide for the common defense"?) There's $7 million to study air pollution—in Mexico City—and $1 million for the bicycle transportation demonstration project in Macomb County, Michigan. And the list goes on and on and on.[8]

One could continue indefinitely just listing one-line descriptions of ludicrous government projects, which in many cases have no real value to anyone except those paid to carry them out. Rarely does the budget contain the *only* kind of projects contemplated by the founders of the nation, namely, those of common benefit (that is, of benefit to *everyone*) that are also within the powers enumerated in the Constitution as allowable government actions.

Needless to say, constitutional limits on government action fell by the wayside years ago. Where economic interventions are concerned, the federal government received the blessing of the Supreme Court, in a series of cases between 1937 and 1942, to do virtually anything authorized by Congress.[9] Given that green light, members of Congress proved time and again that no scheme to buy votes was too outrageous to refuse. Anyone who thinks that taxes must be raised to cut the federal government's deficit, because spending already has been cut to the bone, should spend some time reading the budget documents.

Democracy Versus Rights

Of course, we've been told since childhood that all of this is just the workings of "democracy," as if taking a vote could decide the wisdom or morality of an action. The central purpose of the Constitution in the first place was to put *limits* on the actions of political representatives. A majority vote can do nothing to justify an action. The majority vote of the people or the Congress can no more justify a political action than the majority vote of a gang can justify an assault.

Majority voting is simply a decision rule for selecting the actions that will be taken from the set of all *permissible* actions. Through the years the mantra of "democracy" has been chanted over the most morally offensive actions of American governments, as if majority voting can make everything okay. It cannot. When governments override the rights of individuals, they violate their only *raison d'être*. Under the banner of democracy, the United States has built an engine of oppression so vast that it is doubtful whether it can ever be substantially reduced, much less dismantled.

Are Rights Justifiable?

Is it possible that I am taking too seriously some 200-year-old rhetoric about human rights, and that I have compounded the blunder by supposing that property rights are among the most fundamental of all human rights? After all, didn't Jeremy Bentham tell us that the notion of rights is not only nonsense, it is "nonsense on stilts"?

I admit that I am no philosopher and that, if called upon to supply a proof of the existence of human rights, I cannot provide one. Nor am I persuaded by the attempts I've seen of philosophers far better prepared than I to give the proof. But as an economist, I am trained to ask certain questions: First, what's the alternative? Second, after a choice is made, what happens next, and after that, and after that, as repercussions of the initial choice continue to have indirect effects?

Suppose you tell me, there is no such thing as rights; and I reply, okay, let's agree that there are none. Later, when a mugger accosts you and demands that you surrender your wallet on pain of having your throat slashed, am I supposed to feel that you have been wronged? Of course, you won't like this event, but the mugger will; it's just your personal loss against the mugger's personal gain.

Or suppose you wake up tomorrow morning and discover that a majority vote has been taken, and the majority or its chosen representatives have decided that all people like you—in some respect, it doesn't matter which—are to report for transportation to concentration camps. Well, that's democracy in action. Remember what happened to the Japanese-Americans in 1942.

If there are no rights, then we'll just have to get along without them. But chances are, with no conception of rights, social life will be pretty much as Hobbes thought: brutish and short, et cetera, or else everyone will end up obeying the person who wields the most power at the moment. A society that doesn't take human rights seriously and protect them will turn out sooner rather than later to be hellish. Apart from whatever one may think about the philosophical status of rights, a world without rights would not meet the aspirations of even the most thoroughgoing utilitarian. So, if one doesn't care whether people believe in rights, fine; but one must be prepared to suffer the consequences.

We know from history what happens to societies without genuine individual rights. From sweeping powers of government, unconstrained by silly notions that all individuals have rights to life, liberty, and property, come the Soviet Union and its empire, Nazi Germany, Fascist Italy, and Pol Pot's Cambodia as well as today's China, Vietnam, Cuba, and a lot of other loathsome societies that merit the full measure of our contempt and sorrow.

In due course we shall arrive at something similar in the United States, for this country is fast proceeding in the direction of subjugating all human rights, especially human rights to property, without which the others eventually will prove more or less worthless. When the government controls everybody's access to newsprint and broadcasting channels, freedom of the press won't have any real substance—just consider how shamelessly the news media performed during the recent war when the government controlled reporters' access to the theater of war. When the government controls the conditions on which people can obtain or give employment, freedom of speech won't matter much—who will jeopardize his job by speaking out against the government? When the government controls the manner in which all goods and services must be produced and the terms on which they may be sold, freedom of association won't be worth much—what good will it do to have a meeting under those conditions? A nation without firm private property rights will eventually prove unable to defend any human rights whatever. Only citizens who have secure private property rights possess a protected, autonomous position from which they can challenge their rulers. Our forefathers understood this well, but most Americans have forgotten.

Property Rights Are Human Rights

Property rights have been slandered throughout most of the 20th century, especially by people who contrast property rights and human rights, and pose a choice between them. Now, faced with such a choice, who wouldn't opt for human rights—far better to worry about human beings than about sticks and stones. But this way of posing the question is misleading and utterly unacceptable.

All rights are human rights. It is in the very nature of rights, which are morally justifiable claims on the conduct of other persons, that only human beings can possess them. Property rights don't belong to the factory in which a corporation manufactures its products; they belong to the corporation's shareholders, the individual human beings who have surrendered other property in voluntary transactions to acquire ownership claims on the factory. A related and equally foolish idea is that government can tax "business" rather than individuals. But bricks and mortar can't pay taxes; only persons can. "Taxing business" is just another term for taxing certain people differently from others.

Property rights are the human rights to decide how property will be used, to appropriate the income or other benefits of the property, and to transfer the rights of ownership to others in voluntary transactions. Everyone realizes that some degree of property ownership is essential for sustaining human life in society. But many people suppose that once we go beyond personal property such as clothing, furniture, automobiles, perhaps houses, and arrive at "bigger" property such as land, factories, mines, and railroads, private ownership no longer is essential. The supposition is wrong. Suppression of private property rights at any level tends to have socially destructive consequences.

Property rights must be lodged somewhere. Even societies that pretend to have no private rights in "bigger" property simply lodge the rights in the hands of politicians or bureaucrats. *Someone*, some human being, still decides how the property will be used and who will receive its benefits.

But without private property rights, the link is severed between rational employment of the property and the rewards or punishments of the decision-maker. Irresponsible behavior no longer carries with it an automatic punishment. Politicians or bureaucrats are free to use resources destructively—as they have in socialist economies for decades and as they have in the socialized sectors of the United States such as public education or management of public forests or rangelands or national defense production—and still the decision-makers may thrive.

Private property rights create an incentive to employ resources in their most highly valued uses as determined by consumers. Socialized property arrangements insulate the decision-makers from the preferences of consumers, who invariably suffer, as they have throughout the socialist world since 1917, and as the unfortunate people of those places, some of whom now are free to speak, readily attest.

For Sale: A Precious Birthright

As ever more rules and regulations curtail the decisions individuals may make for themselves, as ever greater proportions of people's income are siphoned off to be used as our leaders decide, as every species of special interest pays tribute to predatory politicos who suck the marrow from the bones of civil society, individuals are reduced to ever more meaningless atoms in the social cosmos. All of life becomes politicized, which means corrupted by power. And as individual liberty and individual rights die, all that is decent in human society dies with them.

Our Revolutionary forebears complained that King George had "erected a multitude of New Offices, and sent hither swarms of Officers to harass our People, and eat out their substance." But Jefferson and Madison could not have dreamed, even in their most horrifying nightmares, of the swarms of bureaucrats upon us now, harassing us and eating our substance. The nation's founders could not have understood how cheaply a wealthy society of their descendants would sell its precious birthright of liberty and justice and respect for individual rights.

No individual, of course, can do much about the state of *the nation.* *But* each of us has a mind, and with some effort one can use it to think. The next time you hear of a proposal to employ the government for still another noble purpose, think! Ask yourself: At what cost to individual liberty will this project operate? And how can we preserve our remaining liberties if we give our assent piecemeal to the thousands of new proposals for enlarging and strengthening government that pour forth each year? What will be the end result of these piranha attacks on human rights? And do you want to live in that kind of world?

---

1. Ludwig von Mises, *The Ultimate Foundation of Economic Science: An Essay on Method* (Kansas City, Kan.: Sheed Andrews and McMeel, 1978), p. 98.

2. Thomas Hobbes, *Philosophical Rudiments Concerning Government,* as reprinted in *Hobbes: Selection,* edited by Frederick J. E. Woodbridge (New York: Charles Scribner's Sons, 1930), p. 267.

3. "Declaration and Resolves of the First Continental Congress," in *Documents of American History,* edited by Henry Steele Commager (New York: Appleton-Century-Crofts, 1948), pp. 83–4.

4. "Declaration of the Causes and Necessity of Taking Up Arms," in *Documents*, pp. 92–5.

5. "The Virginia Bill of Rights," in *Documents*, p. 103.

6. "Massachusetts Bill of Rights," in *Documents*, pp. 107–08.

7. Unified agenda of Federal regulations, as cited in Robert Pear, "In Bush Presidency, the Regulators Ride Again," *The New York Times*, April 28, 1991.

8. The preceding examples, and many more, appear in a series of stories on Congress in *New Dimensions*, March 1991, pp. 22–57.

9. Robert Higgs, *Crisis and Leviathan: Critical Episodes in the Growth of American Government* (New York: Oxford University Press, 1987), pp. 180–94.

A Tale of Two Revolutions

by Robert A. Peterson

The year 1989 marks the 200th anniversary of the French Revolution. To celebrate, the French government is throwing its biggest party in at least 100 years, to last all year. In the United States, an American Committee on the French Revolution has been set up to coordinate programs on this side of the Atlantic, emphasizing the theme, "France and America: Partners in Liberty."

But were the French and American Revolutions really similar? On the surface, there were parallels. Yet over the past two centuries, many observers have likened the American Revolution to the bloodless Glorious Revolution of 1688, while the French Revolution has been considered the forerunner of the many modern violent revolutions that have ended in totalitarianism. As the Russian naturalist, author, and soldier Prince Piotr Kropotkin put it, "What we learn from the study of the Great [French] Revolution is that it was the source of all the present communist, anarchist, and socialist conceptions."[1]

It is because the French Revolution ended so violently that many Frenchmen are troubled about celebrating its 200th anniversary. French author Leon Daudet has written: "Commemorate the French Revolution? That's like celebrating the day you got scarlet fever." An anti-89 movement has even begun to sell mementos reminding today's Frenchmen of the excesses of the Revolution, including Royalist black armbands and calendars that mock the sacred dates of the French Revolution.

The French should indeed be uneasy about their Revolution, for whereas the American Revolution brought forth a relatively free economy and limited government, the French Revolution brought forth first anarchy, then dictatorship.

Eighteenth-century France was the largest and most populous country in western Europe. Blessed with rich soil, natural resources, and a long and varied coastline, France was Europe's greatest power and the dominant culture on the continent. Unfortunately, like all the other countries of eighteenth-century Europe, France was saddled

Mr. Peterson is headmaster of The Pilgrim Academy in Egg Harbor City, New Jersey. This article was originally published in the August 1989 issue of *The Freeman*.

with the economic philosophy of mercantilism. By discouraging free trade with other countries, mercantilism kept the economies of the European nation-states in the doldrums, and their people in poverty.

Nevertheless, in 1774, King Louis XVI made a decision that could have prevented the French Revolution by breathing new life into the French economy: he appointed Physiocrat Robert Turgot as Controller General of Finance. The Physiocrats were a small band of followers of the French physician François Quesnay, whose economic prescriptions included reduced taxes, less regulation, the elimination of government-granted monopolies and internal tolls and tariffs—ideas that found their rallying cry in the famous slogan, "laissez-faire, laissez-passer."

The Physiocrats exerted a profound influence on Adam Smith, who had spent time in France in the 1760s and whose classic *The Wealth of Nations* embodied the Physiocratic attack on mercantilism and argued that nations get rich by practicing free trade.[2] Of Turgot, and the Physiocrats, the great French statesman and author Frederic Bastiat (1801–1850) wrote: "The basis of their whole economic system may be truly said to lie in the principle of self-interest.... The only function of government according to this doctrine is to protect life, liberty, and property."[3]

Embracing the principle of free trade not just as a temporary expedient, but as a philosophy, Turgot got the king to sign an edict in January 1776 that abolished the monopolies and special privileges of the guilds, corporations, and trading companies. He also abolished the forced labor of the peasants on the roads, the hated *corvée*. He then dedicated himself to breaking down the internal tariffs within France. By limiting government expense, he was able to cut the budget by 60 million livres and reduce the interest on the national debt from 8.7 million livres to 3 million livres.

Had Turgot been allowed to pursue his policies of free trade and less government intervention, France might very well have become Europe's first "common market" and avoided violent revolution. A rising tide would have lifted all ships. Unfortunately for France and the cause of freedom, resistance from the Court and special interests proved too powerful, and Turgot was removed from office in 1776. "The dismissal of this great man," wrote Voltaire, "crushes me.... Since that fatal day, I have not followed anything ... and am waiting patiently for someone to cut our throats."[4] Turgot's successors, following a mercantilist policy of government intervention, only made the French economy worse. In a desperate move to find money in the face of an uproar across the country and to re-establish harmony, Louis

XVI agreed to convene the Estates-General for May 1789. Meanwhile, the king's new finance minister, Jacques Necker, a Swiss financial expert, delayed the effects of mercantilism by importing large amounts of grain.

On May 5, the Estates-General convened at Versailles. By June 17, the Third Estate had proclaimed itself the National Assembly. Three days later, the delegates took the famous Tennis Court Oath, vowing not to disband until France had a new constitution.

But the real French Revolution began not at Versailles but on the streets of Paris. On July 14, a Parisian mob attacked the old fortress known as the Bastille, liberating, as one pundit put it, "two fools, four forgers and a debaucher." The Bastille was no longer being used as a political prison, and Louis XVI had even made plans to destroy it. That made little difference to the mob, who were actually looking for weapons.

Promising the guards safe conduct if they surrendered, the leaders of the mob broke their word and hacked them to death. It would be the first of many broken promises. Soon the heads, torsos, and hands of the Bastille's former guardians were bobbing along the street on pikes. "In all," as historian Otto Scott put it, "a glorious victory of unarmed citizens over the forces of tyranny, or so the newspapers and history later said."[5] The French Revolution had begun.

Despite the bloodshed at the Bastille and the riots in Paris, there was some clear-headed thinking. Mirabeau wanted to keep the Crown but restrain it. "We need a government like England's," he said.[6] But the French not only hated things English, they even began to despise their own cultural heritage—the good as well as the bad. On October 5, the Assembly adopted the Declaration of the Rights of Man and the Citizen—a good document all right, but only if it were followed.

Twenty-eight days later, the Assembly showed they had no intention of doing so: all church property in France was confiscated by the government. It was the wrong way to go about creating a free society. Certainly the Church was responsible for some abuses, but seeking to build a free society by undermining property rights is like cutting down trees to grow a forest. Such confiscation only sets a precedent for further violation of property rights, which in turn violates individual rights—the very rights of man and the citizen the new government was so loudly proclaiming. By confiscating church property—no matter how justified—France's Revolutionary leaders showed that they weren't interested in a true free society, only in one created in the image of their own philosophers. As Bastiat later pointed out, they were among the modern world's first social engineers.

Soon France began to descend into an abyss in which it would remain for the next 25 years. In towns where royalist mayors were still popular, bands of men invaded town halls and killed city magistrates. Thousands of people sold their homes and fled the country, taking with them precious skills and human capital. François Babeuf, the first modern communist, created a Society of Equals dedicated to the abolition of private property and the destruction of all those who held property. The king's guards were eventually captured and killed. The Marquis de Sade, from whom we get the term sadism, was released from prison. The Paris Commune took over control of Paris.

Fiat Money Inflation

The actions of the government were even more radical than those of the people at large. In order to meet the continuing economic crisis, the Assembly resorted to paper money—the infamous assignats, backed ostensibly by the confiscated church property. Although most of the delegates were aware of the dangers of paper money, it was thought that if the government issued only a small amount—and that backed up by the confiscated property—the assignats would not create the kind of economic disaster that had accompanied the use of paper money in the past.

But as had happened again and again through history, the government proved unable to discipline itself. As Andrew Dickson White put it in his *Fiat Money Inflation in France*: "New issues of paper were then clamored for as more drams are demanded by a drunkard. New issues only increased the evil; capitalists were all the more reluctant to embark their money on such a sea of doubt. Workmen of all sorts were more and more thrown out of employment. Issue after issue of currency came; but no relief resulted save a momentary stimulus which aggravated the disease."[7]

Writing from England in 1790, long before the French inflation had done its worst, Edmund Burke saw the danger of fiat currency. According to Burke, issuing assignats was the government's pat answer to any problem: "Is there a debt which presses them? Issue assignats. Are compensations to be made or a maintenance decreed to those whom they have robbed of their free-hold in their office, or expelled from their profession? Assignats. Is a fleet to be fitted out? Assignats.... Are the old assignats depreciated at market? What is the remedy? Issue new assignats." The leaders of France, said Burke, were like quack doctors who urged the same remedy for every illness.

Burke saw in the French Revolution not a decrease in the power of the state, but an increase in it: "The establishment of a system of liberty would of course be supposed to give it [France's currency] new strength; and so it would actually have done if a system of liberty had been established." As for the confiscation of property—first that of the Catholic Church then that of anyone accused of being an enemy of the Revolution—Burke said: "Never did a state, in any case, enrich itself by the confiscation of the citizens."[8]

But the issuing of assignats was only the beginning. In the spring of 1792, the first Committee of Public Safety was established, charged with judging and punishing traitors. Soon the streets of Paris began to run with blood, as thousands of people were killed by the guillotine. The following fall, the French government announced that it was prepared to help subject peoples everywhere win their freedom. Thus, instead of peacefully exporting French products and French ideas on liberty, the French began exporting war and revolution ... hence the saying, "When France sneezes, the whole world catches cold."

As more soldiers were needed to "liberate" the rest of Europe, France instituted history's first universal levy—the ultimate in state control over the lives of its citizens. Meanwhile, for opposing the Revolution, most of the city of Lyons was destroyed. And Lafayette, who at first had embraced the Revolution, was arrested as a traitor.

Stifling Controls

Soon a progressive income tax was passed, prices on grain were fixed, and the death penalty was meted out to those who refused to sell at the government's prices. Every citizen was required to carry an identity card issued by his local commune, called, in an Orwellian twist of language, Certificates of Good Citizenship. Every house had to post an outside listing of its legal occupants; the Revolutionary Communes had committees that watched everyone in the neighborhood; and special passes were needed to travel from one city to another. The jails were soon filled with more people than they had been under Louis XVI. Eventually, there flooded forth such a torrent of laws that virtually every citizen was technically guilty of crimes against the state. The desire for absolute equality resulted in everyone's being addressed as "citizen," much as the modern-day Communist is referred to as "comrade."

Education was centralized and bureaucratized. The old traditions, dialects, and local allegiances that helped prevent centralization—and thus tyranny—were swept away as the Assembly placed a mathematical grid of departments, cantons, and municipalities on an unsuspecting France. Each department was to be run exactly as its neighbor. Since "differences" were aristocratic, plans were made to erase individual cultures, dialects, and customs. In order to accomplish this, teachers—paid by the State—began to teach a uniform language. Curriculum was controlled totally by the central government. Summing up this program, Saint-Just said, "Children belong to the State," and advocated taking boys from their families at the age of five.[9]

So much of modern statism—with all of its horror and disregard for individualism—began with the French Revolution. The "purge," the "commune," the color red as a symbol of statism, even the political terms Left, Right, and Center came to us from this period. The only thing that ended the carnage—inside France, at least—was "a man on horseback," Napoleon Bonaparte. The French Revolution had brought forth first anarchy, then statism, and finally, dictatorship. Had it not been for the indomitable spirit of the average Frenchman and France's position as the largest country in Western Europe, France might never have recovered.

Now contrast all of this with the American Revolution—more correctly called the War for Independence. The American Revolution was different because, as Irving Kristol has pointed out, it was "a mild and relatively bloodless revolution. A war was fought to be sure, and soldiers died in that war. But . . . there was none of the butchery which we have come to accept as a natural concomitant of revolutionary warfare. . . . There was no 'revolutionary justice'; there was no reign of terror; there were no bloodthirsty proclamations by the Continental Congress."[10]

A "Conservative Revolution"

The American Revolution was essentially a "conservative" movement, fought to conserve the freedoms America had painstakingly developed since the 1620s during the period of British "salutary neglect"—in reality, a period of laissez-faire government as far as the colonies were concerned. Samuel Eliot Morison has pointed out: "[T]he American Revolution was not fought to *obtain* freedom, but to *preserve* the liberties that Americans already had as colonials. Independence was no conscious goal, secretly nurtured in cellar or jungle by bearded conspirators, but a reluctant last resort, to preserve 'life, liberty, and the pursuit of happiness.' "[11]

A sense of restraint pervaded this whole period. In the Boston Tea Party, no one was hurt and no property was damaged save for the tea. One patriot even returned the next day to replace a lock on a sea chest that had been accidentally broken.[12] This was not the work of anarchists who wanted to destroy everything in their way, but of Englishmen who simply wanted a redress of grievances.

After the Boston Massacre, when the British soldiers who had fired upon the crowd were brought to trial, they were defended by American lawyers James Otis and John Adams. In any other "revolution," these men would have been calling for the deaths of the offending soldiers. Instead, they were defending them in court.

When the war finally began, it took over a year for the colonists to declare their independence. During that year, officers in the Continental Army still drank to "God save the King." When independence was finally declared, it was more out of desperation than careful planning, as the colonists sought help from foreign nations, particularly the French. In the end, it was the French monarchy—not the Revolutionists, as they had not yet come to power—that helped America win its independence.

Through the seven years of the American war, there were no mass executions, no "reigns of terror," no rivers of blood flowing in the streets of America's cities. When a Congressman suggested to George Washington that he raid the countryside around Valley Forge to feed his starving troops, he flatly refused, saying that such an action would put him on the same level as the invaders.

Most revolutions consume those who start them; in France, Marat, Robespierre, and Danton all met violent deaths. But when Washington was offered a virtual dictatorship by some of his officers at Newburgh, New York, he resisted his natural impulse to take command and urged them to support the republican legislative process. Professor Andrew C. McLaughlin has pointed out: "To teach our youth and persuade ourselves that the heroes of the controversy were only those taking part in tea-parties and various acts of violence is to inculcate the belief that liberty and justice rest in the main upon lawless force. And yet as a matter of plain fact, the self-restraint of the colonists is the striking theme; and their success in actually establishing institutions under which we still live was a remarkable achievement. No one telling the truth about the Revolution will attempt to conceal the fact that there was disorder. . . . [Yet] we find it marked on the whole by constructive political capacity."[13]

No Assault on Freedom of Religion

In America, unlike France, where religious dissenters were put to death, there was no wholesale assault on freedom of religion. At the

Constitutional Convention in 1787, there were devout Congregational-
ists, Episcopalians, Dutch Reformed, Lutherans, Quakers, Presbyteri-
ans, Methodists, and Roman Catholics. Deist Ben Franklin asked for
prayer during the Convention, while several months later George
Washington spoke at a synagogue. During the Revolution, many
members of the Continental Congress attended sermons preached by
Presbyterian John Witherspoon, and while Thomas Jefferson worked
to separate church and state in Virginia, he personally raised money
to help pay the salaries of Anglican ministers who would lose their
tax-supported paychecks. In matters of religion, the leaders of America's Revolution agreed to disagree.

Finally, unlike the French Revolution, the American Revolution
brought forth what would become one of the world's freest societies.
There were, of course, difficulties. During the "critical period" of
American history, from 1783 to 1787, the 13 states acted as 13 separate
nations, each levying import duties as it pleased. As far as New York
was concerned, tariffs could be placed on New Jersey cider, produced
across the river, as easily as on West Indian rum. The war had been
won, but daily battles in the marketplace were being lost.

The U.S. Constitution changed all that by forbidding states to levy
tariffs against one another. The result was, as John Chamberlain put
it in his history of American business, "the greatest 'common market'
in history."[14] The Constitution also sought to protect property rights,
including rights to ideas (patents and copyrights) and beliefs (the First
Amendment). For Madison, this was indeed the sole purpose of civil
government. In 1792 he wrote: "Government is instituted to protect
property of every sort. . . . This being the end of government, that alone
is a *just* government which *impartially* secures to every man whatever
is his *own*."[15] Alexander Hamilton, the first Secretary of the Treasury,
helped restore faith in the public credit with his economic program. It
was at his urging that the U.S. dollar was defined in terms of hard
money—silver and gold. (At the Constitutional Convention, the delegates were so opposed to fiat paper money that Luther Martin of
Maryland complained that they were "filled with paper money dread.")

Hamilton's centralizing tendencies would have been inappropri-
ate at any other time in American history; but in the 1790s, his program helped 13 nations combine to form one United States. Had succeeding Treasury Secretaries continued Hamilton's course of strengthening the federal government, at the expense of the states, America's
economic expansion would have been stillborn.

Fortunately, when Jefferson came to power, he brought with him
the Swiss financier and economist Albert Gallatin, who served Jeffer-

son for two terms and Madison for one. Unlike his fellow countryman Necker, whose mercantilist policies only hastened the coming of the French Revolution, Gallatin was committed to limited government and free market economic policies. Setting the tone for his Administration, Jefferson said in his first inaugural address: "Still one thing more, fellow citizens—a wise and frugal government, which shall restrain men from injuring one another, shall leave them otherwise free to regulate their own pursuits of industry and improvement, and shall not take from the mouth of labor the bread it has earned."

For the next eight years, Jefferson and Gallatin worked to reduce the nation's debt as well as its taxes. The national debt was cut from $83 million to $57 million, and the number of Federal employees was reduced. Despite the restrictions on trade caused by Napoleon's Berlin and Milan decrees, and the British blockade of Europe, American businessmen continued to develop connections around the world. By the end of Jefferson's first term, he was able to ask, "What farmer, what mechanic, what laborer ever sees a tax gatherer in the United States?"[16] By 1810, America was well on its way to becoming the world's greatest economic power. France, meanwhile, still languished under the heavy hand of Napoleon.

In his Report to the House of Representatives that same year, Gallatin summed up the reasons for America's prosperity: "No cause ... has perhaps more promoted in every respect the general prosperity of the United States than the absence of those systems of internal restrictions and monopoly which continue to disfigure the state of society in other countries. No law exists here directly or indirectly confining man to a particular occupation or place, or excluding any citizen from any branch he may at any time think proper to pursue. Industry is in every respect perfectly free and unfettered; every species of trade, commerce, art, profession, and manufacture being equally opened to all without requiring any previous regular apprenticeship, admission, or license."[17] The American Revolution was followed by 200 years of economic growth under the same government. By contrast, the French Revolution was followed by political instability, including three revolutions, a directorate, a Reign of Terror, a dictatorship, a restoration of the Bourbon Monarchy, another monarchy, and five republics. Today, socialism has a greater hold in France than it does in America—although America is not far behind. Even though they were close in time, it was the French Revolution that set the pattern for the Russian Revolution and other modern revolutions, not the American.

Bastiat's Opinion

Frederic Bastiat clearly saw the difference between the two. The French Revolution, he argued, was based on the idea of Rousseau that society is contrary to nature, and therefore must be radically changed. Because, according to Rousseau, the "social contract" had been violated early in man's history, it allowed all parties to that contract to return to a state of "natural liberty." In essence, what Rousseau was saying was, "Sweep aside all the restraints of property and society, destroy the existing system. Then you will be free, free to lose yourself in the collective good of mankind, under my care."[18]

The social architects who emerged out of the chaos of the French Revolution included Robespierre and Napoleon. In his analysis of Robespierre, Bastiat said: "Note that when Robespierre demands a dictatorship, it is ... to make his own moral principles prevail by means of terror.... Oh, you wretches! ... You want to reform everything! Reform yourselves first! This will be enough of a task for you."[19]

In Bastiat's opinion, the French Revolution failed because it repudiated the very principles upon which a free society is based: self-government, property rights, free markets, and limited civil government. The American Revolution, however, brought forth the world's freest society: "Look at the United States," wrote Bastiat. "There is no country in the world where the law confines itself more rigorously to its proper role, which is to guarantee everyone's liberty and property. Accordingly, there is no country in which the social order seems to rest on a more stable foundation.... This is how they understand freedom and democracy in the United States. There each citizen is vigilant with a jealous care to remain his own master. It is by virtue of such freedom that the poor hope to emerge from poverty, and that the rich hope to preserve their wealth. And, in fact, as we see, in a very short time this system has brought the Americans to a degree of enterprise, security, wealth, and equality of which the annals of the human race offer no other example.... [In America] each person can in full confidence dedicate his capital and his labor to production. He does not have to fear that his plans and calculations will be upset from one instant to another by the legislature."[20]

Bastiat did see two inconsistencies in the American Republic: slavery ("a violation of the rights of a person") and tariffs ("a violation of the right to property"). According to Bastiat, these were the two issues that would divide America if they were not dealt with speedily.

What was the answer for America as well as France? "Be responsible for ourselves," said Bastiat. "Look to the State for nothing beyond law and order. Count on it for no wealth, no enlightenment. No more holding it responsible for our faults, our negligence, our improvidence. Count only on ourselves for our subsistence, our physical, intellectual, and moral progress!"[21]

On the 200th anniversary of the French Revolution, Frenchmen and Americans can truly become partners in liberty by working toward the principles advocated by Bastiat, America's Founding Fathers, and others: limited government, private property, free markets, and free men.

1. Piotr Kropotkin, *The Great French Revolution* (New York: Putnam's Sons, 1909), Introduction.

2. So strong were the connections between the Physiocrats and Adam Smith that, according to the French economists Charles Gide and Charles Rist, "But for the death of Quesnay in 1774—two years before the publication of *The Wealth of Nations*—Smith would have dedicated his masterpiece to him." Later Frederic Bastiat lumped Smith, Quesnay, and Turgot together as "my guides and masters." Dean Russell, *Frederic Bastiat: Ideas and Influence* (Irvington-on-Hudson. N.Y.: The Foundation for Economic Education, 1969), pp. 58, 19.

3. Russell, p. 20.

4. Peter Gay and R. K. Webb, *Modern Europe to 1815* (New York: Harper and Row, 1973), p. 462.

5. Otto J. Scott, *Robespierre: The Voice of Virtue* (New York: Mason and Lipscomb Publishers, 1974), pp. 59–61.

6. *Ibid.*, p. 54.

7. Andrew Dickson White, *Fiat Money Inflation in France* (Irvington-on-Hudson, N.Y.: The Foundation for Economic Education, 1959), p. 107.

8. Edmund Burke, *Reflections on the Revolution in France* (Indianapolis: The Bobbs-Merrill Co., 1955, originally published in 1790), pp. 275–276, 280.

9. Scott, pp. 223–224.

10. Benjamin Hart, *Faith and Freedom* (Dallas: Lewis and Stanley, 1988), p. 301.

11. Samuel Eliot Morison, *The Oxford History of the American People* (New York: Oxford University Press, 1965), p. 182.

12. Gene Fisher and Glen Chambers, *The Revolution Myth* (Greenville, S.C.: Bob Jones University Press, 1981), p.18.

13. Andrew C. McLaughlin, *The Foundations of American Constitutionalism* (New York: Fawcett, 1932, 1961), pp. 88–89.

14. John Chamberlain, *The Enterprising Americans: A Business History of the United States* (New York: Harper and Row Publishers, 1974, 1981), p. 37.

15. *Letters and Other Writings of James Madison*, Vol. IV (New York: R. Worthington, 1884), p. 478.

16. James Richardson, ed., *A Compilation of the Messages and Papers of the Presidents*, Vol. 1 (New York: Bureau of National Literature, 1897) p. 367.

17. John M. Blum, et al., *The National Experience*, Part I (New York: Harcourt Brace Jovanovich, 1963, 1981), p. 213.

18. George Charles Roche, *Frederic Bastiat: A Man Alone* (New Rochelle, N.Y.: Arlington House, 1971), pp. 146–147.

19. *Ibid.*, p. 148.
20. *Ibid.*, pp. 205–206, 244.
21. *Ibid.*, p. 164.

A Law for Governments

by Clarence B. Carson

According to the lore of our time, business monopolies are highly dangerous—so dangerous in their threat to the commonweal that they must either be prevented or regulated and controlled. For many years, attention has been focused on the supposed untoward character of business activities and of how the innocent may fall victim to them. This emphasis has drawn men's eyes and attention away from both the source of harmful business monopoly and the noncommercial monopoly which poses the greatest threat of all to the peace and well-being of peoples. That is the monopoly which government has—*the monopoly of the use of force in a given jurisdiction.* All other monopolies pale before this one in the potentialities for destructiveness, and it is this power alone which can give to business activities potentialities for continued and concerted damage.

Yet, government is not only a great potential danger but also a necessity. Unless somebody has a monopoly of the use of force in a given jurisdiction, there is likely to be more or less continuous warfare as groups contend for control. That there be a monopoly within a jurisdiction necessary for peace, and government is also charged with keeping the peace—with preventing aggression from abroad, with putting down domestic insurrection, with inhibiting assault, deception, and with settling disputes which may arise. In short, government is not only potentially dangerous but also potentially highly beneficial. In any case, it is necessary.

The dangers of government are manifold: that it will be despotic, arbitrary, tyrannical, confiscatory, dictatorial, weak and ineffective, strong and overbearing, aggressive, destructive of life and property, playing favorites, and so on. Nor is there an abuse of which those who govern are capable that has not many times been practiced. Rulers have from time immemorial perpetrated aggressive war, deceived their own and other peoples, raped and ravished, stolen and confiscated, put the innocent to death, and allowed the guilty to run loose and wreak havoc. To say that governments have also dispensed justice

Dr. Carson has written and taught extensively, specializing in American intellectual history. This article was first published in the January 1970 issue of *The Freeman*.

and maintained the peace is equally true, but it should not mislead as to the inherent dangers of such an instrument.

The existence of government poses a grave and recurring danger. It poses a problem, too, which may be stated in various ways. How shall this force of government be contained and restrained? How shall those who govern—for after all, the danger that government poses arises from those who govern—be kept from acting arbitrarily and despotically? How shall those who make, administer, and interpret the laws themselves be brought under the law? This last is, in essence, the question as it should ever be posed. It should be clear that there is no easy answer to it, nor is it likely that the problem will be finally solved. Government operates by the exercise of power. To do its job effectively, it must have a monopoly of the use of force in a jurisdiction. Yet such a monopoly makes it most difficult to bring government under the law. There must first be a law for governments. Then, devices must be found for inducing those who govern to abide by the law.

Natural Law and Constitutions

In modern (post Renaissance) Western civilization two intertwined devices have been employed to bring those who govern under the law—to establish a law for governments. The first—and most fundamental—of these is the natural law theory. The second is the device of having a written constitution.

These methods did not arise in a vacuum. Instead, there were compelling circumstances for coming up with some means of bringing rulers under the law. The major political trend in many European countries was toward absolute monarchy in the sixteenth and seventeenth centuries. This meant, in theory, that all power issued from the monarch and might be claimed by him. Also, it tended to mean that there was nobody to hold the monarch in check, or make him subject to the law. The inevitable result was rule at the whim of the monarch—arbitrary and despotic government. Not everywhere and at all times was it equally the case, but it was certainly the dominant trend.

The natural law theory provided the foundation, in these circumstances, for bringing government under the rule of law, for delimiting the powers of the monarch most particularly. Here was a law above and beyond the power of monarchs to alter and to which they, like other men, were subject. Natural law theory was not, of course, new to the sixteenth and seventeenth centuries. It had been effectively formulated by the Roman Stoics, and following that formulation became a part of the heritage of Western civilization. It received new impetus not only from the need to find some means for circumscribing the powers of monarchs but also from Renaissance humanism and the scientific developments of the seventeenth century.

Some of the early spokesmen for natural law theory on the continent of Europe were Hugo Grotius (1583–1645), Samuel Pufendorf (1632–1694), and Jean Bodin (1530–1596); in England, Richard Hooker (1554–1600), James Harrington (1611–1677), and Algernon Sidney (1622–1683). From these, and others, it entered a general stream of thought to be espoused by such continental European, English, and American thinkers as Burlamaqui, Vattel, Beccarai, Locke, Blackstone, Montesquieu, John Wise, Jonathan Mayhew, and Thomas Jefferson, until it was the dominant mode of thought in the eighteenth century.

A Law Antecedent to Man

Basically, the modern natural law theory held that there is a law antecedent to man, society, and government, that this law is from God, that it is a law which must be observed if each of these is to reach its true form and fulfillment. It is discovered by attending to the nature of things, and when one attends rightly to the nature of things, he is using right reason. When man's nature and the nature of the universe are viewed in this fashion, it is found that man has certain natural rights: namely, the right to life, to the use of one's faculties, and to the fruits of one's labors. Society is natural to man—man is a social being—for within society he can make those exchanges which satisfy and complete him. In like manner, government is necessary for man, for it enables him to live in peace, to have fruitful relations with others, and keep what is his.

The great thrust of modern natural law thought was to limit government to its proper sphere. One historian of natural law says, "Now the primary practical object pursued by the theorists of Natural Law was the delimitation of an area within which objective Right should be withdrawn from the caprice of the legislator, and subjective Right should escape the attacks of the State's authority.... It was thus with a new and unprecedented force that the theory of Natural Law was able to enter the domain of public law...."[1]

That the natural law set bounds to the actions of government was the import of what many of the theorists had to say. Hugo Grotius declared that "it is beyond controversy among all good men that if the persons in authority command anything contrary to Natural Law or the divine precepts, it is not to be done.... First, those rulers who are subject to the people ... , if they transgress against the laws of the State, may not only be resisted, but put to death. ... "[2] Burlamaqui maintained that "if the abuse of the legislative power proceeds to excess, and to the subversion of the fundamental principles of the laws of nature, and of the duties which it enjoins, it is certain that under such circumstances, the subjects are by the laws of God not only authorized, but even obliged to refuse obedience to all laws of this kind."[3] John Locke particularized "the bounds which the trust that is put in them by the society, and the law of God and nature have set to the legislative power of every commonwealth, in all forms of government."[4]

Natural law theory would not, of itself, bring governments under the law. Natural law has presumably been in existence since the beginning of time. Nor have great thinkers from time to time been wanting in their understanding of its precepts. But as a theory, the natural law does not and has not prevented arbitrary and despotic government. The second step in bringing under the law those who govern was to specify the laws for those who rule in a particular state—to have a constitution.

The British Model

The British pointed the way to constitutional government. Indeed, the British had a long history of attempting to subject their government to the law. Most of this effort was devoted to making the king rule by and observe the law. The question was usually phrased in this way: Is the king above the law? Sir John Fortescue, the leading legal mind of fifteenth century England, maintained that the king was not above the law. But Fortescue was not taking a novel position in English history, though he may have taken it more pointedly than had his predecessors. It had been made dramatically clear at least two centuries before that the king should not be considered above the law. The main thrust of the Magna Carta which King John signed in 1215 was his acknowledgment that he must observe the established legal procedures in his acts.

The matter came to a head once more in the seventeenth century, and more famous documents were added to the English constitution. The Stuart kings claimed absolute powers, and their subjects took action to restrain them. Charles I subscribed to the Petition of Right which spelled out new limitations on his power. The Bill of Rights, proclaimed in the latter part of the seventeenth century, settled the matter definitively. The king was brought decisively under the law.

It was never made so clear, by documents, however, that the other branches of government were under the law. The great model of a constitution which set forth a thoroughgoing law for government is the U. S. Constitution, supplemented by the constitutions of the states. Here, for the first time effectively, a law for all branches of government was committed to paper. That the U. S. Constitution is a law for the government it authorizes must not be generally understood. Yet that is what it is. Every one of the original passages deals with the powers of government, with the authority of those who govern, or with how they shall be chosen, for how long they shall serve, what their qualifications shall be, and how the Constitution shall be ratified and amended. The Constitution is not a law for the citizenry, except in respect to how they shall be governed and what political procedures shall be followed. It is a fundamental law for government.

Limitations upon Government

This character of the Constitution may be clearly shown by quoting a few passages from it. Article I, section 1, reads: "All legislative Powers herein granted shall be vested in a Congress of the United States, which shall consist of a Senate and House of Representatives." The remainder of that portion deals with qualifications of legislators, the conduct of their business, and the extent of the legislative authority. Article II, section 1, reads: "The executive Power shall be vested in a President of the United States of America. He shall hold his Office during the Term of four Years, and, together with the Vice President, chosen for the same Term, be elected, as follows. . . ." There follows a description of the mode of election, the qualifications for the office, how the President may be replaced, and a listing of his powers and duties. Article III, section 1, begins: "The judicial Power of the United States, shall be vested in one supreme Court, and in such inferior Courts as the Congress may from time to time ordain and establish." This, too, is followed by an account of the authority and jurisdiction of the Federal courts.

Article IV as well as parts of Article I deal with prescriptions for and limitations on state governments. For example, Article IV, section 1, says: "Full Faith and Credit shall be given in each State to the public Acts, Records, and judicial proceedings of every other State. And the Congress may by general Laws prescribe the Manner in which such Acts, Records and proceedings shall be proved, and the Effect thereof." Article I, section 10, contains such points as these: "No State shall enter into any Treaty . . . ; coin Money; emit Bills of Credit; pass any ... Law impairing the Obligation of Contracts...." Article V sets forth procedures for amendment.

Article VI proclaims all earlier debts of the United States valid, declares that all laws and treaties made under the authorization of the Constitution the supreme law of the land, and prescribes the oath binding upon all officers of the United States and of the several states. Article VII simply prescribes the method and how many states shall be necessary for ratification of the Constitution.

It is the fact that the Constitution is a law for governments that makes it so important that its provisions be rigorously observed. It is important, of course, that private individuals abide by the law. It is even more important that those who govern abide by the law, for when they act lawlessly they do so with the full force of government.

Separation of Powers

Drawing up a law for governments was one thing; getting it observed was something else. The answer to monopolistic abuses in private industry is competition. If a company does not serve well or its products are exorbitantly priced, in a free market others may enter the field and subject that company to the discipline of the marketplace. There is not so ready a solution to the problem posed by a government's monopoly of the use of force. Direct competition among governments is a thing to be avoided rather than sought, for direct competition in the use of force is warfare.

Yet, it is possible to use the competition principle in a modified form without inviting perpetual warfare. One way that this has been done is by the separation of powers within the government so that those who govern may check and restrain one another. The famous formulation of this doctrine was made by Montesquieu in *The Spirit of the Laws*. He reasoned in this fashion:

> When the legislative and executive powers are united in the same person, or in the same body of magistrates, there can be no liberty; because apprehensions may arise lest the same monarch or senate should enact tyrannical laws, to execute them in a tyrannical manner.
>
> Again, there is no liberty if the power of judging be not separated from the legislative and executive powers. Were it joined with the legislative, the life and liberty of the subject would be exposed to arbitrary control; for the judge would

then be the legislator. Were it joined to the executive power, the judge might behave with all the violence of an oppressor.[5]

Looking at it in another way, the separation of powers principle may be seen as a means of inhibiting tyrannical power by bringing those who govern under the law. Whereas, if the powers are joined in a single body, there would be nobody to see that it observed the law.

American Federalism

The British government was thought by Montesquieu to embody the separation-of-powers principle in the eighteenth century. So it did, for the monarch was reduced mainly to the execution of the laws, Parliament enacted the laws, and there was a more or less independent judiciary. Americans accepted Montesquieu's formulation as an article of belief and separated the powers of government both in the United States Constitution and in those of the states.

Americans went further than this in retaining as much of the competitive principle as practicable in order to keep government under the law. They set up a federal system of government, one in which the powers of government were dispersed among the general and the state governments. Each of these governments was to have a jurisdiction over the citizenry under it. This made it so that a grasp for power by those in one government would tend to endanger the powers of those in the other. They might be expected in their own interest to resist expansions of power and hence restrain each other.

Checks and Balances

An even more subtle form of competition is inherent in the republican form of government established in the United States. Those who govern derive their tenure from the consent of the people, either directly or indirectly. That government be under the law is a condition of the liberty of the people. That is, an increase in the powers of government will be at the expense of the people, or some portion of them. Hence, the electorate may be jealous of their own prerogatives and resist the extension of government power. At the least, they may turn out of power those politicians who have displeased them when they come up for election.

Under the influence of Britain and the United States other peoples turned with a will to the task of establishing a law for their governments in the nineteenth century. Constitutions were drawn up, elective legislatures set up or buttressed, powers balanced and checked, and arbitrariness restrained. Limited governments provided for more liberty than most peoples had ever known. In many ways, this movement toward constitutional government reached its peak—and its virtual culmination—in the wake of World War I when the old autocratic governments were overturned, the territories of empires carved up into nation-states, and constitutions adopted which were supposed to provide extensive liberties for the inhabitants.

Twentieth-Century Reformers Revert Toward Tyranny

But a counter tendency had already set in, one which would eventuate in new tyrannies, arbitrary governments, dictatorships, and oppression. The first peoples to fall under the new despotism were the Russians, with the establishment of the Soviet Union in the early 1920s. They were followed by the Italians, Germans, and many others in various degree. Behind much of this thrust was not only the age-old desire of those who govern to be unlimited in their exercise of power but also a rationale for the concentration and exercise of power. That rationale can be called, generically, socialism, though it is known also as communism, fascism, collectivism, syndicalism, and "liberalism." The animating idea behind it is the determination to use government power to make over man and society according to an ideological vision of what they should be. The effort to accomplish this is made by massive applications of government power. This power is applied in order to attempt to manage and control the economy, redistribute the wealth of the land, provide favors for the indigent, empower certain groups, disable certain others, and bring the whole under the sway of government. In some lands, this has been done directly, brutally, and dictatorially. In others, such as the United States, the effort has been made much more subtly, with a minimum of the show of force, and in the framework of other forms of government. In all cases, however, the effort has been made by unloosing those who govern and restricting and restraining the general populace.

That tyrannies have made their appearance in some places in our century is well known. That some peoples have fallen under the yoke of oppression is rather generally recognized. All too often, however, this has been attributed to certain evil men—as, for example, Adolf Hitler and Joseph Stalin—and not to the more basic development. When this latter character is recognized, it should be clear that the task is to bring governments under the law. It is, or should be, the pressing issue of our times. There has been much talk in recent years in the United States of the need to restore law and order. Undoubtedly, there is such a need. It is important that citizens obey the law that order may prevail. But if it is only the inhabitants who obey the law, their obedience will quite often simply aid the establishment of tyranny. Those who govern must also obey the law, the law for governments. All governments are subject to law—the natural law. Beyond that, they may have their particular constitutions which establish the laws for those who govern. Rigorous adherence to these is necessary for government to be limited so that the citizenry may be free.

---

1. Otto Gierke, *Natural Law and the Theory of Society*, Ernest Barker, trans. (Boston: Beacon Press, 1957), p. 39.

2. Wilson O. Clough, ed., *Intellectual Origins of American National Thought* (New York: Corinth Books, 1961), pp. 174–75.

3. *Ibid.*, p. 194.

4. *Ibid.*, p. 159.

5. *Ibid.*, p. 186.

The Fruits of Independence

by Clarence B. Carson

The Constitution of 1787 was a culmination. It was the culmination of a decade of constitution making in the states and for the United States. It was the culmination of several long traditions. For one, it was the culmination of a British tradition of having written acknowledgements and guarantees of rights and liberties. For another, it was the culmination of a colonial tradition of having governments based upon charters. And for yet another, it was the fruition of the Judeo-Christian and Protestant practice of appealing to the precise written word. The Constitution brought to fertile fruition, too, the natural law philosophy. The natural rights doctrine, which held a central place in the justification of revolt against British rule, now served as a basis for protecting rights and freeing people under independence.

That is a way of saying that liberty was the great motivating theme of these years. The desire to preserve and extend their liberty moved the Patriots to break from England, to fight a War for Independence, and to establish their own governments. The constitution making of these years was animated by the determination to establish liberty more firmly upon these shores. Of course, those who participated in these activities were under the sway of a whole range of motives, ranging from the noble to ordinary to sometimes base ones, as people always are. But what distinguished them, surely, was the steadfast determination to establish liberty.

Limited Government

The Founders believed that for people to have liberty and enjoy their rights governments must be limited and restrained. They believed that government is necessary, of course. It is necessary because men without government would do violence to one another; the strong would prey upon the weak; the clever would take unjust advantage of others; disorder would prevail. Or, to put it another way, man is a fallen creature and must be restrained from harming others.

This article is reprinted from Dr. Carson's book series, *A Basic History of the United States*, and appeared in the September 1984 issue of *The Freeman*.

But governments are made up of men as well, and those who govern are given unusual power over others. It is especially important, then, that government be limited and restrained. If men were angels, Madison observed, they would have no need of government. And if they had angels to govern them, there would be no need of limiting the government. But those are not the conditions that prevail: there are fallible men to be governed and fallible men to govern them. That being the case, they believed that government should be limited.

Indeed, there probably have never been a people more jealous of their rights or more aware of the dangers of government to them than were Americans in the late eighteenth century. The documents of this period are replete with warnings about the dangers of extensive or unrestrained government power. John Dickinson stated that it was his conviction "that every free state should incessantly watch and instantly take alarm on any addition being made to the power exercised over them."[1] Thomas Jefferson maintained that "The natural progress of things is for liberty to yield and government to gain ground."[2] John Adams wrote Thomas Jefferson in 1777 congratulating him on the fact that Virginia had been able to fill its quota for the Continental Army without resorting to the draft, for he said that a draft "is a dangerous Measure, and only to be adopted in great Extremities, even by popular Governments." He had observed, he said, that kings gathered armies in this fashion as a means of realizing their own ambitions.[3] Power was the danger, not simply the form of government, according to Richard Henry Lee. He thought "that unbridled passions produce the same effect, whether in a king, nobility, or a mob. The experience of all mankind has proved the ... disposition to use power wantonly. It is therefore as necessary to defend an individual against the majority in a republic as against the king in a monarchy."[4]

The dangers of government were fully rehearsed in the Constitutional Convention. For example, Rufus King of Massachusetts objected to setting a date for Congress to meet each year because he "could not think there would be a necessity for a meeting every year. A great vice in our system was that of legislating too much."[5] Roger Sherman wanted to make the President absolutely dependent on Congress because "An independence of the Executive ... was in his opinion the very essence of tyranny...."[6] Benjamin Franklin opposed salaries for those in the executive branch because, he said, "there are two passions which have a powerful influence on the affairs of men. These are ambition and avarice; the love of power, and the love of money. Separately, each of these has great force in prompting men to action; but when united ... in the same object, they have in many minds the most violent effects. Place before the eyes of such men, a post of *honour* that shall be at the same time a place of *profit,* and they will move heaven and earth to obtain it."[7]

James Madison pointed out the dangers of unrestricted majority rule: "In all cases where a majority are united by a common interest or passion," he said, "the rights of the minority are in danger."[8]

This awareness of the dangers of governmental power, an awareness sharpened by the history of the abuse of those powers over the years, provided the framework for the American limitation of government. It was this that so moved them to separate the powers of government into three branches—the legislative, executive and judicial—, to divide the legislature into two houses, to give the states a check on the government through the Senate, and to disperse power between the general government and the states. But the Founders went beyond separating and dispersing power; they made it necessary for branches to act in concert to accomplish their ends and required a *consensus* for great and important changes.

Legislation has to pass each of the houses separately and be approved by the President to become law. In addition to that, any act is supposed to be in keeping with the powers granted under the Constitution, and the courts may refuse to enforce it. Thus, ultimately, all acts may require the approval of all three branches. That would be majority rule, however. But if the President vetoes a bill, it can only become a law by being passed in each house by at least two-thirds of those voting. That moves closer to the requirement of consensus for government action. For major changes in the government—constitutional changes—there is, in effect, a required consensus. The ordinary route of amendment is for each of the houses to approve a proposed amendment by two-thirds of those voting. Then, the amendment must be submitted to the states, and three-fourths of them must approve the change. All these are procedural requirements which limit the government.

The United States government is limited in two other ways by the Constitution. First, it is a government of enumerated (named) powers. The government is not clothed with all powers but only such as are named in the Constitution or necessary to put into effect those that are named. James Madison described the situation this way: "The powers delegated by the proposed Constitution to the federal government are few and defined. Those ... will be exercised principally on external [foreign] objects, as war, peace, negotiation, and foreign commerce; with which last the power of taxation will, for the most part, be connected."[9]

All legislative powers in the United States government are vested by the Constitution in the Congress. Thus, the powers granted to the government are mostly named in the grant of these powers. They are listed in Section 8 of Article I, and include the following:

> The Congress shall have Power to lay and collect Taxes. . . .
> To borrow Money on the credit of the United States;
> To regulate Commerce with foreign Nations, and among the several States, and with the Indian Tribes;
> To establish a uniform Rule of Naturalization.

The going assumption at the time of the drawing and ratification of the Constitution was that the general government had only such powers as were granted. But it was not left as an assumption; the 10th Amendment spells out the point. It reads, "The powers not delegated to the United States by the Constitution, nor prohibited by it to the States, are reserved to the States respectively, or to the people."

The second way the United States government is limited is by specific prohibitions. For example, taxation is limited in various ways in the Constitution. It required that all direct taxes be apportioned on the basis of population (altered later by the 16th Amendment). Other taxes must be levied uniformly throughout the United States. All taxation must be for the common defense and/or general welfare of the United States, which was not a grant of power but a limitation upon it. Section 9, Article I contains these among other limitations:

> The Privilege of the Writ of *Habeas Corpus* shall not be suspended, unless when in Cases of Rebellion or Invasion the public Safety may require it.
> No Tax or Duty shall be laid on articles exported from any State. . . .
> No Title of Nobility shall be granted by the United States.

In addition to such prohibitions as these the Bill of Rights or first ten amendments to the Constitution consists of limitations on the United States government. As already noted, the fear of government generally, and especially of a central government, resulted in the move for a bill of rights. Many were emphatic about the need for such a list to limit the new government. Thomas Jefferson declared that it was a matter of principle with him "that a bill of rights is what the people are entitled to against every government . . . , and what no just government should refuse."[10] Patrick Henry insisted that "If you intend to reserve your inalienable rights, you must have the most express stipulation . . ."[11]

At any rate, the Bill of Rights specifically restricts and limits the United States government. The first Amendment begins in a way to make that crystal clear: "*Congress shall make no law* respecting an establishment of religion, or prohibiting the free exercise thereof; or abridging the freedom of speech," etc. (Italics added.) The others do not point to a specific branch of government that may not act, but it is clear from the language that government is being restricted by them. For example, the fourth Amendment states that "The right of the people to be secure in their persons, houses, papers, and effects, against unreasonable searches and seizures, shall not be violated, and no Warrants shall issue, but upon probable cause. . . ." Since governments are the only body that may legally do such things, the article clearly is limiting government. So it is with the other parts of the Bill of Rights.

Not only is the United States government limited by the Constitution, but the state governments are as well. They are limited, in the first place, by the grant of powers to the United States government, powers which, ordinarily, states may only exercise, if at all, with the approval of Congress. Second, some powers are absolutely denied to the states, e.g., No State shall enter into any Treaty, Alliance, or Confederation; grant Letters of Marque and Reprisal; coin Money; emit Bills of Credit; make any Thing but gold and silver *Coin* a Tender in Payment of Debts; pass any . . . Law impairing the Obligation of Contracts, or grant any Title of Nobility."

The central feature of the United States Constitution, then, is the limitation of government.

Freeing the Individual

A major fruit of independence was the freeing of the individual from a variety of government compulsions. Governments were restrained that individuals might be free. That was the thrust of the making of constitutions during these years. The state constitutions were already limiting state governments before the U. S. Constitution was written. States frequently had their own bills of rights which had as their main purpose the protection of their inhabitants from government. Moreover, many of the restraints which had been imposed under British rule were removed as independence was achieved. Indeed, Americans used the occasion offered by the break from England to remove those restraints on the individual that did not accord with their outlook.

One of those restraints on the individual was compulsory church attendance and the associated taxation and other restrictions supporting an established church. In the main, these restrictions were removed by disestablishing churches. The establishment most readily dispensed with was that of the Church of England. While that church was established in several colonies, it was not popular in most of them, many of its clergy remained loyal to England, and dissenters were numerous in most states. The movement to disestablish the Church of England was greatly aided, too, by the fact that it was a national church; membership in it was tied to loyalty to the king of England. Since Americans could not accept that any longer, the church was speedily disestablished. Several states had no established churches: namely, New Jersey, Rhode Island, Pennsylvania, and Delaware. Even so, they used the opportunity afforded by independence to reduce religious restraints.

The established Congregational church was maintained for several decades in Massachusetts, Connecticut, and New Hampshire. There was, however, some lightening of the load of religious restrictions in these states. The Massachusetts constitution of 1780 affirmed that every man had the right to worship in his own way, that all churches were equal before the law, and tax monies could be used to pay ministers of churches generally. However, attendance in some Christian church was still required, and people were still taxed to pay ministers. New Hampshire made much the same provisions as Massachusetts, but Connecticut clung to as much as the leaders dared of the established church. They did allow a dissenter from it to avoid payment of taxes if he could present a certificate from an officer of the church showing that he attended. But the days of formally established churches were ending in New England, too, though disestablishment in the last of these states was not completed until the 1830s.

The constitutions of New Jersey, Georgia, North and South Carolina, Delaware, and Pennsylvania provided that none should be compelled to pay taxes to churches nor attend any service except such as they chose. Virginia, however, made the most thoroughgoing effort to establish freedom of conscience. This might have been a reaction to the fact that Virginia had the oldest established church in English America and the most rigorously established. Thomas Jefferson, James Madison, and George Mason were leading advocates of religious liberty, but they did not succeed in getting their ideas into law until 1786. This was done by the Virginia Statute of Religious Freedom, which proclaimed religious liberty a natural right. The legally effective portion of the statute reads this way:

That no man shall be compelled to frequent or support any religious worship, place, or ministry whatsoever, nor shall be enforced, restrained, molested, or burdened in his body or goods, nor shall otherwise suffer on account of his religious opinions or belief; but that all men shall be free to profess and by argument to maintain, their opinion in matters of religion, and that the same shall in no wise diminish, enlarge, or affect their civil capacities.[12]

In large, this was what Americans were coming to think of as religious liberty.

The Constitution of the United States left to the states the power to determine as they would whether they would have an established church or to what extent religious liberty would prevail. The first Amendment simply prohibited Congress to establish a religion or interfere with its free exercise. The states did, however, move to disestablish churches and to reduce religious restrictions, as already noted, thus freeing people in the matter of conscience.

Many of the provisions in the state bills of rights, as well as the Bill of Rights for the United States, were guarantees of legal practices protecting the freedom of the individual that were a part of the British tradition. The Virginia Bill of Rights, adopted June 12, 1776, was both a model for such documents and illustrates the point. It guaranteed trial by jury in both criminal and civil cases, prohibited excessive bail and fines, declared general warrants to be oppressive, and acknowledged freedom of the press. The protections of persons accused of a crime were stated in detail:

That in all capital or criminal prosecutions a man hath a right to demand the cause and nature of his accusation, to be confronted with the accusers and witnesses, to call for evidence in his favour, and to a speedy trial by an impartial jury of his vicinage [the vicinity of where he lives], without whose unanimous consent he cannot be found guilty, nor can he be compelled to give evidence against himself; that no man may be deprived of his liberty, except by the law of the land or the judgment of his peers.[13]

In addition to these protections, the Massachusetts Declaration of Rights of 1780 provided for the right to bear arms, the right of peaceful assembly, the prohibition of *ex post facto* laws and bills of attainder, among others. Most of the above provisions are also in the United States Constitution.

Property Rights

There were some major changes from British practice, however, particularly in the matter of ownership of real property. Several feudal restraints on property were removed. Primogeniture—the legal provision requirement that if the owner died without a will the bulk of the estate went to the eldest son—was abolished generally. The most general encumbrance on property was the quitrent, an annual payment due to king or proprietors on land. Such claims as still existed at the time of independence were speedily extinguished, and land thereafter was generally owned in "fee simple." Entail—legal provisions that estates could not be broken up—, where it existed, was abolished. Such royal prerogatives as the right of the monarch to white pines (for shipbuilding) on private land were, of course, nullified.

A part of the freeing of the individual, then, was making real property ownership free of government restraints and disposable at will by the individual. Indeed, property in general was carefully protected both in state constitutions and in the U. S. Constitution. Some later commentators have claimed that the Founders distinguished between what they call "human rights" and property rights and attached greater significance to the former. The evidence for that does not appear in the documents or pronouncements of the time. If anything, they placed more emphasis on property than on other rights of humans, but they certainly did not declare one variety higher than the other.

For example, the Massachusetts Declaration of Rights states:

> All men are born free and equal, and have certain natural, essential, and unalienable rights; among which may be reckoned the right of enjoying and defending their lives and liberties; that of acquiring, possessing, and protecting property; in fine, that of seeking and obtaining their safety and happiness.[14]

The Declaration went on to provide that "No part of the property of any individual can, with justice, be taken from him, or applied to public uses, without his consent, or that of the representative body of the people. . . ."[15] With even greater clarity, the Virginia Bill of Rights says that people "cannot be taxed or deprived of their property for public uses, without their own consent or that of their representatives so elected."[16]

Slavery

In any case, the tendency of the declarations and constitutions of these years was the freeing of individuals from governmental control of their affairs and protecting them in their rights. It has rightly been pointed out, of course, that where Negro slavery continued to exist it was a glaring exception to this tendency. Some have even gone so far as to accuse the Founders of hypocrisy in professing to believe in the equal rights of all men and acquiescing in the continuation of slavery. It strikes us as strange that Thomas Jefferson, who penned the stirring statement "that all men are created equal," should have been himself a slaveholder. But even in the case of chattel slavery the trend of the 1780s was toward the freeing of the individual, and if the trend and sentiment in the direction of ending slavery had continued apace the apparent contradiction would have been resolved.

Some states began to act with the purpose of eventually ending slavery almost as soon as independence from Britain was declared. In 1776, Delaware prohibited the importation of slaves and removed all restraints on their manumission (freeing by the owner). Virginia stopped slave imports in 1778; Maryland adopted a similar measure in 1783. Both states permitted manumission. In 1780, Pennsylvania not only prohibited further importation of slaves but also provided that after that date all children born of slaves should be free. Similar enactments were made in the early 1780s in New Hampshire, Connecticut, and Rhode Island. In Massachusetts, the supreme court ruled that on the basis of that state's constitution of 1780 slavery was abolished there. Even North Carolina (the greatest resistance to freeing slaves was in the lower South) moved to discourage the slave trade in 1786 by taxing heavily such slaves as were imported after that time. In order to protect free Negroes, Virginia made it a crime punishable by death for anyone found guilty of selling a freed Negro into slavery. As already noted, the Northwest Ordinance of 1787 prohibited slavery in the Northwest territory.

Jefferson had written a warning about the continuation of slavery, which he abhorred, in his *Notes on Virginia*. It was a violation of their most basic rights to keep some people in perpetual bondage. "And can the liberties of a nation be thought secure when we have removed their only firm basis, a conviction in the minds of the people that these liberties are the gift of God? That they are not to be violated but with his wrath? Indeed I tremble for my country," he said, "when I reflect that God is just: that his justice cannot sleep forever. . . ."[17]

Madison, writing in defense of the Constitution, said that it would no doubt have been better if the slave trade had been prohibited by the Constitution rather than delaying action until 1808, but he looked forward to the time when "a traffic which has so loudly upbraided the barbarism of modern policy . . . may terminate forever. . . ."[18]

There is no reason to doubt the sincerity of many of the Founders in wishing an end both to slavery and the slave trade. Moreover, at the earliest date that it could constitutionally Congress prohibited the importation of slaves. Although slaveholders in the lower South were still tenaciously attached to slavery, they were holding out against a tide running in the opposite direction in the 1780s. Even in the lower South, the crops which were so dependent on slave labor—rice and indigo—declined in importance once the break from England was made. Unfortunately, for the abolition of slavery, the cotton gin was invented in the 1790s; cotton became an important fiber; and slavery was revived by the expansion into the Old Southwest.

Free Trade

One of the fruits of independence was the freeing of trade both within the United States and with other peoples around the world. Independence from Britain removed British imposed mercantile restrictions in one swoop. That is not to say that Britain did not continue in various ways to limit American trade after the break. They did, well into the 1790s, at least. But British mercantilism was no longer legally binding on Americans; they could trade with whomever they could and would around the world. Initially, too, the states adopted various restrictions which limited trade within the United States. But the Constitution of 1787 put an end to that.

American belief and sentiments were tending more and more to favor free trade. The freedom of people to trade with whomever they would on mutually agreeable terms seemed to them to be of a piece with freedom for the individual in general. Benjamin Franklin said that "it seems contrary to the nature of Commerce, for Government to interfere in the Prices of Commodities. Trade is a voluntary Thing between Buyer and Seller, in every article of which each exercises his own Judgment, and is to please himself."[19] Pelatiah Webster, an American economic thinker of this period, declared: "I propose . . . to take off every restraint and limitation from our commerce. Let trade be as free as air. Let every man make the most of his goods in his own way and then he will be satisfied."[20] Jefferson said that "the exercise of a free trade with all parts of the world" was "possessed by the American as of natural right...."[21]

Actually, the freedom to trade is a corollary of private property. The right to dispose of property on whatever terms he will to whomever he will is necessarily a part of the full ownership of property. At its fully extended development, it involves for the seller the right to find anywhere in the world that buyer who will make the best offer for his goods, his time, or his services. For the buyer of these, it involves his right to locate the most attractive goods at prices he is willing to pay.

Aside from the break from England, the greatest stride by Americans toward free trade was the ratification of the Constitution. The Constitution provided for a common market throughout the United States. The power to regulate commerce among the states was vested in the United States. Thereafter, the states could not obstruct commerce, and the whole country became in effect, a free trading area. Further, the Constitution provided that states may not tax imports or exports, except for carrying out inspection laws, without the consent of Congress. But to discourage any of that, all money collected had to be paid into the U.S. Treasury.

A Common Currency

The Constitution contains several other provisions promoting a common market throughout the country. Congress is empowered to pass uniform bankruptcy laws, set up standard weights and measures, and establish post offices and post roads. A common currency (or money) is also important for trade to take place easily. So far as the Constitution provides for a common currency, however, it does so by indirection. It authorizes the government to coin money and to regulate its value. It does not authorize the passing of any tender laws (laws making any currency or money legal tender or forcing its acceptance), and it prohibits states to make anything legal tender except gold and silver coins.

Paper money had a well deserved bad reputation at the time of the making of the Constitution. Not only did Americans generally have the recent unsettling experience with the Continental currency, which became worthless, but also several states had in the 1780s flooded the market with virtually worthless paper money. When the states, most notably Rhode Island, adopted laws to force the paper money into circulation, it not only obstructed trade but also endangered property in debts. The subject of paper money came up twice for extended discussion in the Constitutional Convention. It arose once over a proposal to authorize Congress to emit bills of credit (issue paper money). The delegates were overwhelmingly opposed to the proposal. The tenor of the opposition may be gathered from these delegate comments. Oliver Elsworth of Connecticut declared that he "thought this a favorable moment to shut and bar the door against paper money. . . . The power may do harm, never good."[22] George Read of Delaware "thought the words [emit bills of credit], if not struck out, would be as alarming as the mark of the Beast in Revelations." John Langdon of New Hampshire "had rather reject the whole plan [the Constitution] than retain the . . . words."[23] Voting by states, the delegates omitted the power by a vote of 9 to 2.

Paper money came up again in connection with a proposal to permit the states to emit bills of credit with the consent of Congress. That, too, was overwhelmingly rejected. The states are prohibited to issue paper money. Thus, the only provision for a common currency is in the power of the United States to coin money and the reserved power of the states to make those of gold and silver legal tender.

While the Constitution does not specifically provide for free trade with the rest of the world, its provisions lean in that direction. It does provide that "No Tax or Duty shall be laid on Articles exported from any State." Thus, tariffs on exports are prohibited. Congress is authorized to levy tariffs on imports. In any case, the widespread sentiment in favor of freeing trade set the stage for low tariffs in the early decades of the Republic, and many Americans had come to dislike British mercantilistic restraints too much to wish to impose them on their own trade.

The Voluntary Way

The story of America after 1789, until well into the twentieth century, is not so much the story of the doings of government as of people generally. It is the story of freed individuals working, building, growing crops, building factories, clearing the land for farms, organizing churches, providing for families, and doing all those things that make up the warp and woof of life. They did this singly as individuals, as families, and in voluntary groups. This is always to some degree true, of course. The world's work is done by people generally and very little by governments. But governments often play a dominant role in the economic, social, religious, educational, recreational, and community lives of a people. This had been so in the European countries from which American settlers came. It has become the rule once again in most places in the world in the twentieth century.

The constitution-making cleared the ground for the triumph of the voluntary way in America in the late eighteenth century. Governments were restrained and individuals were freed to pursue their own devices alone or in voluntary cooperation with others. There is no need to exaggerate the extent of this change, however. The British colonists generally enjoyed considerable liberty, as a result of British tradition and law, of British neglect, and of the remoteness of many people from the oversight of government. The Americans continued much of what they considered to be the best of their British heritage under their new constitutions. Nor was everyone freed nor to the same degree under them. Slaves were still in bondage where slavery was continued and could hardly participate in the voluntary way. Children were, as they usually are, under the authority of their parents or other adults. Women generally were still under the protection and in some respects the authority of men—fathers, older brothers, and husbands—, partners, as adults, ordinarily to men, though in some ways subordinate ones. But these last were family matters, not things under the direction of government.

In large, then, the voluntary way triumphed. Governments still issued charters for some undertakings, but these more often confirmed some voluntary undertaking than initiating it. Even the registry of births and deaths was much more apt to be done in the family Bible than in some government office. As churches were disestablished, religion became a voluntary affair. Attendance, participation, the payment of the clergy, what structures would be built, what services would be held, were matters left to individual and family choice and voluntary cooperation. Education had never been firmly established by government in America. There had been some faltering attempts to do so in New England and New York, but not much came of them. The education of children was largely left to parents, and schools and colleges were set up, when they were, by churches or other voluntary associations or simply by some schoolmaster. So it was, too, in the matter of providing for those in temporary or some longer term need. Most often, extended families provided for orphans, for widows, for the sick, and for the disabled. Institutional charity, such as it was, was most apt to be provided by churches or private gifts.

Under mercantilism, governments had attempted to direct economic activity for their own ends. The British had not only restricted and controlled economic activity but also granted monopolies to chartered companies to engage in specified production or trade. American colonies had sometimes imitated some of these mercantilistic practices. There were still residues of mercantilism at the time of the founding of the United States, but in general Americans preferred voluntary economic activity to that which was government directed. Mostly men started and operated businesses without asking the leave or aid or charters from government. They built ships and plied the seas in trade as they could and would. In short, they tended to follow the voluntary in their economic life.

How America flourished and grew by voluntary cooperation is a story to be told in detail elsewhere. Suffice it to say here that numerous voluntary societies came into being, that religious denominations multiplied and congregations were organized in virtually every community, that schools and colleges became commonplace, and that there were no more enterprising people in the world than were Americans in the nineteenth century.

1. John Dickinson, *Letters from a Farmer in Pennsylvania* in *Empire and Interest*, Forrest McDonald, intro. Englewood Cliffs, N.J.: Prentice-Hall, 1962), p. 73.

2. Edward Dumbauld, ed., *The Political Writings of Thomas Jefferson* (New York: Liberal Arts Press, 1955), p. 138.

3. Lester J. Cappon, ed., *The Adams-Jefferson Letters*, vol. I (Chapel Hill: University of North Carolina Press, 1959), p. 5.

4. Jack P. Greene, ed., *Colonies to Nation* (New York: McGraw-Hill, 1967), p. 562.

5. James Madison, *Notes in the Debates in the Federal Constitutional Convention of 1787*, Adrienne Koch, intro. (Athens, Ohio: Ohio University Press, 1966), p. 398.

6. *Ibid.*, p. 48.

7. *Ibid.*, p. 53.

8. *Ibid.*, p. 76.

9. Alexander Hamilton, *et. al.*, *The Federalist Papers* (New Rochelle, N.Y.: Arlington House, n.d.), p. 292.

10. Alfred Young, ed., *The Debate over the Constitution* (Chicago: Rand McNally, 1965), p. 49.

11. Quoted in Moses C. Tyler, *Patrick Henry* (Boston: Houghton Mifflin, 1887), p. 290.

12. Green, *op cit.*, p. 391.

13. Henry S. Commager, ed., *Documents of American History*, vol I (New York: Appleton-Century-Crofts, 1962, 7th ed., 1962), p. 104.

14. *Ibid.*, p. 107.

15. *Ibid.*, p. 108.

16. *Ibid.*, p. 104.

17. Greene, *op cit.*, p. 391.

18. Hamilton, *op cit.*, p. 19.

19. Quoted in Virgle G. Wilhite, *Founders of American Economic Thought* (New York: Bookman, 1958), p. 308.

20. *Ibid.*, p. 172.

98 / *Clarence B. Carson*

21. Dumbauld, *op. cit.*, p. 19.
22. Charles C. Tansill, ed., *Formation of the Union of American States* (Washington: Government Printing Office, 1927), p. 557.
23. *Ibid.*

III. IN DEFENSE OF LIBERTY

Against All Enemies

by Robert Bearce

Part I

The elected and appointed officials of our federal government take an oath of office before undertaking their constitutional duties. Let's take a look at that oath, expressed as a question and answered by "I do."

Do you solemnly swear that you will support and defend the Constitution of the United States against all enemies, foreign and domestic; that you will bear true faith and allegiance to the same; that you take this obligation freely, without any mental reservation or purpose of evasion; and that you will well and faithfully discharge the duties of the office on which you are about to enter: So help you God?

In response to their oath of office, our Congressmen and Senators answer "I do," but do they really mean it?

Unfortunately for the cause of freedom, the oath of office has often become only a hollow formality. Too many members of the administrative, legislative, and judicial branches of the federal government have failed to "support and defend the Constitution of the United States" and "bear true faith and allegiance to the same."

The Constitution has been misinterpreted, abused, and subverted. As it continues to be violated, we should see how freedom is gradually being destroyed.

The word "destroyed" might appear to be somewhat harsh, but it is appropriate. We ought to heed a warning made by Patrick Henry in 1775, not long before the opening shots of the War for Independence were fired at Lexington and Concord. Henry clearly understood how freedom was being threatened by oppressive government rule. He warned against indifference, complacency, and apathy.

"It is natural to man to indulge in the illusions of hope. We are apt to shut our eyes against a painful truth, and listen to the song of that siren, till she transforms us into beasts. Is this the part of wise men, engaged in a great and arduous struggle for liberty? Are we disposed to be of the number of those who, having eyes, see not, and

---

This article was originally published as a three-part series in the September, October, and November 1980 issues of *The Freeman*.

having ears, hear not, the things which so nearly concern their temporal salvation? For my part, whatever anguish of spirit it may cost, I am willing to know the whole truth; to know the worst and provide for it."

By "temporal salvation," Patrick Henry meant the preservation of freedom—the freedom to work and provide for our personal lives as we best see fit. Henry and other patriots believed that freedom meant individuals had the ability and responsibility to plan their own lives without unnecessary government intervention. That freedom was being threatened, and Henry was telling the colonists to wake up and confront the danger before them. His admonition applies to us today.

If we truly want to strengthen freedom and regain what we have already lost, we will pledge ourselves to defending the Constitution. We cannot support our Constitution, however, unless we face the fact that it is being continually ignored and betrayed. It is time that we give some serious thought to the Constitution.

Protection from Enemies—Foreign and Domestic

The Founding Fathers who framed our Constitution in 1787 knew that individuals have certain unalienable rights—"life, liberty, and the pursuit of happiness," as earlier expressed in the Declaration of Independence. These rights were God-given rights. No government or constitution gave them to the individual. Rather, the purpose of governments and constitutions was to protect these basic, God-given rights.

The Founding Fathers comprehended how and why people behave the way they do. Men like James Madison and Alexander Hamilton understood human nature. They saw that some human beings would always resort to force, deceit, war, stealing, and killing to get what they wanted. Thus, there was an obvious need for government—legitimate, just government to carry out two main functions:

1. protecting free people from foreign enemies and invaders;
2. protecting honest, self-responsible, hard working citizens within the nation from domestic lawbreakers who would use coercion, fraud, or force to deprive others of "life, liberty, and the pursuit of happiness."

Good government would do the above, and the Founding Fathers outlined that kind of government in our Constitution. Just as they gave the government certain authority, they also placed limitations on government power. The framers of the Constitution realized that while government was needed to protect individual freedom, government itself had to be placed within limited, strictly defined boundaries. If government was not restrained, it would destroy individual liberty and lead to tyranny. Government had to be controlled. James Madison explained the matter:

> It may be a reflection on human nature that such devices should be necessary to control the abuses of government. But what is government itself but the greatest of all reflections on human nature? If men were angels, no government would be necessary. If angels were to govern men, neither external nor internal controls on government would be necessary. In framing a government which is to be administered by men over men, the great difficulty lies in this: you must first enable the government to control the governed, and in the next place oblige it to control itself.

When Madison wrote that government should "control the governed," he was thinking about necessary government laws required to maintain impartial law and order—law and order that protected individual liberty. This issue of defending individual rights and limiting the power of government is the central theme of the Constitution.

Preserving Personal Liberty

Four aspects of the Constitution show the Founding Fathers' concern for preserving personal liberty within the boundaries of limited government.

First, we have a *written* constitution. Having the powers of government and the rights of the citizenry spelled out in print is no assurance that freedom will be observed, but a written constitution does act as a safeguard to liberty. When the Constitution is snubbed or disregarded, we can at least hold up a warning hand and say something to the effect: "Stop, government bureaucrats! The law you have just passed is unconstitutional. The Fifth Amendment says...."

Second, our Constitution provides for a republic. That is, we have a republican form of government based upon the citizenry electing representatives to carry out the functions of government. The Founding Fathers did not frame a constitution that would set up a democracy—a kind of government where political power lay directly in the hands of the people. Under a pure democracy, the citizens of the state would exercise popular vote to decide what laws should be made. The majority view would be registered and then carried out by the administrative hand of the central government. There would be no representation (legislative branch of government) between the citizenry and the administrative branch of government.

A democracy might appear to be more "democratic" than a republic, but the authors of the Constitution knew that a democracy would lead to a loss of individual freedom followed by anarchy or tyranny. While the Constitution was being considered for ratification by the Massachusetts Convention, Moses Ames observed: "It has been said that a pure democracy is the best government for a small people who assemble in person. . . . It may be of some use in this argument . . . to consider, that it would be very burdensome, subject to faction and violence; decisions would often be made by surprise, in the precipitancy of passion, by men who either understand nothing or care nothing about the subject; or by interested men, or those who vote for their own indemnity. It would be a government not by laws, but by men."

The Dangers of Democracy

Seeing the dangers of a democracy, the Founding Fathers adopted a republican form of government. It is true that the history of our nation shows that a republic can suffer the very weaknesses of a democracy that Ames described, but the fact remains that a republic comes nearer to preserving individual rights than does a democracy.

Madison and others rejected popular vote as the method of making laws. Instead, Article I of the Constitution provides for representation through the election of Senators and Congressmen to the Senate and House of Representatives. These legislators would represent us and make laws—laws that should protect and promote individual freedom. The government was to be guided by clearly defined laws, not by direct majority rule, which would lead to oppression.

Although Thomas Jefferson did not participate in the work on the Constitution, he understood why a republic was superior to a democracy. He also knew what the basic purpose of a republic was: "The true foundation of republican government is the equal right of every citizen, in his person and property, and in their management."

A republic meant a government that allowed the people of the United States to work freely, associate freely, and otherwise plan their own lives in the way they pleased—equal rights shared by all citizens. Speaking of the national or central government of the United States, Article IV, Section 4 of the Constitution says: "The United States shall guarantee to every State in this Union a *Republican Form of Government*, and shall protect each of them against Invasion. . . .(emphasis added).

A third principle of our Constitution that defends individual liberty is federalism. When we speak today about the "federal government," we refer to the executive, legislative, and judicial branches of the central government located in Washington, D.C. In the minds of the Founding Fathers, though, federal government was an all-encompassing term used to describe a nation made up of sovereign states—a nation composed of a central or national government (the folks in Washington, D.C.) and state governments (Delaware, South Carolina, Connecticut, etc.).

Notice that the Constitution recognizes that the United States *are,* not "is," a union of sovereign states. Article III, Section 3 reads: "Treason against the United States, shall consist only in levying War against *them,* or in adhering to *their* Enemies. . ."(emphasis added). Although the Founding Fathers considered themselves as Americans and citizens of a unified nation, they also considered themselves citizens of separate, self-governing states. The United States were considered in the plural, not the singular. Thus, treason against the United States was against them, not it. This fact stresses the federalist nature of the government established by the Constitution.

The Separation of Powers to Protect the Citizenry

The Constitution provides for federalism that grants some powers to the national government and other powers to the states. This federal separation of powers acts as a safeguard to personal freedom. Federalism places the burden of law-making and political decisions upon power units close to the supervision of the citizenry. The Founding Fathers did not want the national government in Washington, D.C., telling the people of Virginia or North Carolina what to do.

Thus, political power was distributed among the different state, county, and local governments, enabling the people to govern themselves. This widespread distribution of authority makes it more difficult for one power unit to infringe upon the constitutional rights of the citizens.

The Founding Fathers provided for another form of separation of powers. This is the fourth aspect of the Constitution's defense of individual liberty. The national government, or, as we say, the federal government, was split up into three separate branches with each branch having distinct, limited powers.

Basically, the executive branch of government headed by the President and his Cabinet carries out constitutional laws and duties. The legislative branch made up of the Senate and House of Representatives makes the laws, while the judicial branch (the Supreme Court and federal courts) decides whether or not laws have been violated in light of the Constitution.

Three Branches of Government

The authority and powers of the three branches of the federal government are balanced and checked by one another. For example, the President can veto laws passed by Congress. Congress, on the other hand, can withhold funds from executive agencies. Although Congress can pass legislation, the Supreme Court has the power to declare certain laws unconstitutional, making them null and void. The President appoints federal judges and various civil servants, but the Senate can refuse to ratify major appointments. The federal judiciary can find individuals guilty of crimes, but the President has power to grant pardons and reprieves.

This separation of powers, like federalism, should act as a checks and balances system to keep government from going beyond the boundaries of its constitutional authority. No single branch of government should have the combined power to make, interpret, and enforce laws.

The United States Constitution is really a remarkable document. It is a monument to personal freedom. The Founding Fathers distrusted government, and they attempted to shackle political power when they adopted the Constitution. It restricts government to the primary responsibilities of providing for the common defense, maintaining domestic security and peace, and protecting individual rights.

The Bill of Rights

When we think of individual rights, we usually have in mind the first ten amendments to the Constitution, the Bill of Rights. Much has been written about the first eight amendments which include assurances of freedom of religion, speech, and press ... the right to bear arms ... the right to trial by jury, etc. Not enough is said, though, about the Ninth and Tenth Amendments.

The Ninth Amendment states that "The enumeration in the Constitution of certain rights, shall not be construed to deny or disparage others retained by the people."

This amendment assures the individual that he has other rights besides those listed in the Constitution and previous eight amendments. These unnamed rights cannot be taken away just because they are not mentioned in the Constitution. We have such rights as "the pursuit of happiness," not included in the Constitution but stated earlier in the Declaration of Independence.

Now look at the Tenth Amendment: "The powers not delegated to the United States by the Constitution, nor prohibited by it to the States, are reserved to the States respectively, or to the people."

This important amendment says that all powers not granted by the Constitution to the national government are retained either by the states or individual citizens. Likewise, all powers not prohibited by the Constitution to the states are left in the hands of the states or people themselves.

Unfortunately, many of our government officials today act as if the Ninth and Tenth Amendments do not exist. They have twisted the meaning of the Constitution and the role of government. They look upon the Bill of Rights as rights granted to us by a supposedly benevolent government. In reality, the first ten amendments are a list of prohibitions against government *interfering* with those rights. Our legislators should listen to Daniel Webster.

Webster was only a youngster when the Constitution was ratified in 1788, but in later years he earned the reputation of being "The Defender of the Constitution." During a Senate speech in 1830, he declared: "The people, then, Sir, erected this government. They gave it a Constitution, and in that Constitution they have enumerated the powers which they bestow on it. They have made it a limited government. They have defined its authority. They have restrained it to the exercise of such powers as are granted; and all others, they declare, are reserved to the states or the people."

A Framework for Freedom

The Founding Fathers knew that the basic responsibility of government was to serve as a "watchdog" to maintain a free society of free individuals working together freely. Improved working conditions ... better education ... good health care ... material progress— all of these are goals that people work toward. The purpose of government is to ensure the necessary freedom that will permit individuals to work for those goals through self-responsibility, individual initiative, the free market, and voluntary exchange. Government has the responsibility of providing a framework that will allow individuals to achieve prosperity and dignity on their own.

The Founding Fathers were not men who felt that the purpose of government was to plan, formulate, and then implement specific ways to achieve the goals of a nation. Government was not to be in the business of providing public housing or job training through its political, economic, or social legislation. Government was not to mold society but, instead, allow society to mold itself freely.

Let's consider some advice from Jefferson: "... Still one thing more, fellow citizens—a wise and frugal Government, which shall restrain men from injuring one another, shall leave them otherwise free to regulate their own pursuits of industry and improvement, and shall not take from the mouth of labor the bread it has earned. This is the sum of good government.... "

We need to see how far we have strayed away from the Constitution. Not only is government poking its bureaucratic nose into where it should not be, it is not fulfilling one of its primary constitutional responsibilities—deterring crime. Government is supposed to prevent, prosecute, and punish crime, but now government itself has become the lawbreaker of the Constitution.

The Enemy Within

Many of our public officials have broken their oath of office. They affirm or swear that they will support the Constitution and defend it "against all enemies, foreign and domestic." There is the foreign threat of Marxist subversion and aggression. More dangerous, however, are the domestic enemies—individuals whose actions and attitudes are corrupting the Constitution. Those individuals include some of the very government officials sworn to uphold the Constitution.

Actions by the executive, legislative, and judicial branches of the federal government have proven that many officeholders apparently do not understand the Constitution. If they do know what the Constitution stands for, then we should hold them responsible for willfully repudiating their oath of office.

Two tasks are before us. First, we must have a firm appreciation for the Constitution. Second, we must have a clear understanding how and why the Constitution is being defied. Until we face the truth, we will slide steadily towards the eventual destruction of freedom in the United States.

Part II

John Quincy Adams, sixth President of the United States, once observed: "Our Constitution professedly rests upon the good sense and attachment of the people. This basis, weak as it may appear, has not yet been found to fail."

Up until President Adams' administration and for many years afterwards, our Constitution did indeed work in the manner it was meant to work. Times have changed, though. Although the principles of the Constitution of the United States remain as strong as ever, we have seriously neglected and forsaken them. The Constitution itself is a rugged, foresighted document, but, as President Adams said, its effectiveness lies in how well we observe its provisions.

Tragically, too many Americans today have abandoned the faith of the Founding Fathers. Our Constitution has been trampled upon by government officials, members of the mass media, educators, other public-opinion molders, as well as the average citizen.

Consider for a moment how some Americans (particularly those serving in Congress) have manipulated the "general welfare" clause of the Constitution. The "general welfare" is mentioned in the preamble and in Article I, Section 8.

The preamble reads: "WE THE PEOPLE of the United States, in Order to form a more perfect Union, establish Justice, insure domestic Tranquility, provide for the common defense, promote the general Welfare, and secure the Blessings of Liberty to ourselves and our Posterity, do ordain and establish this Constitution for the United States of America."

Article I, Section 8 of the Constitution mentions the "general welfare" in this way: "The Congress shall have the Power to lay and collect Taxes, Duties, Imposts and Excises, to pay the Debts and provide for the common defense and general welfare of the United States. . . ."

The preamble clearly defines the two major functions of government: (1) ensuring justice, personal freedom, and a free society where individuals are protected from domestic lawbreakers and criminals, (2) protecting the people of the United States from foreign aggressors.

No Special Privileges

When the Founding Fathers said that "WE THE PEOPLE" established the Constitution to "promote the general Welfare," they did not mean the federal government would have the power to aid education, build roads, and subsidize business. Likewise, Article I, Section 8 did not give Congress the right to use tax money for whatever social and economic programs Congress might think would be good for the "general welfare."

James Madison stated that the "general welfare" clause was not a freeway for Congress "to exercise every power which may be alleged to be necessary for the common defense or general welfare." If by the "general welfare," the Founding Fathers had meant any and all social, economic, or educational programs Congress wanted to create, there would have been no reason to list specific powers of Congress such as establishing courts and maintaining the armed forces. Those powers would simply have been included in one all-encompassing phrase, to "promote the general welfare."

Writing about the "general welfare" clause in 1791, Thomas Jefferson saw the danger of misinterpreting the Constitution. The danger in the hands of Senators and Congressmen was "that of instituting a Congress with power to do whatever would be for the good of the United States; and, as they would be the sole judges of the good or evil, it would be also a power to do whatever evil they please."

The Founding Fathers said in the preamble that one reason for establishing the Constitution was to "promote the general welfare." What they meant was that the Constitution and powers granted to the federal government were *not* to favor special interest groups or particular classes of people. There were to be no privileged individuals or groups in society. Neither minorities nor the majority was to be favored. Rather, the Constitution would promote the "general welfare" by ensuring a free society where free, self-responsible individuals—rich and poor, bankers and shopkeepers, employers and employees, farmers and blacksmiths—would enjoy "life, liberty, and the pursuit of happiness," rights expressed in the Declaration of Independence.

Quoting the Tenth Amendment, Jefferson wrote: "I consider the foundation of the Constitution as laid on this ground: That 'all powers not delegated to the United States, by the Constitution, nor prohibited by it to the States, are reserved to the States or to the people.' To take a single step beyond the boundaries thus specially drawn around the powers of Congress is to take possession of a boundless field of power, no longer susceptible of any definition."

A Monstrous Bureaucracy

Jefferson was correct in fearing that Congress could "take possession of a boundless field of power," but he was wrong in saying that such unlimited power could not be defined. It can indeed be defined by simply looking at the federal government of the United States today. There we see a "boundless field of power" in both little and big matters.

Unlike public officials during Jefferson's time, our modern-day legislators have a very loose interpretation of the Constitution. The result is that government has snowballed into a monstrous bureaucracy. Consider the power given to Congress by the Constitution in Article I, Section 8, clause 8: "To promote the Progress of Science and useful Arts. . . ."

Does that mean Congress has the right *to* use our tax dollars to finance agencies like the National Science Foundation and the National Foundation on the Arts and Humanities?

Definitely not! The complete clause reads: "To promote the Progress of Science and useful arts, *by securing for limited Times to Authors and inventors the exclusive Right to their respective Writings and Discoveries*" (emphasis added).

That's what the Founding Fathers meant by encouraging science and the arts. An appropriate Copyright Office was set up. Article I, Section 8, clause 8 is just one example of how the Constitution protects individual freedom and assures the individual the right to enjoy the fruits of his own labor, energy, and abilities.

Our present-day legislators, however, have ignored the Constitution as they pass legislation to help science and the arts. We now have the federally funded National Science Foundation, National Endowment for the Arts, and National Endowment for the Humanities. How do these federal programs spend our tax monies? Well, it has been reported that $130,000 from the National Science Foundation was used to study the evolution of the cricket. Another $46,000 was evidently spent by the National Endowment for the Arts to finance a film documentary on the history of the toilet. On the other hand, we are informed that for only $2,500 the National Endowment for the Humanities was able to finance a study on why tennis players are rude on tennis courts. A real bargain!

Undoubtedly, federal programs like the National Science Foundation have had some worthy results, but the benefits received are not the issue for discussion or debate. The problem is that such federal programs are unconstitutional. Rather than depending upon free individuals to encourage science and the arts through voluntary contributions to private foundations, Congress is taking money from some citizens and giving it to whomever it judges to be needy of federal handouts.

Congress Assumes Powers Beyond Intent of Founders

Congress is continually usurping its constitutional power, spending more of our tax dollars, and otherwise assuming obligations the Founding Fathers never meant it to undertake. For example, our generous government offers us such helpful publications as *And Now a Word About Your Shampoo, Keeping Your Pet Healthy,* and *Imaginative Ways With Bathrooms.* The really nice thing about these publications is that they are "free."

Now, it might be heartening to some people to know that our government wishes to advise us on how to plan or remodel our bathrooms, but are we to believe that federal funding for such publications is provided for in the Constitution?

The Constitution is being twisted and manhandled as our legislators toil in Congress to do what we can and should do for ourselves. One prominent Senator proudly lists in his legislative newsletter laws and proposals he has worked for in our behalf. These include a National Technology Act ... federal subsidies for mass transit ... a child abuse act ... aid for bilingual education ... a legal Services Corporation ... an Arthritis Act ... a Drug Utilization Improvement Act ... subsidies for solar energy ... monies for public service jobs, and so forth and so on.

The Senator's constituency, as well as all American citizens, should recall Jefferson's advice: " ... Still one thing more, fellow citizens—a wise and frugal Government, which shall restrain men from injuring one another, shall leave them otherwise free to regulate their own pursuits of industry and improvement, and shall not take from the mouth of labor the bread it has earned. This is the sum of good government."

Yet, our federal government today rumbles on, disavowing the Constitution and taking from our "mouth of labor the bread it has earned" through taxation. Government grows bigger and more comprehensive as federal funds are spent for cooperative farm extension work ... urban mass transit ... child-nutrition programs ... public housing ... elementary and secondary education ... air and water pollution control ... rural-housing grants ... minority business development ... public broadcasting ... adolescent health services and pregnancy prevention ... boating safety assistance ... new-community assistance grants ... urban renewal, and so forth and so on.

A Free Economy

America's past progress in achieving material prosperity in a climate of freedom and human dignity did not come as a result of government intervention into social/economic matters. Our nation has prospered because we were true to the Constitution. The Founding Fathers believed that the role of government was to provide a political framework that would permit individuals to work together in voluntary cooperation, pursuing their own destinies. Individual initiative and personal responsibility—not government social and economic intervention—were the basis for stability and growth.

The critical question for us is how many of the federal government's departments, boards, projects, and agencies are constitutional. We should remember that elected and appointed public servants are sworn to support and defend the Constitution of the United States. Consider what the Constitution has to say about private property, and then think about how government has abused its authority.

The Fourth Amendment states: "The right of the people to be secure in their persons, houses, papers, and effects, against unreasonable searches and seizures, shall not be violated. . . ."

The Fifth Amendment assures us that we will not "be deprived of life, liberty, or property, without due process of law. . . ."

The 14th Amendment states that citizens will not be deprived of "life, liberty, or property, without due process of law. . . ."

Few government officials, if any, will deny that private property is a basic principle or right enjoyed by Americans. Yet, these same public officials support laws that have the effect of infringing upon our liberty and property.

Without the right to dispose of our property as we best see fit, the right to private property is meaningless. Our property includes everything from our homes or the business we might own to our earnings at whatever job or profession we have. Our pay checks are just as much a matter of private property as are our homes, automobiles, and TV sets. Government deprives us of liberty and property to the extent that it (1) tries to manage our economic lives for us; and (2) prevents us from reaping the rewards of hard work and enjoying the fruits of our own property. Through unnecessary government regulations as well as excessive taxation we are not in full control of our property.

Private Property Protected

James Madison, known as the Father of the Constitution, understood that government interference threatens freedom and private property:

"That is not a just government, nor is property secure under it, where arbitrary restrictions, exemptions, and monopolies deny to part of its citizens that free use of their faculties, and free choice of their occupations, which not only constitute their property in the general sense of the word; but are the means of acquiring property so called."

Madison, Roger Sherman, and other men who wrote our Constitution achieved a wise, firm balance between personal liberty and government power. The Constitution has proven itself to be a stable but flexible document. Our problem today is that we have allowed flexibility to be interpreted as a blank check for government to do whatever it wishes. This is seen in the misinterpretation of the "general welfare" clause and the so-called "elastic clause" of Article I, Section 8 which says Congress shall have the power:

"To make all laws which shall be necessary and proper for carrying into Execution the foregoing Powers, and all other Powers vested by this Constitution in the Government of the United States, or in any Department or Office thereof."

Our government officials continually distort the meaning of the Constitution's "elastic clause." In doing so, they have stepped beyond the boundaries of limited, constitutional government. If he were alive today, James Madison would tell us that many government laws and programs might be useful, but they are certainly not "necessary and proper" according to the Constitution. He would remind us that no law is constitutional unless it is "necessary and proper" to carry out *specifically enumerated* powers given to the executive, legislative, or judicial branches of government by the Constitution.

The duty of the federal judiciary—the Supreme Court and lower federal courts—is to determine whether laws are constitutional and whether they have been broken. Just as both the executive and legislative branches of government have shown their contempt for the Constitution, so the judiciary has failed to carry out its legitimate responsibilities. Instead of rightfully interpreting the Constitution as a bulwark defending individual freedom against government oppression, many judges in our federal courts reject the Constitution and interpret it to agree with what *they* believe to be politically, economically, morally, or socially correct.

Meanwhile, Congress flouts the Constitution by not only making laws but also interpreting them and enforcing them—responsibilities of the judicial and executive arms of government. Countless agencies, commissions, departments, and boards set up by Congress issue burdensome, unconstitutional guidelines, regulations, and laws. What would the Founding Fathers think of this federal bureaucracy? They would recall what the Declaration of Independence had to say about government and the King of England. "The history of the present King of Great Britain is a history of repeated injuries and usurpations, all having in direct object the establishment of an absolute Tyranny over these States.... He has erected a multitude of New Offices, and sent hither swarms of Officers to harass our people, and eat out their substance."

Freedom Threatened

The patriots of the War for Independence fought to preserve freedom against a "multitude of New Offices" and "swarms of Officers." Later, the people of the United States adopted a Constitution designed to limit government authority and protect individual liberty. That freedom is threatened today, not so much from foreign aggression as from many of our own citizens who do not want to live by the principles of the Constitution.

Senators, members of the House of Representatives, and other government officeholders have sworn that they will support and defend the Constitution "against all enemies, foreign and domestic." Our public officials have also sworn to "bear true faith and allegiance" to the Constitution.

Are they living up to their oath of office? Are other citizens, "WE THE PEOPLE of the United States," bearing "true faith and allegiance" to the Constitution?

Part III

Our Constitution and the principles of freedom are being steadily eroded today. Too many Americans evidently disagree with Thomas Jefferson's basic political philosophy: "Every man wishes to pursue his occupation and to enjoy the fruits of his labors and the produce of his property in peace and safety and with the least possible expense. When these things are accomplished, all the objects for which government ought to be established are answered."

According to Jefferson and other Americans who fought for freedom, the purpose of government was to assure the God-given rights of individuals to work freely, create, build, invent, succeed, fail, and plan their own lives ... without needless government interference. Government should intervene to prevent, prosecute, and punish crime. Government was also responsible for organizing the defense of the nation from foreign aggressors. The two major roles of government were designed to allow free individuals to rise to the heights of individual potential consistent with their own abilities, energy, will power, and personal accountability.

The United States Constitution has worked very well in the past as a bulwark for personal liberty. Now, though, we are faced by a loss of individual rights and a growth of government power. Two views of the Constitution by two past Presidents illustrate a partial cause for our present difficulties.

President William Taft wrote that: " ... the President can exercise no power which cannot be reasonably and fairly traced to some specific grant of power ... in the Constitution or in an act of Congress."

Taft's *strict* interpretation of the Constitution contrasts with President Theodore Roosevelt's *liberal* interpretation of the powers of the Presidency: " ... My belief was that it was not only his (the President's) right but his duty to do anything that the needs of the nation demanded unless such action was forbidden by the Constitution or by the laws."

Over the years since President Theodore Roosevelt wrote about the Presidency, the "liberal" interpretation of the Constitution has gained an ever increasing acceptance by all three branches of the government—executive, legislative, and judicial. This "liberal" concept of government authority tramples upon the Tenth Amendment of the Bill of Rights: "The powers not delegated to the United States by the Constitution, nor prohibited by it to the States, are reserved to the States respectively, or to the people."

The problem is twofold: (1) "WE THE PEOPLE of the United States," as stated in the preamble, have deserted the Constitution. (2) The people's elected and appointed officials have debased the Constitution. If we truly value what freedom we have left, and if we wish to regain what rights we have lost, we must understand the destructive mentality or philosophy that has gripped so many Americans.

The Santa Claus Complex

First, a greater number of Americans are accepting what has been called the "Santa Claus" complex. Some people might want to term it the Big Daddy or Great Uncle Sam complex. At any rate, when citizens look upon the federal government as Santa Claus, they will continue to expect supposedly "free" presents from the government.

While large numbers of businesses, special interest groups, professions, and average citizens are looking to the federal Santa Claus for goodies, their elected officials have an affliction called the "Robin Hood" complex. Actually, the Santa Claus mentality and the Robin Hood philosophy work together to assault the Constitution. In order to play Santa Claus and give to the citizenry federal subsidies, grants, and other aid, government officials must also assume the role of a benevolent Robin Hood.

They do this with a great deal of enthusiasm and sense of morality. Before they can distribute gifts to different segments of the populace, they must first take money from other people. Thus, government plays Robin Hood, taking from the "rich" and giving to the "poor"—the "poor" classified as whomever the federal government so chooses.

The fact is that government cannot create wealth. It cannot give away anything it hasn't first confiscated from the "rich" (industries, businessmen, hard-working individuals) or the citizenry as a whole. Robin Hood does this through taxation. The only other way the federal government can pay for its handouts is simply to create money it cannot or will not bring into the Treasury through taxation. When it creates the new money from the federal printing presses, we suffer inflation.

Although the average citizen decries inflation and excessive taxation, he continues to vote for more government interference in the economic and social life of the United States. Legislators are quite willing to play the parts of Santa Claus and Robin Hood. To do so is the best way to get elected and reelected. They learn by experience and continue to promote the idea that government is motivated by compassion and humanitarianism.

To some extent that is true. A large number of public servants are probably motivated by a desire to do good. Although playing Santa Claus is mostly a matter of self-interest, many government officials honestly believe they are doing what is best for the citizenry of the United States after they assume public office. They believe they can use the authority of government to devise and then carry out plans to bring "social justice," good housing, health care, and the like, to the people. Frankly, they feel that government has a moral obligation to manage our lives. Their goodness in our behalf, however, profanes the Constitution.

Instead of showing loyalty to the principles of the Constitution—limited government and personal liberty—they attempt to create the "good society" according to their own designs. Again, their intentions are good, but they still refuse to have faith in the individual. They really do not think individuals are capable of achieving dignity, economic stability, and justice on their own—within the framework provided by the Constitution.

Holding Officials Responsible

Those government leaders who scorn the principles of the Constitution should be held accountable. On the other hand, the question should be asked as to who put such Robin Hoods in office. The American people, of course, are the ones who vote for the politicians who head for Washington, D.C., to continue the task of planning and regulating our lives. A nation-wide survey reported that 94 percent of those surveyed believed that the main duty of a Congressman was "making sure his district gets its fair share of government money and projects."

The survey shows that Americans are quite willing to accept the idea that their elected officials are in the business of distributing monies from the federal Treasury. Apparently, few citizens think the responsibility of their Senators and Congressmen is to cut back on the growth of government.

We—legislators and average citizens—need to reexamine the Constitution and realize the extent to which we have degraded it. We should think about a proposal made by Nobel Prize-winning economist Milton Friedman. Considering the fact that people in government are trying to do good with other people's money, Dr. Friedman suggests that we need an eleventh amendment to the ten already in the Bill of Rights. The new amendment would ensure that every individual would have the right to do good—*with his or her own money.*

In reality, we already have the right to do good for others at our own expense, although it can be said that this right is being hindered due to oppressive taxation and government-sponsored inflation. We cannot very well help other people if we do not have the money to do so.

Regardless of stifling taxation, our right to help others is being neglected or rejected as we place charity, human concern, and humanitarianism in the hands of the government.

Parental Guidance

For example, some Americans are concerned that advertising and some children's programming on TV is bad for the kiddies and the stability of the family. Advertisers, they say, take advantage of innocent young viewers. The youngsters are brainwashed and led astray to clamor for toys, candy, or other items that they do not need. The duped children are more or less forced by the commercials to demand the products seen on TV.

Thus, we have the tragic spectacle (as some Americans see it) of boys and girls strong-arming their helpless parents into buying the trivial products advertised on TV. If the parents should refuse, havoc arises in the family. Adults and children suffer emotional trauma. If the parents agree to the children's demands, then the families waste money on the supposedly useless products.

The answer for the above problems, as suggested by those who dislike the quality of children's programs and advertising, is either government regulation or "social conscience" on the part of business. "Social conscience" means that companies that manufacture children's products should sponsor their programs without showing ads for toys, cereals, and other products. We could then have commercial-free children's TV ... which would eventually mean government subsidy of children's programs at taxpayers' expense.

Now then, if you ask the proponents of government intervention whether or not they allow their own kids to watch what they, the parents, say is bad children's TV, they might very well answer with an emphatic "No!" That being the case, we should ask such people why they feel so superior to their fellow Americans. In other words, why is it that they presumably have enough concern for their children to turn off the booby tube, but other parents apparently cannot make the same decision in behalf of their own children?

Other questions we might ask are these: If changes really need to be made in children's TV, why don't those who want the changes use their own money to establish a private foundation to bring about whatever improvements they feel are necessary? Why don't those concerned about little Johnny's appetite for candy launch a nationwide campaign—paid for out of their own pockets and through voluntary contributions—to inform parents that they are perfectly capable of doing two things: (1) saying "No!" to their children, and (2) turning off the TV set or making certain that their children do so.

The fact is that we will always have our goodhearted, well-intentioned crusaders who want to bring about what they believe to be a better society. Their moral failure lies in the fact that they basically have faith only in their *own* intentions and the power of government to implement those good intentions for *all our good* ... regardless of whether we agree or not.

Those who support more government regulations, "guidelines," and laws tend to believe that the ordinary citizen is not capable of making intelligent decisions on his own. This distrust of individual responsibility illustrates some of America's alienation from the Constitution. The principle of limited government authority is spurned. Individual freedom and the Bill of Rights are belittled.

The Bill of Rights

The Bill of Rights was meant to be a steadfast safeguard to individual liberty These ten amendments were *prohibitions* against excessive government power. They upheld individual rights against government interference. Now, though, an increasing number of Americans are accepting and encouraging a different concept of human rights. They would accept a new bill of rights that would not *restrict* government power, but instead authorize more government intrusion into our daily affairs.

As the federal government expands and becomes more intensive, we proceed further down the path toward servitude. Willingly or unknowingly, most Americans accept their fate. Our future was somewhat prophesied by James Madison: "There are more instances of the abridgment of the freedom of the people by gradual and silent encroachments of those in power than by violent and sudden usurpation."

Madison realized that freedom was threatened by the gradual, often deceptive growth of government power. Whenever government steps beyond its constitutional duties, society begins to deteriorate. When government tries to arrange and direct society in defiance of the Constitution, a type of class warfare begins. As government attempts to pay for its various programs, it must resort to increased redistribution of the wealth. Society and politics become a battle ground where everyone demands "his share" of the funds in the federal Treasury.

Along with the continual struggle by lobbyists, special interest groups, and other beneficiaries for a cut of the federal pie, there is a corresponding loss of integrity. When the government takes from some (or all) to give to others, the redistribution of wealth hurts all segments of society—both the productive and the not so productive.

For example, a businessman finds himself in financial trouble due to his own incompetence or mismanagement. He looks to the federal government for help, and he receives it. A second economic crisis hits him, and he again finds himself rescued by government aid. Soon, he has lost his sense of self-responsibility. He has become dependent upon a paternalistic government. In this state of dependence, there is very little guilt about having his own failure subsidized by money taken from the productive elements of society.

Dependence and Servitude

Likewise, the productive people—whether they be corporations or individuals—slowly lose their sense of accountability, initiative, and self-reliance. They ask themselves why they should continue striving so hard, only to have the fruit of their labors taxed away for the benefit of others. Thus, there is a growing tendency for the thrifty, energetic, and hard-working people in society to work less and eventually become dependent upon government.

Government intervention is the first step towards dependence upon government. After dependence comes servitude.

If we are to escape the servitude of a socialistic type of government, we must act upon the advice of Patrick Henry: "No free government, or the blessings of liberty can be preserved to any people but by a firm adherence to justice, moderation, temperance, frugality and virtue, and by a frequent recurrence to fundamental principles."

For the United States in the 1980s, "fundamental principles" should be the Constitution. Although the work of the Founding Fathers in 1787 is far from perfect, the Constitution does reflect an honest, firm adherence to certain basic truths about freedom and the purpose of government. One of the worst mistakes we can make is to believe that the Constitution is not relevant for today. The opposite is true.

More than ever, we need to uphold the Constitution with the realization that it is based upon certain wise, unchanging principles—principles that should be understood and obeyed today as much as they were during Madison's day. The Constitution is not an outmoded document to be shrugged off as something that cannot or should not direct our political, economic, and moral life today.

Regardless of how durable the Constitution is, it cannot protect freedom unless "WE THE PEOPLE of the United States" heed George Washington when he said: "The preservation of the sacred fire of liberty and the destiny of the republican model of government are justly considered, perhaps, as deeply, as finally, staked on the experiment intrusted to the hands of the American people."

Identifying Those Who Corrupt the Constitution

If we have an understanding of how the Constitution can protect our freedom from government encroachment, we must first identify those individuals and groups who are corrupting the Constitution. Are they federal bureaucrats who place their faith in larger and more powerful government? Yes, but who puts them in office in the first place?

"WE THE PEOPLE of the United States"!

Before we can think about the bad guys holding public office, we have to ask ourselves how unfaithful we have been to the Constitution. The average American's desire for urban renewal, aid to education, price supports, and other handouts is the root of oppressive government. When we stop asking for needless government intervention, the constitutional renegades in Congress will not be reelected.

As soon as we have our own houses in order regarding allegiance to the Constitution, we can turn our attention to those people in government who want to continue spending our tax money, regulating our lives, and seducing other segments of society with their programs of government aid. Having a profound understanding of the Constitution, we can judge how well our elected and appointed officials are living up to their oath of office.

Sometimes it is possible to detect hostility toward the Constitution simply by knowing what government officials say in speeches, interviews, press conferences, or by the written word. More important, however, are their voting records and daily actions in office. Can your own Congressman and Senators answer a truthful "I do" to the oath of office?

Do you solemnly swear that you will support and defend the Constitution of the United States against all enemies, foreign and domestic; that you will bear true faith and allegiance to the same; that you take this obligation freely, without any mental reservation or purpose of evasion; and that you will well and faithfully discharge the duties of the office on which you are about to enter: So help you God?

Politicians come and go. New Congresses are sworn in as our political process carries on year by year. New administrations take over, and new Cabinets are appointed. Regardless of who our elected and appointed officials are—whether they be defenders or betrayers of the Constitution—the tasks before us always remain the same. We are to comprehend the meaning of the Constitution and uphold it by accepting responsibility for planning our own lives. Once our own allegiance to the Constitution is firm and true, we can scrutinize our government officials with Thomas Jefferson's wisdom in mind:

"In questions of power let no more be heard of confidence in man, but bind him down from mischief by the chains of the Constitution."

IV. "BY THE CHAINS OF THE CONSTITUTION"

The Political Economy of the U.S. Constitution

by Dwight R. Lee

During the bicentennial of the U.S. Constitution it is appropriate to reflect on the political wisdom of our Founding Fathers. No written constitution in history has established a more durable or successful democracy than has the U.S. Constitution. A full appreciation of the Founding Fathers, however, requires an understanding of the economic as well as the political consequences of our Constitution. Every economy is a political economy and the enormous success of the U.S. economy has been as dependent on our political system as on our economic system.

Indeed, many of the problems that currently plague the U.S. economy are the result of our failure to hold on to the political wisdom that guided our Founding Fathers. Economic knowledge is obviously important in the effort to promote economic growth and development. But no matter how sound our economic understanding, economic performance will continue to suffer until we once again recognize that political power is a force for progress only when tightly constrained and directed toward limited objectives.

The genesis of the political and economic wisdom of our Founding Fathers is found in the fact that they distrusted government while fully recognizing the necessity of government for a beneficent social order. The cautious embrace the Founders gave government is reflected in their view of democracy as necessary but not sufficient for the proper control of government.

The concerns that led to the colonists' break with Great Britain were very much in the public mind when the Constitutional Convention met in Philadelphia during the summer of 1787. The well known prerevolution rallying cry, "No taxation without representation," reflected a clear understanding of the dangers that accompanied any exercise of government power not answerable to those who are governed. That the government established by the Constitution would be democratic in form was not in doubt. Unchecked democratic rule, however, was anathema to the most thoughtful of the Founding Fa-

Dr. Lee is a professor of economics at the University of Georgia. This article was originally published in the February 1987 issue of *The Freeman*.

127

thers. A grievance against English rule rivaling that of "taxation without representation" concerned the sovereign authority assumed by the English Parliament in 1767. In that year Parliament decreed that, through its democratically elected members, it had the power to pass or strike down any law it desired. The colonists had brought with them the English political tradition, which dated back at least to the Magna Carta of 1215: the people have certain rights that should be immune to political trespass regardless of momentary desires of a democratic majority. The concern was not only that the colonists were unrepresented in Parliament but, more fundamentally, that Parliament assumed unlimited power to meddle in the private lives of individuals whether they were represented or not.

Although the Founding Fathers were determined to establish a government that was democratic in the limited sense that political decisions could not ignore citizen input, they had no intention of creating a government that was fully responsive to majority interests. In many ways the Constitution is designed to frustrate the desire of political majorities to work their will through the exercise of government power. The most obvious example of this is the first ten amendments to the Constitution, or the Bill of Rights. These amendments guarantee certain individual freedoms against political infringement regardless of majority will. If, for example, freedom of speech and the press was dependent on majority vote many unpopular but potentially important ideas would never be disseminated. How effectively would a university education expose students to new and controversial ideas if professors had to submit their lectures for majority approval?

Other examples exist of the undemocratic nature of the government set up by the Constitution. There is very little that can be considered democratic about the Supreme Court. Its nine members are appointed for life, and their decision can nullify a law passed by the Congress and supported by the overwhelming majority of the American public. In a five to four decision one member of the court, insulated from the democratic process, can frustrate the political will of a nearly unanimous public. The arrangement whereby the President can reverse the will of the Congress through his veto power is certainly not a very democratic one. Neither is the Senate where the vote cast by a senator from Wyoming carries weight equal to the vote by the senator from California, even though the California senator represents a population 50 times larger than does the Wyoming senator. The senators from the 26 least populated states can prevent a bill from clearing Congress, even though it has incontestable popular support in the country at large. Congress is actually less democratic than just indicated once it is recognized that popular bills can be prevented from ever being considered in the full House of Representatives or Senate by a few representatives who serve on key congressional committees.

It is safe to say that the chief concern of the framers of the Constitution was not that of insuring a fully democratic political structure. Instead they were concerned with limiting government power in order to minimize the abuse of majority rule. In the words of R. A. Humphreys, "they were concerned not to make America safe for democracy, but to make democracy safe for America."[1]

Prelude to the Constitutional Convention

Fear of the arbitrary power that could be exercised by a strong central government, democratically controlled or otherwise, was evident from the Articles of Confederation. The Articles of Confederation established the "national government" of the thirteen colonies after they declared their independence from England. There is some exaggeration in this use of the term national government, since the Articles did little more than formalize an association (or confederation) of thirteen independent and sovereign states. While the congress created by the Articles of Confederation was free to deliberate on important issues and pass laws, it had no means of enforcing them. The Articles did not even establish an executive branch of government, and congressional resolutions were nothing more than recommendations that the states could honor if they saw fit. The taxes that states were assessed to support the Revolutionary War effort were often ignored, and raising money to outfit and pay the American army was a frustrating business.

Because of the weakness of the national government, the state governments under the Articles of Confederation were strong and often misused their power. Majority coalitions motivated by special interests found it relatively easy to control state legislatures and tramp on the interests of minorities. Questionable banking schemes were promoted by debtors, with legislative assistance, in order to reduce the real value of their debt obligations. States often resorted to the simple expedient of printing money to satisfy their debts. Trade restrictions between the states were commonplace as legislators responded to the interests of organized producers while ignoring the concerns of the general consumers. There was a 1786 meeting in Annapolis, Maryland, of the five middle states to discuss ways to reduce trade barriers between the states. At this meeting the call was made for a larger meeting in Philadelphia in the following year to discuss more general problems with the Articles of Confederation. This meeting became the Constitutional Convention.

Achieving Weakness Through Strength

It was the desire of Madison, Hamilton, and other leaders at the Constitutional Convention to replace the government established by the Articles of Confederation with a central government that was more than an association of sovereign states. The new government would have to be strong enough to impose some uniformity to financial, commercial, and foreign policy and to establish some general protections for citizens against the power of state governments if the new nation was to be viable and prosperous. In the words of James Madison, we needed a "general government" sufficiently strong to protect "the rights of the minority," which are in jeopardy "in all cases where a majority are united by a common interest or passion."[2] But this position was not an easy one to defend. Many opponents to a genuine national government saw little merit in the desire to strengthen government power at one level in order to prevent the abuse of government power at another level. Was there any genuine way around this apparent conflict? Many thought not, short of giving up on the hope of a union of all the states. There were those who argued that the expanse and diversity of the thirteen states, much less that of the larger continent, were simply too great to be united under one government without sacrificing the liberty that they had just fought to achieve.[3]

Madison, however, saw no conflict in strengthening the national government in order to control the abuses of government in general. In his view the best protection against arbitrary government authority was through centers of government power that were in effective competition with one another. The control that one interest group, or faction, could realize through a state government would be largely nullified when political decisions resulted from the interaction of opposing factions within many states. Again quoting Madison,

> The influence of factious leaders may kindle a flame within their particular States but will be unable to spread a general conflagration through the other States.... A rage for paper money for an abolition of debts, for an equal division of property, or for any other improper or wicked project, will be less

apt to pervade the whole body of the Union than a particular member of it. . . .[4]

A central government strong enough to unite a large and diverse set of states would weaken, rather than strengthen, the control that government in general could exercise.

To the framers of the Constitution weakening government in the sense just discussed meant making sure that government was unable to extend itself beyond a relatively limited role in the affairs of individuals. This does not imply, however, impotent government. The referees in a football game, for example, certainly are not the strongest participants on the field and have limited control over specific outcomes in the game. Yet in enforcing the general rules of the game the decisions of the referees are potent indeed. Government, in its role as referee, obviously cannot lack the authority to back up its decisions. In addition to performing its refereeing function, it is also desirable for government to provide certain public goods; goods such as national defense that will not be adequately provided by the private market. Again this is a duty which requires a measure of authority; in this case the authority to impose taxes up to the limit required to provide those public goods which are worth more than they cost.

How to Impose Control?

In granting government the power to do those things government should do, the Founding Fathers knew they were creating a power that had to be carefully controlled. But how could this control be imposed? It could not be imposed by specifying a particular list of government do's and don't's. Such a list would be impossibly detailed and even if it could be drafted it would need to be revised constantly in response to changes in such considerations as population size, age distribution, wealth, and the state of technology. Instead, government has to be controlled by a general set of constitutional rules within which governmental decisions are made, with specific government outcomes determined through the resulting political process. It was the hope of those at the Constitutional Convention to establish a political process, through constitutional reform, that brought government power into action only when needed to serve the broad interests of the public.

This hope was not based on the naive, though tempting, notion that somehow individuals would ignore their personal advantages

and concentrate on the general advantage when making political decisions. While noble motives are seldom completely absent in guiding
individual behavior, whether private or public, the Founding Fathers
took as a given that most people, most of the time, maintain a healthy
regard for their private concerns. The only way to prevent self-seeking
people from abusing government power was to structure the rules of
the political game in such a way that it would be costly for them to
do so. The objective of the framers was to create a government that
was powerful enough to do those things that received political approval but to establish a political process that made it exceedingly
difficult to obtain political approval for any action that lacked broad
public support.

There were, of course, some powers that the national government
was not constitutionally permitted to exercise. The national government was created by the states, and until the Constitution all governmental power resided in the states. Through the Constitution the states
relinquished some of their powers to the national government, e.g.,
the power to impose taxes on the citizens, establish uniform rules of
naturalization, raise an army and navy, and declare war. In addition
the states agreed to refrain from exercising certain powers; e.g., the
power to coin money, pass laws impairing the obligation of contracts,
and pass retroactive laws. Important government powers remained
in the states, however, with some of them located in the local governments. Thus the powers that could be exercised by government were
limited, and the powers that did exist were diffused over three levels
of government. The Constitution further diffused power at the national level by spreading it horizontally over three branches of government, the power of each acting as a check and balance on the power
of the others.

The intent of the Founding Fathers was to so fragment government power that it would be extremely difficult for any narrowly
motivated faction to gain sufficient control to work its political will.
Only those objectives widely shared and consistent with constitutional limits would be realized through the use of government power.
The beauty of the political process established by the Constitution is
that it is cumbersome and inefficient. According to Forrest McDonald
the process is "So cumbersome and inefficient ... that the people,
however virtuous or wicked, could not activate it. It could be activated
through deals and deceit, through bargains and bribery, through log-
rolling and lobbying and trickery and trading, the tactics that go with
man's baser attributes, most notably his greed and his love of power.
And yet, in the broad range and on the average, these private tactics

and motivations could operate effectively only when they were compatible with the public good, for they were braked by the massive inertia of society as a whole."[5] Or, as Clinton Rossiter has said of the Founding Fathers' motives in creating the system of checks and balances, "Liberty rather than authority, protection rather than power, delay rather than efficiency were the concern of these constitution-makers."[6]

The Economic Success of the Constitution

It is hard to argue with the success of the U.S. Constitution. The history of the United States in the decades after the ratification of the Constitution was one of limited government and individual liberty, major increases in the size of the U.S. in terms of population and geography, and unprecedented growth in economic well-being. With the major exception of (and to a large extent, in spite of) the unfortunate legacy of slavery and the Civil War, millions of diverse people were able to pursue their individual objectives through harmonious and productive interaction with one another. The opportunities created by the process of specialization and exchange made possible by limited and responsible government motivated an outpouring of productive effort that soon transformed a wilderness into one of the most prosperous nations in the world. The role the U.S. Constitution played in this transformation was an important one and can be explained in terms of both negative and positive incentives.

Broadly speaking there are two ways an individual can acquire wealth: (1) capture existing wealth through nonproductive transfer activities, or (2) create new wealth through productive activities. A major strength of the Constitution is that it established positive incentives for the latter activities and negative incentives for the former.

The most obvious form of nonproductive transfer activity is private theft. The thief simply takes through force or stealth something that belongs to someone else. A primary purpose for establishing government is to outlaw private theft. But the power that government necessarily possesses if it is to enforce laws against private theft is a power that affords individuals or groups the opportunity to benefit through public "theft" (legal transfer activity to phrase it more gently). The more vague and ineffective the limits on government authority, the less difficult it is to acquire legal transfers through political activity, and the larger the number of people who will find this activity offering them the greatest profit opportunity.

While those who are successful at the transfer game can increase their personal wealth, in some cases significantly, it is obvious that the country at large cannot increase its wealth through transfer activity. What one person receives is what another person, or group, loses. No net wealth is created, and for this reason transfer activity is often referred to as a zero-sum game. In fact, it is more accurately described as a negative-sum game. The attempts of some to acquire transfers, and the predictable efforts of others to protect their wealth against transfers, require the use of real resources. These resources could be productively employed creating new wealth rather than wasted in activities that do nothing more than redistribute existing wealth. For every dollar that one person receives from a transfer activity the rest of the community sacrifices more than a dollar.

Incentives to Produce

A major virtue of the U.S. Constitution was that it discouraged people from playing the transfer game. By establishing a governmental apparatus that was very difficult to put in motion for narrowly motivated purposes, the Constitution dampened the incentive to use government as a means of acquiring the wealth of others. This is not to say that the government was not used as a vehicle for transfer in the early days of our constitutional government. Every political decision results in some redistribution of wealth, and no governmental structure will ever completely insulate the political process against the transfer activities of some.[7] But the opportunity for personal enrichment through political activity was limited. Most people found that the best way to increase their wealth was through wealth-producing activities.

It was here that the political structure established by the Constitution created positive incentives. Not only did the Constitution establish a climate in which it was difficult to profit from transfer activities, it also created a setting in which productive effort was rewarded. By providing protection against the arbitrary taking of private property (the Fifth Article of the Bill of Rights) people were given assurance that they would not be denied the value generated by their efforts. This provided people with strong incentives to apply themselves and their property diligently. In the words of M. Bruce Johnson, "America was a place where if you were ready to sow, then by God you could reap."[8]

But the motivation to work hard is not enough for a productive economy. Also needed is information on the objectives toward which effort and resources are best directed, as well as incentives to act on this information. It is the protection of private property that provides the foundation for a system of price communication and market interaction which serves to guide effort and resources into their most valuable employments. To complete this system the concept of private property rights has to be expanded to include the right to transfer one's property to others at terms regulated only by the mutual consent of those who are party to the exchange. The lower the cost of entering into transactions of this type, the more effectively the resulting market prices will allow people to communicate and coordinate with each other to the advantage of all. The U.S. Constitution lowered these transaction costs by reducing government's ability to interfere with mutually acceptable exchanges and by putting the weight of the national government behind the sanctity of the contracts that resulted from these exchanges.

In what has become known as the "contract clause" of the Constitution, the states are forbidden from passing any "law impairing the obligation of contracts...." In the same clause the states are also forbidden from imposing tariff duties on imports or exports (unless absolutely necessary for enforcing inspection laws). In the "commerce clause" the national government was given the power to regulate commerce "among the several states." Though the commerce clause can be interpreted (and indeed has been in recent decades) as providing the central government the authority to substitute political decisions for market decisions over interstate commerce, the U.S. Congress ignored this possibility until it passed the Interstate Commerce Act in 1887. Prior to the Civil War the commerce clause was used instead by the U.S. Supreme Court to rule unconstitutional state laws that attempted to regulate commerce. After 1868 the Supreme Court made use of the doctrine of due process as expressed in the fourteenth amendment to strike down many government attempts to violate the sanctity of contracts through their regulation of such things as prices, working hours, working conditions, and pay.

In summary, the Constitution created an environment in which private advantage was best served by engaging in productive positive-sum activities. The specialization and exchange facilitated by the constitutional rules of the game is a system in which individuals can improve their own position only by serving the interests of others. When private property is protected against confiscation, an individual becomes wealthy only by developing skills, creating new products, or innovating better technologies and thereby providing consumers with more attractive options than they would otherwise have. In a truly free enterprise economy, with the minimum government role envisioned by the framers of the Constitution, the rich are the benefactors of the masses, not the exploiters as commonly depicted. Wealth through exploitation becomes possible only when unrestricted government allows negative-sum transfer activity to become more profitable than positive-sum market activity.

Constitutional Erosion and the Rise of Political Piracy

The early success of the Constitution, and the economic system that developed under it, is reflected in the fact that relatively few people felt any urgency to worry about politics. Political activity offered little return as there was little chance to exploit others, and little need to prevent from being exploited by others, through political involvement. People could safely get on with their private affairs without having to worry about the machinations and intrigues of politicians and bureaucrats in faraway places. But this very success can, over time, undermine itself as a politically complacent public increases the opportunities for those who are politically involved to engage in political chicanery.

Motivating people to maintain the political vigilance necessary to protect themselves against government is always a difficult task. The individual who becomes involved in political activity incurs a direct cost. By devoting time and resources in attempting to realize political objectives he is sacrificing alternative objectives. The motivation to become politically active will be a compelling one only if the expected political outcome is worth more to the individual than the necessary personal sacrifices. This will typically not be the case when the objective is to prevent government from undermining the market process that it is government's proper role to protect. The benefits that are realized from limited government are general benefits. These benefits accrue to each individual in the community whether or not he personally works to constrain government.

Over the broad range of political issues, then, people quite rationally do not want to get involved. This is not to say, however, that everyone will be apathetic about all political issues. This clearly is not the case, and it is possible to predict the circumstances that will motivate political activism. Often a relatively small number of individuals will receive most of the benefit from a particular political decision, while the community at large bears the cost. Members of such a special interest group will find it relatively easy to organize for the purpose of exerting political influence. The number of people to organize is comparatively small; the group is probably already somewhat organized around a common interest, and the political issues that affect this common interest will be of significant importance to each member of the group.

Of course, the free rider problem exists in all organizational efforts, but the smaller the group and the narrower the objective the easier it is to get everyone to contribute his share. Also, the benefits of effective effort can be so great to particular individuals in the group that they will be motivated to work for the common objective even if some members of the group do free-ride. Not surprisingly then, narrowly focused groups commonly will have the motivation and ability to organize for the purpose of pursuing political objectives.[9] The result is political piracy in which the politically organized are able to capture ill-gotten gains from the politically unorganized.

The constitutional limits on government imposed effective restraints on political piracy for many years after the Constitution was ratified. There are undoubtedly many explanations for this. The vast frontier rich in natural resources offered opportunities for wealth creation that, for most people, overwhelmed the opportunities for personal gain through government transfer activity. Also, it can take time for politically effective coalitions to form after the slate has been wiped clean, so to speak, by a social upheaval of the magnitude of first the Revolutionary War and then the Civil War.[10] Public attitudes were also an important consideration in the control of the government.

Much has been written about how the pervasive distrust of government power among the American people shaped the framing of a Constitution that worked to limit government.[11] What might be more important is that the Constitution worked to limit government because the public had a healthy distrust of government power. For example, in the 1860s the Baltimore and Ohio railroad had its Harpers Ferry bridge blown up many times by both the Confederate and Union armies, and each time the railroad rebuilt the bridge with its own funds without any attempt to get the government to pick up part of the tab. Or consider the fact that in 1887 President Grover Cleveland vetoed an appropriation of $25,000 for seed corn to assist drought-stricken farmers with the statement, "It is not the duty of government to support the people."[12] There is little doubt that Cleveland's view on this matter was in keeping with broad public opinion.

The constitutional safeguards against government transfer activity unfortunately have lost much of their effectiveness over the years. The western frontier disappeared, and a long period of relative stability in the political order provided time for factions to become entrenched in the political process. Of more direct and crucial importance, however, in the move from productive activity to transfer activity has been the weakening judicial barrier to the use of government to advance special interests. The 1877 Supreme Court decision in *Munn v. Illinois* is often considered to be a watershed case. This decision upheld a lower court ruling that the Illinois state legislature had the authority to determine the rates that could be charged for storing grain. This decision, by sanctioning an expanded role for government in the determination of prices, increased the payoff to political activity relative to market activity and established an important precedent for future increases in that payoff.

In *Chicago Milwaukee and St. Paul Railroad Co. v. Minnesota*, decided in 1890, the Supreme Court imposed what appeared to be limits on state regulation of economic activity by ruling that such regulation must be reasonable. Unfortunately, this reasonableness doctrine put the effectiveness of judicial restraint on government at the mercy of current fashion in social thought. What is considered unreasonable at one time may be considered quite reasonable at another.[13] It was unreasonable for the Baltimore and Ohio railroad to consider requesting government funds to repair its Harpers Ferry bridge, destroyed by government forces, during the Civil War. In the 1980s it was considered reasonable for Chrysler Corporation to request and receive a federal government bailout because Chrysler was not competing successfully for the consumer's dollar.

Undermining Constitutional Law

The idea of reasonable regulation significantly undermined the concept of a higher constitutional law that established protections needed for the long-run viability of a free and productive social order. Once the notion of reasonable regulation stuck its nose into the judicial tent it was just a matter of time before the courts began seeing their task as that of judging particular outcomes rather than overseeing the general rules of the game. Illustrative of this changing emphasis was the legal brief submitted by Louis Brandeis, then an attorney for the state of Oregon, in the 1908 case *Muller v. Oregon*. At issue was the constitutionality of an Oregon law which regulated the working hours of women. The Brandeis brief contained only a few pages addressing constitutional considerations and well over one hundred pages of social economic data and argumentation attempting to establish the unfortunate consequences of women working long hours. It was a judgment on the reasonableness of a particular outcome, women working long hours, rather than constitutional considerations, which were considered of paramount importance and led to a Supreme Court ruling in favor of Oregon.[14] When the constitutionality of legislation stands or falls on the "reasonableness" of the particular outcomes it hopes to achieve, opportunities increase for people to increase their wealth through nonproductive political activity.

In the 1911 case *United States v. Grimand,* the Supreme Court handed down a decision that significantly increased the private return to obtaining transfers through political influence. Prior to this decision, the U.S. Congress had increasingly moved toward granting administrative agencies the authority to promulgate specific rules in order to implement the general policy objectives outlined by Congress. In *United States v. Grimand* the high court empowered these administrative rulings with the full force of law. After this decision, the cost of successfully using government authority to transfer wealth decreased significantly as special interest groups seeking preferential treatment could concentrate their influence on a few key members of a particular administrative board or agency. The typical result of this has been the development of symbiotic relationships between bureaucratic agencies and their special interest clients. A special interest group can thrive on the benefits transferred to it by the ruling of a bureaucracy, and the bureaucracy's budget and prestige will depend on a thriving special interest group demanding its services.[15]

What we have observed over the years is a slow, somewhat erratic, but unmistakable breakdown in the protection the Constitution provides the public against arbitrary government power. Those who want to get on with the task of creating new wealth have much less assurance today then they did in the past that significant portions of the wealth they create will not be confiscated by government and transferred to those who have specialized in political influence.

Maintaining constitutional constraints on government transfer activity is a task requiring constant vigilance. Once a breakdown in these constraints begins, it can initiate a destructive dynamic of increasing government transfers that is difficult to control. Any change that makes it easier to obtain transfers through government will motivate some people to redirect their efforts away from productive enterprises and into transfer enterprises. As this is done, those who continue to create new wealth find the payoff from doing so is somewhat diminished as more of this wealth is being taken from them. This further reduction in the relative return to productive activity motivates yet more people to use government power to benefit at the expense of others. Furthermore, the burdens and inefficiencies created by one government program will be used as "justification" for yet additional government programs which will create new burdens and inefficiencies.[16] This dynamic can lead to what is best characterized as a "transfer society."[17]

Political Piracy and the Transfer Society

Once we start down the road to the transfer society we can easily find ourselves trapped in a situation almost everyone will disapprove of, but which no one will be willing to change. The analogy of piracy is appropriate here. When all ships are productively employed shipping the goods, a large amount of wealth can be generated. But if sanctions against piracy are eased a few shippers may find it to their personal advantage to stop shipping and start pirating the merchandise being shipped by others, even though this reduces the total wealth available. This piracy by the few will reduce the return the others receive from shipping, and there will be an increase in the number finding the advantage in piracy. Eventually the point may be reached where everyone is sailing the seas looking for the booty that used to be shipped but is no longer. No one is doing well under these circumstances, and indeed, all would be much better off if everyone would return to shipping the goods. Yet who will be willing to return to productive shipping when everyone else is a pirate?

Obviously we have not yet arrived at the point of being a full-blown transfer society; not everyone has become a political pirate. There are plenty of people who remain productive, and they still receive a measure of protection against the confiscation of the returns to their efforts by the constitutional limitations that remain on government power. But there can be no doubt that these limitations are less effective today than they were in the past. This erosion is in large measure due to a change in the prevailing attitude toward government. The fear of unrestrained government power that guided the Founding Fathers has been largely replaced with the view that discretionary government power is a force for social good. If there is a problem, government supposedly has the obligation and ability to solve it. Such public attitudes have a decisive influence on the effectiveness of constitutional limitations.

Simply writing something down on a document called the Constitution does not by itself make it so. And, because of this fact, Alexis de Tocqueville, writing in the 1830s, predicted that the U.S. Constitution would eventually cease to exercise effective restraint on government. According to Tocqueville, "The government of the Union depends almost entirely upon legal fictions." He continued that it would be difficult to imagine that it is possible by the aid of legal fictions to prevent men from finding out and employing those means of gratifying their passions which have been left open to them."[18]

But controlling our passions is what constitutional government is all about. In the absence of government we have the anarchy of the Hobbesian jungle in which those who control their passion for immediate gratification and apply their efforts toward long-run objectives only increase their vulnerability to the predation of those who exercise no control or foresight. Granting government the power to enforce general rules of social interaction is surely a necessary condition if a productive social order is to emerge from a state of anarchy. But without strict constitutional limits on the scope of government activity, the existence of government power will only increase the scope of effective predation. The notion that government can solve all problems becomes a convenient pretense for those who would solve their problems, not in cooperation with others, but at the expense of others. Unlimited government reduces the personal advantage to the productive pursuit of long-run objectives just as surely as does anarchy. In such a case, government is little more than the means of moving from the anarchy of the Hobbesian jungle to the anarchy of the political jungle.

The American experience, however, demonstrates convincingly that with a healthy fear of government power and a realistic understanding of human nature, a constitution can be designed that, over a long period of time, will effectively constrain government to operate within the limits defined by the delicate balance between proper power and prudent restraint. All that is needed to restore the U.S. Constitution to its full effectiveness is a return to the political wisdom that guided our Founding Fathers 200 years ago.

Conclusion

The United States is a wealthy country today in large part because our Founding Fathers had what can be quite accurately described as a negative attitude toward government. They had little confidence in the ability of government to promote social well-being through the application of government power to achieve particular ends. In their view, the best that government can realistically hope to achieve is the establishment of a social setting in which individuals are free, within the limits of general laws, to productively pursue their own objectives. This negative view of government contrasts sharply with the dominant view today; the view that government is the problem solver of

142 / Dwight R. Lee

last resort and has an obligation to provide a solution to any problem not resolved immediately in the private sector. Unfortunately, this positive view of government is less conducive to positive consequences than the negative view of the Founders. According to F. A. Hayek:

> The first [positive view] gives us a sense of unlimited power to realize our wishes, while the second [negative view] leads to the insight that there are limitations to what we can deliberately bring about, and to the recognition that some of our present hopes are delusions. Yet the effect of allowing ourselves to be deluded by the first view has always been that man has actually limited the scope of what he can achieve. For it has always been the recognition of the limits of the possible which has enabled man to make full use of his powers.[19]

The exercise of government can, without doubt, be used to accomplish particular ends. Neither can it be denied that many of the specific outcomes realized through government programs provide important benefits and advance worthy objectives. But, as is always the case, those accomplishments are only realized at a cost, and the pervasive truth about government accomplishments is that those who benefit from them are seldom those who pay the cost. Indeed, much of the motivation for engaging in political actions is to escape the discipline imposed by the market where individuals are accountable for the cost of their choices.

The escape from market discipline is the inevitable consequence of reducing the constitutional limits on the use of government power. The immediate and visible benefits that are generated by wide-ranging government discretion are paid for by a shift in the incentive structure that, over the long run, will reduce the amount of good that can be accomplished. More, much more, has been accomplished by the American people because our Founding Fathers had a strong sense of the limits on what can be accomplished by government.

---

1. R. A. Humphreys, "The Rule of Law and The American Revolution," *Law Quarterly Review* (1937). Also quoted in F. A. Hayek, *The Constitution of Liberty* (Chicago: University of Chicago Press, 1960), p. 474.

2. *Records of the Federal Convention of 1787*, Max Ferrand, ed. (New Haven: Yale University Press, 1937), Vol. 1., p. 57 and pp. 134–35.

3. See Herbert J. Storing, *What the Anti-Federalists Were for: The Political Thought of the Opponents of the Constitution* (Chicago: The University of Chicago Press, 1981).

4. Madison in Federalist 10, *The Federalist Papers* (New York: New American Library Edition, 1961).

5. Forrest McDonald, *E Pluribus Unum: The Foundation of the American Republic 1776–1790* (Indianapolis: Liberty Press, 1979), p. 316.

6. Clinton Rossiter, *Seedtime of the Republic: The Origin of the American Tradition of Political Liberty* (New York: Harcourt, Brace and World, 1953), p. 425.

7. For a discussion of the use of government to transfer wealth throughout American history, see Jonathan R. T. Hughes, *The Governmental Habit: Economic Controls from Colonial Times to the Present* (New York: Basic Books, 1977).

8. M. Bruce Johnson , ed., *Resolving the Housing Crisis: Government Policy, Decontrol, and the Public Interest* (San Francisco: Pacific Institute for Public Research, 1982), p. 3.

9. According to Milton Friedman, "The most potent group in a democracy like ours is a small minority that has a special interest which it values very highly, for which it is willing to give its vote, regardless of what happens elsewhere, and about which the rest of the community does not care very strongly." See Milton Friedman, "Special Interest and His Law," *Chicago Bar Record* (June 1970).

10. Mancur Olson, *The Rise and Decline of Nations* (New Haven: Yale University Press, 1982).

11. Gordon S. Wood, *The Creation of the American Republic 1776–1787* (Chapel Hill: The University of North Carolina Press, 1969), especially chapter 1.

12. Quoted in A. Nevins, *Grover Cleveland: A Study in Courage* (New York: Dodd Mead, 1932).

13. In spite of the two decisions just cited, between 1897 and 1937, the Supreme Court made use of the due process clause of the Fourteenth Amendment to reach decisions that served to protect the market process against political intrusions. See Bernard Siegan, Economic Liberties and the Constitution (Chicago: University of Chicago Press, 1981). Unfortunately, this pattern of judicial decision was not solid enough to prevent these decisions from being ignored or overruled when the political climate and prevailing notions of reasonableness changed.

14. For a brief but useful discussion of this case see Thomas K. McCraw, *Prophets of Regulation* (Cambridge: The Belknap Press of Harvard University Press, 1984), pp. 87–88.

15. The relationship between the U.S. Department of Agriculture and the farm bloc is but one of the many illustrative examples that could be cited here. It is clear that those employed by the Department of Agriculture support the agricultural price support and subsidy programs that transfer literally billions of dollars every year from the American consumer and taxpayer to the nation's farmers (most of this transfer goes to the wealthiest farms: see Bruce L. Gardner, *The Governing of Agriculture* [Lawrence: Regents Press of Kansas, 1981]). It is by expanding these programs that the Department of Agriculture can justify bigger budgets and more employees, something it has been quite successful at doing. In 1920 when the farm population was approximately 31 million, the Department of Agriculture employed 19,500 people. By 1975 the farm population had declined to less than 9 million, but the Department of Agriculture had increased its employment to 121,000 people. This trend toward fewer agricultural workers relative to agricultural bureaucrats has continued into the 1980s.

16. Our federal farm programs are a perfect example of this process. See Gardner, *ibid.* Early on James Madison recognized the possibility of this type of legislative chain reaction. In Federalist 44 Madison states, "that legislative interference, is but the first link of a long chain of repetitions; every subsequent interference being naturally produced by the effects of the preceding."

17. For a detailed and compelling analysis of how the breakdown in constitutional limitations on government activity has moved the U.S. away from a positive-sum economic activity and toward negative-sum activity, see Terry L. Anderson and Peter J. Hill, *The Birth of a Transfer Society* (Stanford, Calif: Hoover Institution Press, 1980).

18. Quoted in Felix Morley, *Freedom and Federalism* (Chicago: Regnery, 1959), pp. 138–139.

19. Friedrich A. Hayek, *Law, Legislation and Liberty*, Vol 1, *Rules and Order* (Chicago: University of Chicago Press, 1973), p. 8.

Constitutional Restraints on Power

by Edmund A. Opitz

American political institutions presuppose certain convictions about human nature, the worth and prerogatives of persons, the meaning of life, the distinction between right and wrong, and the destiny of the individual. The Colonists came to their understanding of these matters as heirs of the intellectual and religious heritage of Christendom—the culture whose shaping forces sprang from ancient Israel, Greece, and Rome.

Given the consensus of two centuries ago—which regarded man as a sovereign person under God—it was only logical to structure government so as to expand opportunities for the exercise of personal freedom. The Constitution is clearly designed to maximize each individual's equal right to pursue his own peaceful goals and enjoy the benefits and responsibilities of ownership.

The Declaration of Independence put into words what nearly everyone was thinking, that personal rights and immunities are ours because we are created beings, that is, we manifest a major purpose and intent of this universe. This implies a firm rejection of the alternative, which is to assume that we are the mere end products of natural and social forces, adrift in a meaningless cosmos. For if the universe is meaningless, then no way of life is any more meaningful than any other; in which case Power has no limits.

Our forebears had firm convictions about the purpose of life, and knew that in order to achieve life's transcendent end Power must be limited: "Resistance to tyrants is obedience to God," they declared. If life is viewed in these terms, how shall we conceive the proper scope and competence of government? What is its role in society? What functions should we assign to it?

Government is the power structure of a society. This is the first and most important fact about the political agency that it has the legal authority to coerce. The second thing is to inquire whether the power wielded by government is self-sprung, or delegated by a more com-

The Reverend Mr. Opitz, a member of the staff of the Foundation for Economic Education, is a contributing editor of *The Freeman*. He is the editor of *Leviathan at War*. This article was originally published in the April 1978 issue of *The Freeman*.

145

prehensive authority than the merely political. Does government rule autonomously or by divine right; or is the real power located elsewhere and merely loaned to government? The Constitution is clear on this point; the power is in the people to lay down the laws which Power must obey. They set it up; they tell it what to do.

"We, the People of the United States," reads the Preamble, "do ordain and establish this Constitution for the United States of America."

Specific Limitations

The people empower an agency to do certain things for them as a nation, but if we isolate the provisions they laid down to limit government the prevailing intent or consensus which made the Constitution its political tool becomes clearer.

> The powers not delegated to the United States by the Constitution, nor prohibited by it to the States, are reserved to the States respectively, or to the people.
>
> *Amendment X*

The people, furthermore, possess a body of rights by native endowment above and beyond those mentioned in the Constitution.

> The enumeration in the Constitution of certain rights, shall not be construed to deny or disparage others retained by the people.
>
> *Amendment IX*

These sovereign people shall be free to worship, speak, and publish freely.

> Congress shall make no law respecting an establishment of religion, or prohibiting the free exercise thereof.
>
> *Amendment I*

> Congress shall make no law abridging the freedom of speech.
>
> *Amendment I*

> Congress shall make no law abridging the freedom ... of the press.
>
> *Amendment I*

Voluntary association is the corollary of individual liberty, and this is emphasized, as well as the right of petition.

> Congress shall make no law abridging ... the right of the people peaceably to assemble.
>
> *Amendment I*

> Congress shall make no law abridging the right of the people ... to petition the Government for a redress of grievances.
>
> *Amendment I*

The old world divisions of mankind into castes and orders of rank are to be no more.

> No title of nobility shall be granted by the United States.
>
> *Article I, 9*

Every citizen shall have a right to participate in the processes by which the nation is governed; and, should he desire to run for public office he shall not be put to a creedal test.

> The right of the citizens of the United States to vote shall not be denied or abridged. ...
>
> *Amendments XV and XIX*

> No religious test shall ever be required as a qualification to any office or public trust under the United States.
>
> *Article VI*

Freedom to Trade; No Special Privilege

Commerce makes for a free and prosperous people, so restraints on trade shall be removed.

> No tax or duty shall be laid on articles exported from any State. ...
>
> *Article I, 9*

> No preference shall be given by any regulation of commerce or revenue to the ports of one State over those of another.
>
> *Article I, 9*

Progressive taxation violates the principle of equal treatment under the law—penalizes ability, and lowers productivity, so it is forbidden.

> No capitation, or other direct, tax shall be laid, unless in proportion to the census. . . .
>
> *Article I, 9*

The public treasury shall be inviolate; government shall not confer economic privilege on some at the expense of others.

> No money shall be drawn from the Treasury, but in consequence of appropriations made by law.
>
> *Article I, 9*

Personal privacy shall be respected and jealously guarded.

> The right of the people to be secure in their persons, houses, papers, and effects . . . shall not be violated.
>
> *Amendment IV*

Conflict is a built-in feature of human action, and when collisions of interest do occur in society, the rights of the individual must be maintained.

> No person shall . . . be deprived of life, liberty, or property, without due process of law.
>
> *Amendment V*

> Nor shall private property be taken for public use without just compensation.
>
> *Amendment V*

Strings on the Military

In some nations, the civilian life is a mere appendage to the military. This will not happen here because civilians control the purse strings.

> No appropriation of money (to raise and support military and naval forces) shall be for a longer term than two years.
>
> *Article I, 8*

As a further safeguard against any future militarization of this nation, the civilian sector must have the means for defending itself.

> The right of the people to keep and bear arms, shall not be infringed.
>
> *Amendment II*

In some countries, criminal proceedings are used to entrap citizens, whose guilt is assumed; the burden of proof is on them to show their innocence. Here, the innocence of the accused is assumed, until his guilt is proved. The law shall not reach backward to designate as criminal an action which until then was innocent.

> No ... *ex post facto* law shall be passed.
>
> *Article I, 9*

There shall be no Star Chamber proceedings.

> No person shall be held to answer for a capital, or otherwise infamous crime, unless on a presentment or indictment of a Grand Jury.
>
> *Amendment V*

Protecting the Accused

The accused is protected against illegal imprisonment, and must be informed of the charges against him.

> The privilege of the writ of *habeas corpus* shall not be suspended.
>
> *Article I, 9*

Punishment shall fit the crime; it shall not mean extinction of civil rights, forfeiture of property, or penalties against kin.

> No bill of attainder ... shall be passed.
>
> *Article I, 9*

The accused is entitled to be tried by his peers.

> ... the right of trial by jury shall be preserved.
>
> *Amendment VII*

There is to be no forced self-incrimination.

> Nor shall [he] be compelled in any criminal case to be a witness against himself.
>
> *Amendment V*

The rights of the accused are summarized:

1. . . . a speedy and public trial, by an impartial jury;
2. . . . Within the district wherein the crime shall have been committed;
3. . . . to be informed of the nature and cause of the accusation;
4. . . . to be confronted with the witnesses against him;
5. . . . to have compulsory process for obtaining witnesses in his favor;
6. . . . and to have the assistance of counsel for his defense.

Amendment VI

Even when found guilty, the accused is protected.

1. Excessive bail shall not be required;
2. Nor excessive fines imposed;
3. Nor cruel and unusual punishments inflicted.

Amendment VIII

Treason

Treason is a crime against the nation, so serious that it must be defined with special care.

> Treason against the United States, shall consist only in levying war against them, or in adhering to their enemies, giving them aid and comfort.
>
> *Article III, 3*

The person judged guilty of treason is personally responsible for his crime, and therefore his family and kin shall not be punished.

> No attainder of treason shall work corruption of blood.
>
> *Article III, 3*

Impeachment is a special case.

The Senate shall have the sole power to try all impeachments ... and no person shall be convicted without the concurrence of two-thirds of the members present.

Judgment ... shall not extend further than to removal from office, and disqualification to hold any office of honor, trust or profit under the United States.

Article I, 3

A blind spot in the original Constitution is corrected.

Neither slavery, nor involuntary servitude, except as punishment for crime. . . .

Amendment XIII

No state shall ... deny to any person within its jurisdiction the equal protection of the laws.

Amendment XIV

The separate states are not wholly sovereign.

No state shall enter into any treaty ... coin money ... pass any law impairing the obligation of contracts.

Article I, 10

The Method of Freedom

There is a strong penchant in human nature which impels people who feel strongly about something—a good cause, say—to group their forces and use the power of government to fasten their panacea on those they've been unable to persuade. The Constitution is a prime example of the limitations placed upon governmental power so that people with a cause to advance must resort to education, persuasion, and example only. This is the method of freedom, and a people committed to the method of freedom find the Constitution still an apt instrument for structuring a society which maximizes freedom and opportunity for all persons. It was designed to establish a national government internally controlled by checks and balances between the separate powers. And government was to be further limited by the federal structure itself, in which the centripetal power of Washington was to be offset by the centrifugal powers of the separate states. It was not a perfect document, but it carried the means of its own correction, and it did embody the consensus of the people for whom freedom was the prime political good. It was workable. And it will work again whenever a significant number of people have the force of intellect to comprehend sound ideas, and the force of character to make them prevail.

Not in the Constitution

by George W. Nilsson

The Constitution of Vermont reminds us:

> ... that frequent recurrence to fundamental principles and a firm adherence to justice, moderation, temperance, industry, and frugality are absolutely necessary to preserve the blessings of liberty and keep government free.

In addition to the threats of danger from outside of the United States, and subversion within, the constitutional republic of the United States is being threatened by the concentration of power in the federal government in spite of, and contrary to, the "checks and balances" of the Constitution.

Much of such concentration has been due to two World Wars and the Korean War, but more especially by twisting out of shape the interstate commerce clause of the Constitution (Article 1, Section 8, Clause 3), using taxing power for punitive purposes instead of for raising revenue as authorized, and by misusing the general welfare clause.

More and more power is being seized by, or surrendered to, the federal government under the guise of the alleged general welfare clause of Article 1, Section 8, Clause 1 of the Constitution, which contains the following language:

> The Congress shall have power to lay and collect taxes, duties, imposts and excises, to pay the debts and provide for the common defense and general welfare of the United States. ...

This clause is followed by 16 other clauses specifying the various powers of Congress—Clause 2, to borrow money; Clause 3, to regulate foreign and interstate commerce, etc.; then Clause 18 gives the Congress power "to make laws necessary to carry into execution the fore-

Mr. Nilsson was an attorney and a member of the American Bar Association's Committee on American Citizenship. This article first appeared in the *ABA Journal* in January 1961 and was reprinted in *The Freeman*, July 1961.

going powers." This last clause would have been unnecessary if Clause 1 gave "general welfare power."

For 140 years it was generally recognized that the quotation from Clause 1 was not a grant of "general welfare power." Many Presidents vetoed acts passed by Congress for that reason.

For instance, president Andrew Jackson, when he vetoed a bill for public improvements, stated:

> We are in no danger from violations of the Constitution from which encroachments are made upon the personal rights of the citizen. . . . But against the dangers of unconstitutional acts which, instead of menacing the vengeance of offended authority, proffer local advantages and bring in their train the patronage of the government, we are, I fear, not so safe.

Early in the 1930s some individual "discovered" that the clause granted "general welfare power," and more and more this has been used to pass legislation based solely on this alleged grant of general welfare power.

The rush to pass "welfare" legislation for various pressure groups calls to mind an item in the joke column of *Pay Dirt*, a mining magazine published in Phoenix, Arizona (unfortunately, it is more tragic than humorous):

> If a politician tries to buy votes with private money, he is a dirty crook; but if he tries to buy them with the people's own money, he's a great liberal.

As an illustration of how this alleged "welfare" clause is being misused, here is a quotation from a resolution passed June 15, 1959, at the conference of mayors held in Los Angeles, requesting additional federal funds for urban renewal. It begins as follows:

> WHEREAS, The redevelopment of the blighted and deteriorating sections of American cities is vital to the welfare and prosperity of the entire nation. . . .

This, of course, is not a statement of fact but is a self-serving declaration, because the deterioration of cities is due to the failure of the cities to enforce their building and health regulations, and its correction is purely a local matter. That statement is just as illogical as to say that this article is printed with white ink on black paper.

On July 8, 1960, during the Democratic Convention at Los Angeles, the newspapers reported that the mayors of five substantial cities had appeared before the Democratic Platform Committee and requested a statement in the platform recommending the establishment in the federal government of a "Department of Urban Affairs" which would have jurisdiction over "such problems as inadequate housing, residential and industrial slums, double shift schools, inefficient mass transit systems, congested streets, water shortages, and sewage disposal."

Everyone of these problems is purely local. If the local communities are unable to take care of them, that tragic conclusion is an acknowledgment that the people are unable to govern themselves, and that the principles stated in the Declaration of Independence, the Constitution, and the Bill of Rights are incorrect. With such a hypothesis no American lawyer will agree.

When the Constitution was completed and ready to be signed, Benjamin Franklin made a speech in the course of which he said:

> I think a General Government necessary for us, and *there is no form of government, but what may be a blessing to the people if well administered;* and believe further, that this is likely to be well administered for a course of years, and *can only end in despotism, as other forms have done before it, when the people shall become so corrupted as to need despotic government, being incapable of any other.*

Rules for Interpretation

There is a general rule of law that where the statement of a general proposition is followed by specific provisions, the latter prevail. This rule is stated by James Madison in *Federalist Paper* No. 41 and by Alexander Hamilton in *Federalist Paper* No. 83. It is applied by Mr. Justice Story to Article 1, Section 8 of the Constitution, enumerating the powers of Congress, in his book on the Constitution in Sections 909, 910, and 911. He shows that by Clauses 2 to 17, inclusive, specific powers limit Clause 1, referring to general welfare. Section 910 reads in part:

> 910 ... Nothing is more natural or common than first to use a general phrase, and then to qualify it by a recital of particulars. But the idea of an enumeration of particulars, which neither explain, nor qualify the general meaning, and can have no

other effect than to confound and mislead, is an absurdity which no one ought to charge on the enlightened authors of the Constitution. It would be to charge them either with premeditated folly or premeditated fraud.

Another yardstick to be used in determining the meaning of the general welfare clause is discussed below; i.e., that the powers delegated to the United States by the Constitution are few, defined, and limited.

Here let us read a relatively modern statement of that rule:

Justice Frankfurter, in the opinion in *Polish Alliance v. National Labor Relations Board*, 322 U. S. 643, 650 (1943), said:

The interpenetrations of modern society have not wiped out state lines. It is not for us to make inroads upon our federal system either by indifference to its maintainence or excessive regard for the unifying forces of modern technology. Scholastic reasoning may prove that no activity is isolated within the boundaries of a single state, but that cannot justify absorption of legislative power by the United States over every activity.

Climate of Opinion in 1787

In 1787, when the Constitution was adopted, the colonists had been through eight years of war and four years of "a critical period." Knowing what led up to the war, and reading the charges in the Declaration of Independence, can anyone for a minute think that the colonists generally, and the members of the convention specifically, would have adopted a constitution which granted general welfare powers to the federal government?

The resistance to the adoption of the Constitution, which will be discussed hereafter, shows what the people generally felt.

This is summarized by Albert J. Beveridge in his great biography, *The Life of John Marshall*, in Volume I, Chapter 10, where he writes about the convention called in the State of Virginia for the purpose of discussing the ratification of the proposed United States Constitution. At page 371 he describes the general feeling of the people about a strong central government in these words:

They [who resisted the Constitution] had on their side the fears of the people who, as has appeared, looked on all government with hostility, and on a great central Government as some distant and monstrous thing, too far away to be within their reach, too powerful to be resisted, too high and exalted for the good of the common man, too dangerous to be tried. It was, to the masses, something new, vague and awful; something to oppress the poor, the weak, the debtor, the settler; something to strengthen and enrich the already strong and opulent, the merchant, the creditor, the financial interests.

True, the people had suffered by the loose arrangement under which they now lived; but, after all, had not they and their "liberties" survived? And surely they would suffer even more, they felt, under this stronger power; but would they and their "liberties" survive its "oppression"? They thought not.

Thomas Jefferson made the same point in a letter in 1823:

I have been blamed for saying that a prevalence of the doctrine of consolidation would one day call for reformation or revolution. *I answer by asking if a single State of the Union would have agreed to the Constitution had it given all powers to the General Government? If the whole opposition to it did not proceed from the jealousy and fear of every State* being subjected to the other States in matters merely its own? And also is there any reason to believe the States more disposed now than then to acquiesce to this general surrender of all their rights and powers to a consolidated government, one and undivided? [Italics added]

On February 16, 1783, four years before the Constitutional Convention, Pelatiah Webster published a pamphlet containing his idea of a proposed constitution for the United States. The whole draft can be found in *The Origin and Growth of the American Constitution,* by Hannis Taylor, in an appendix beginning at page 529. In paragraph 7 of his proposed Constitution, Pelatiah Webster says:

I propose further that the powers of Congress, and all other departments acting under them, shall all be restricted to such matters only of *general necessity and utility to all the States as cannot come within the jurisdiction of any particular State, or to which the authority of any particular State is not competent,* so that each particular State shall enjoy all sovereignty and supreme authority to all intents and purposes, excepting only those high authorities and powers by them delegated to Congress for the purposes of the general union. [Italics added]

Articles of Confederation

Article VIII of the Articles of Confederation begins with the following language: "All charges of war and of expences that shall be incurred for the common defence and general welfare...."

James Madison pointed out in a letter to Edmund Pendleton, dated January 21, 1792, that the "general welfare clause" had been copied from the Articles of Confederation, and then said:

> ... Where it was always understood as nothing more than a general caption to specific powers, and it is a fact that it was preferred in the new instrument for that very reason as less than any other to misconstruction. [See *Jefferson and Madison*, by Adrienne Koch, pp. 128 and 129, and Irving Brant's *Madison*, Volume 3, *Father of the Constitution*, p. 138.]

Constitutional Convention Debates

A summary of the day-by-day proceedings of the Constitutional Convention of 1787 is found in Charles Warren's book, *The Making of the Constitution*.

From a study of the records of the Convention, it will appear that from time to time efforts were made by some delegates to have the Constitution grant broad general powers to the federal government. Each time such proposal was advanced, it was rejected. Beginning on page 464 is a discussion of "The Taxing Power and the General Welfare Clause." At page 474 occurs this statement:

> In Governor Livingston's Committee Report of August 21, these words had been used with reference to prior debts, and merely described them as having been incurred during the late war "for the common defence and general welfare...."

On page 475 Mr. Warren says:

> Some words evidently had to be added that would make clear the power of Congress to levy taxes *for all the National purposes set forth in the grants of power subsequently specified in this section.* Evidently the Committee selected these words, "to provide for the common defence and general welfare," as comprising all the other purposes for which Congress was to be empowered to levy and collect taxes. *They selected these words as embracing*

all the subsequent limited grants of power which the Committee of Detail, in its Report of August 6, had specified as constituting that amount of common defence and general welfare which the National Government ought to control and as to which ought to have power of legislation. In other words, the phrase "to provide for the general welfare" *is merely a general description of the amount of welfare which was to be accomplished by carrying out those enumerated and limited powers vested in Congress—and no others.* [Italics added.] [See also *James Madison* by Irving Brant, Volume 3, *Father of the Constitution,* Chapter 10, beginning at page 132, which is entitled "General Power or Enumeration."]

Debates in the Various States

History tells us that in 1787 there was great opposition to the adoption of the proposed new Constitution. As a matter of fact, it squeaked through by a very few votes in a number of states. For instance, Massachusetts 187 to 168, Virginia 89 to 79, and New York 30 to 27, and then only on condition that a Bill of Rights be added.

The Federalist Papers were written by Alexander Hamilton, James Madison, and John Jay in support of the adoption of the Constitution, principally in connection with the debates in New York, where there was strong opposition to the adoption of the Constitution.

In *Federalist Paper* No. 41, James Madison said (after pointing out the objections to the clause "to raise money for the general welfare"):

But what color can the objection have, when a specification of the objects alluded to by these general terms immediately follows and is not even separated by a longer pause than a semicolon? If the different parts of the same instrument ought to be so expounded as to give meaning to every part which will bear it, shall one point of the same sentence be excluded altogether from a share in the meaning; and shall be the more doubtful and indefinite terms be retained in their full extent, and the clear and precise expressions be denied any signification whatsoever? *For what purpose could the enumeration of particular powers be inserted, if these and all others were meant to be included in the preceding general power?* Nothing is more natural or common than first to use a general phrase, and then to explain and qualify it by a recital of particulars. [Italics added.]

Only Limited Powers

In considering the question of whether this "general welfare" clause of Article I, Section 8, Clause I is a grant of power, we must also remember that the powers granted to the federal government were few and defined. James Madison, in *Federalist Paper* No. 45, said:

> The *powers* delegated by the proposed Constitution to the Federal Government are *few and defined.* Those which are to remain to the State governments are numerous and indefinite. The former will be exercised principally on external objects, as war, peace, negotiations and foreign commerce; with which last the power of taxation will, for the most part, be connected. The powers reserved to the several States will extend to all the objects which, in the ordinary course of affairs, concern the *lives, liberties* and *properties* of the people and the *internal order, improvement* and *prosperity* of the State [Italics added.]

Alexander Hamilton, himself, who argued in the Constitutional Convention for general instead of particular enumeration of powers, nevertheless said in *Federalist Paper* No. 83:

> The plan of the Convention declares that the power of Congress or, in other words, of the "national legislature," shall extend to certain enumerated cases. *This specification of particulars evidently excluded all pretension to a general legislative authority, because an affirmative grant of special powers would be absurd, as well as useless, if a general authority was intended.* [Italics added.]

Since the people were persuaded to adopt the Constitution on the basis that the federal government was being given only limited and specified powers, how dare anyone, in good conscience, now take the position that the words "general welfare" give the federal government unlimited power?

This principle was restated by Franklin D. Roosevelt on March 2, 1930, while he was Governor of New York, in a speech which was entitled "An Address on State Rights" (*Collected Papers,* Volume I, p. 569). He said in part:

> The preservation of this home rule by the states is a fundamental necessity if we are to remain a truly united country . . .

to bring about government by oligarchy masquerading as democracy it is fundamentally essential that practically all authority and control be centralized in our national government, the individual sovereignty of our states must first be destroyed. . . .

We are safe from the danger of any such departure from the principles upon which this country was founded just so long as the individual home rule of the states is scrupulously preserved and fought for whenever they seem in danger. Thus it will be seen that this home rule is a most important thing—a most vital thing if we are to continue along the course on which we have so far progressed with such unprecedented success.

Bill of Rights

In many of the states, the Constitution was adopted only when it was accompanied by a resolution demanding that a Bill of Rights be added to the Constitution. If the people of the various states were satisfied with the Constitution as written, they certainly would not have demanded the added protection of the Bill of Rights.

As pointed out above, certainly no state would have adopted the Constitution if the Congress had been given *carte blanche* to pass any law or do anything which it desired or which it felt was for the "general welfare."

This demand for a Bill of Rights, therefore, should be sufficient to prove that the Constitution, and particularly Article I, Section 8, Clause I, did not grant general welfare power to the federal government.

True to his promise, James Madison, in the First Congress, which met in 1789, caused to be passed a Bill of Rights containing twelve sections, ten of which were adopted and went into effect December 15, 1791.

This Bill of Rights, and particularly the Ninth and Tenth Amendments, are further and conclusive proof that the clause that we are discussing did not grant any authority to the federal government to pass any laws based on "general welfare powers."

Statements by Contemporaries

On December 5, 1791, Secretary of the Treasury Alexander Hamilton presented to the Congress his "Report on Manufactures."

Madison delivered an address in Congress against the Report, in which he said in part:

> If Congress can apply money indefinitely to the general welfare, and are the sole and supreme judges of the general welfare, they may take the care of religion into their own hands; they may establish teachers in every State, county and parish, and pay them out of the public treasury; they may take into their own hands the education of children, establishing in like manner schools throughout the Union; they may undertake the regulation of all roads, other than post roads. In short, everything, from the highest object of State legislation, down to the most minute object of policy, would be thrown under the power of Congress; for every object I have mentioned would admit the application of money, and might be called, if Congress pleased, provisions for the general welfare.

The report was pigeonholed, the first major defeat for one of Hamilton's most cherished policies. (*Jefferson and Madison*, by Adrienne Koch, p. 129.)

Further on the same question, James Madison, on January 1, 1792, in a letter to Henry Lee, Governor of Virginia, said in part:

> What think you of the commentary ... on the term "general welfare"? ... The federal government has been hitherto limited to the specified powers, by the Greatest Champions for Latitude in expounding those powers.... *If not only the means, but the objects are unlimited, the parchment had better be thrown into the fire at once.* [Italics added.]

And in a letter to Edmund Randolph (January 21, 1792), Madison said:

> *If Congress can do whatever in their discretion can be done by money, and will promote the general welfare, the government is no longer one possessing enumerated powers, but an indefinite one subject to particular exceptions.* [Italics added.] (*Jefferson and Madison*, by Adrienne Koch, p. 128.)

Thomas Jefferson had the same views. He wrote to Albert Gallatin in 1817, about the General Welfare Clause, of which he said:

You will have to learn that an act for internal improvement, after passing both houses, was negatived by the President. The act was founded, avowedly, on the principle that the phrase in the Constitution which authorizes the Congress "to lay taxes, to pay the debts and provide for the general welfare," *was an extension of the powers specifically enumerated to whatever would promote the general welfare; and this, you know, was the Federal doctrine.* Whereas our tenet ever was, and, indeed, it is almost the only landmark which now divides the Federalists and the Republicans, that Congress had not unlimited powers to provide for the *general welfare, but was restrained to those specifically enumerated;* and that, as it was never meant that they should provide for that welfare but the exercise of the enumerated powers, so it could not have meant that they should raise money for purposes which the enumeration did not place under their action; consequently, that the specification of powers is a limitation on the purposes for which they may raise money. [Italics added.] (See *Undermining the Constitution*, by Thomas James Norton, p. 191.)

Abraham Baldwin, a member of the Constitutional Convention, while a member of Congress, on June 17, 1798, said in the Congress:

. . . to provide for the common defence and general welfare had never been considered as a source of legislative power, as it is only a member introduced to limit the other parts of the sentence. (*Undermining the Constitution*, by Thomas James Norton, p. 189.)

Conclusion

(a) In a book recently published, analyzing some of the decisions of the modern Supreme Court, the writer says: "Enthroned at last, were Hamilton's bold nationalistic views. . . ."

To say these modern ideas of "general welfare power" are those of Alexander Hamilton is to malign him. Alexander Hamilton was a great patriot and statesman. His ideas of a new government were far different from those embodied in the Constitution, but after the Constitution was adopted, he faithfully and enthusiastically supported it. For instance, he wrote most of *The Federalist Papers*.

Even though Alexander Hamilton had espoused such ideas as are now ascribed to him, such ideas were not accepted as part of the

Constitution as finally adopted and, therefore, must not be used to interpret the Constitution.

Since Alexander Hamilton's views were rejected by the Constitutional Convention of 1787 (not even being referred to a committee, Hannis Taylor, p. 200); since Alexander Hamilton was absent from the Convention about one-half of the time, once from June 29 to the middle of August 1787, and since his views against the inclusion of a Bill of Rights were rejected, the foregoing statement that his views are now being accepted is a clear acknowledgment that the spirit and letter of the Constitution as written are now being perverted.

Against this view attention is called to *The Federalist Papers* which are referred to and quoted in this article. It is therefore clear from history, common sense, the records of the Constitutional Convention, *The Federalist Papers*, the debates in the state ratification conventions, and precedents followed for more than 140 years, that *there is no grant of general welfare power in the Constitution of the United States.*

(b) While it would seem that such general welfare power is not needed, if it should be determined that it is necessary, then the amending clause of the Constitution should be followed, as was pointed out by George Washington in his Farewell Address:

> If in the opinion of the people the distribution or modification of the constitutional powers be in any particular wrong, let it be corrected by an amendment in the way which the Constitution designates. But let there be no change by usurpation; for though this in one instance may be the instrument for good, *it is the customary weapon by which free governments are destroyed.* The precedent must always greatly overbalance in permanent evil any partial or transient benefit which the use can at any time yield. [Italics added.]

The dire results of undermining the Constitution were pointed out by Daniel Webster in his eulogy of George Washington in 1832, where he said in part: ʼ

> Other misfortunes may be borne, or their effects overcome. . . .
> *But who shall reconstruct the fabric of demolished government? Who shall rear again the well-proportioned columns of constitutional liberty?* Who shall frame together the skillful architecture which unites national sovereignty with State rights, individual security and Public prosperity?

(c) Every lawyer when he is admitted to the Bar takes an oath to "uphold, defend, and protect the Constitution of the United States."

Since the Constitution is being ignored, misconstrued, or bypassed by legislation, by court decisions, and by executive action, it is time that fundamental principles of the Constitution be re-examined, and that every citizen, as well as every lawyer, take his place on the battle line in a new crusade to re-establish the principles and the spirit of the Declaration of Independence, the Constitution, and the Bill of Rights.

The Constitution and Paper Money

by Clarence B. Carson

The United States Constitution does not mention paper money by that name. Nor does it refer to paper currency or fiat money in those words.[1] There is only one direct reference to the origins of what we, and they, usually call paper money. It is in the limitations on the power of the states in Article I, Section 10. It reads, "No State shall ... emit Bills of Credit. ..." Paper that was intended to circulate as money but was not redeemable in gold and silver was technically described as bills of credit at that time. The description was (and is) apt. Such paper is a device for expanding the credit of the issuer. There is also an indirect reference to the practice in the same section of the Constitution. It reads, "No State shall ... make any Thing but gold and silver Coin a Tender in Payment of Debts. ..." Legal tender laws, in practice, are an essential expedient for making unredeemable paper circulate as money. Except for the one direct and one indirect reference to the origin and means for circulating paper money, the Constitution is silent on the question.

With such scant references, then, it might be supposed that the makers of the Constitution were only incidentally concerned with the dangers of paper money. That was hardly the case. It loomed large in the thinking of at least some of the men who were gathered at Philadelphia in 1787 at the Constitutional Convention. There were two great objects in the making of a new constitution: one was to provide for a more energetic general government; the other was to restrain the state governments. Moreover, the two objects had a common motive at many points, i.e., to provide a stronger general government which could restrain the states.

Measures to Prevent a Flood of Unbacked Paper Money

One of the prime reasons for restraining the state governments was to prevent their flooding the country with unbacked paper money. James Madison, one of the leaders at the convention, declared, in an introduction to his notes on the deliberations there, that one of

---

This article was originally published in the July 1983 edition of *The Freeman*.

the defects they were assembled to remedy was that "In the internal administration of the States, a violation of contracts had become familiar, in the form of depreciated paper made a legal tender.... "[2] Edmund Randolph, in the introductory remarks preceding the presentation of the Virginia Plan to the convention, declared that when the Articles of Confederation had been drawn "the havoc of paper-money had not been foreseen."[3]

Indeed, as the convention held its sessions, or in the months preceding it, state legislatures were under pressure to issue paper money. Several had already yielded, or taken the initiative, in issuing the unbacked paper. The situation was out of control in Rhode Island, and had been for some time. Rhode Island refused to send delegates to the convention, and the state's reputation was so bad that the delegates there were apparently satisfied to be spared the counsels of her citizens. Well after the convention had got underway, a motion was made to send a letter to New Hampshire, whose delegates were late, urging their attendance. John Rutledge of South Carolina rose to oppose the motion, arguing that he "could see neither the necessity nor propriety of such a measure. They are not unapprized of the meeting, and can attend if they choose." And, to clinch his argument, he proposed that "Rhode Island might as well be urged to appoint & send deputies."[4] No one rose in defense of an undertaking of that character.

The ill repute of Rhode Island derived mainly from that state's unrestrained experiments with paper money. Rhode Island not only issued paper money freely but also used harsh methods to try to make it circulate. The "legislature passed an act declaring that anyone refusing to take the money at face value would be fined £100 for a first offense and would have to pay a similar fine and lose his rights as a citizen for a second."[5] When the act was challenged, a court declared that it was unconstitutional. Whereupon, the legislature called the judges before it, interrogated them, and dismissed several from office. The legislature was determined to have its paper circulate.

The combination of abundant paper money and Draconian measures to enforce its acceptance brought trade virtually to a halt in Rhode Island. A major American constitutional historian described the situation this way:

> The condition of the state during these days was deplorable indeed. The merchants shut their shops and joined the crowd in the bar-rooms; men lounged in the streets or wandered aimlessly about.... A French traveller who passed through Newport about this time gives a dismal picture of the place:

idle men standing with folded arms at the corners of the streets; houses falling to ruins; miserable shops offering for sale nothing but a few coarse stuffs ... ; grass growing in the streets; windows stuffed with rags; everything announcing misery, the triumph of paper money, and the influence of bad government. The merchants had closed their stores rather than take payment in paper; farmers from neighboring states did not care to bring their produce.... Some ... sought to starve the tradesmen into a proper appreciation of the simple laws of finance by refusing to bring their produce to market.[6]

But there was more behind the Founders' fears of paper money than contemporary doings in Rhode Island or general pressures for monetary inflation. The country as a whole had only recently suffered the searing aftermath of such an inflation. Much of the War for Independence had been financed with paper money or, more precisely, bills of credit.

A Surge of Continentals

Even before independence had been declared the Continental Congress began to emit bills of credit. These bills carried nothing more than a vague promise that they would at some unspecified time in the future be redeemed, possibly by the states. In effect, they were fiat money, and were never redeemed. As more and more of this Continental currency was issued, 1776–1779, it depreciated in value. This paper was joined by that of the states which were, if anything, freer with their issues than the Congress. In 1777, Congress requested that the states cease to print paper money, but the advice was ignored. They did as Congress did, not what it said.

At first, this surge of paper money brought on what appeared to be a glow of prosperity. As one historian described it, "the country was prosperous.... Paper money seemed to be the 'poor man's friend'; to it were ascribed the full employment and the high price of farm products that prevailed during the first years of the war. By 1778, for example, the farmers of New Jersey were generally well off and rapidly getting out of debt, and farms were selling for twice the price they had brought during the period 1765–1775. Trade and commerce were likewise stimulated; despite the curtailment of foreign trade, businessmen had never been so prosperous."[7]

The pleasant glow did not last long, however. It was tarnished first, of course, by the fact that the price of goods people bought began to rise. (People generally enjoy the experience of prices for their goods rising, but they take a contrary view of paying more for what they buy.) Then, as now, some blamed the rise in prices on merchant profiteering.

As the money in circulation increased and expectations of its being redeemed faded, a given amount of money bought less and less. This set the stage for speculative buying, holding on to the goods for a while, and making a large paper profit on them. There were sporadic efforts to control prices as well as widespread efforts to enforce acceptance of the paper money in payment for debts. These efforts, so far as they succeeded, succeeded in causing shortages of goods, creditors to run from debtors trying to pay them in the depreciated currency, and in the onset of suffering.

Runaway Inflation

By 1779, the inflation was nearing the runaway stage. "In August 1778, a Continental paper dollar was valued (in terms of gold and silver) at about twenty-five cents; by the end of 1779, it was worth a penny." "Our dollars pass for less this afternoon than they did this morning," people began to say.[8] George Washington wrote in 1779 that "a wagon load of money will scarcely purchase a wagon load of provisions."[9] It was widely recognized that the cause was the continuing and ever larger emissions of paper money. Congress resolved to issue no more in 1779, but it was all to no avail. Runaway inflation was at hand. In 1781, Congress no longer accepted its own paper money in payment for debts, and the Continentals ceased to have any value at all.

A good portion of the dangers of paper money had been revealed, and reflective people were aware of what had happened. Josiah Quincy wrote George Washington "that there never was a paper pound, a paper dollar, or a paper promise of any kind, that ever yet obtained a general currency but by force or fraud, generally by both."[10] A contemporary historian concluded that the "evils which resulted from the legal tender of the depreciated bills of credit" extended much beyond the immediate assault upon property. "The iniquity of the laws," he said, "estranged the minds of many of the citizens from the habits and love of justice.... Truth, honor, and justice were swept away by the overflowing deluge of legal iniquity...."[11]

But the economic consequences of the inflation did not end with the demise of the Continental currency. Instead, it was followed by a deflation, which was the inevitable result of the decrease in the money supply. The deflation was not immediately so drastic as might be supposed. Gold and silver coins generally replaced paper money in 1781. Many of these had been out of circulation, in hiding, so long as they were threatened by tender law requirements to exchange them on a par with the paper money. Once the threat was removed, they circulated. The supply of those in hiding had been augmented over the years by payments for goods by British troops. Large foreign loans, particularly from the French, increased the supply of hard money in the United States in 1781 and 1782. A revived trade with the Spanish, French, and Dutch brought in coins from many lands as well. In addition, Robert Morris's Bank of North America provided paper money redeemable in precious metals in the early years of the decade.

The Impact of Depression

By the middle of the 1780s, however, the deflation was having its impact as a depression. Trade had reopened with Britain, and Americans still showed a distinct preference for British imports. That, plus the fact that the market for American exports in the British West Indies was still closed, resulted in a large imbalance in trade. Americans made up the difference either by borrowing or shipping hard money to Britain. Prices fell to reflect the declining money supply. Those who had gone into debt to buy land at the inflated wartime prices were especially hard hit by the decline in the prices of their produce. Foreclosures were widespread in 1785–1786. This provided the setting for the demands for paper money and other measures to relieve the pressure of the debts. Some people were clamoring for the hair of the dog that had bit them in the first place—monetary inflation—and several state legislatures had accommodated them.

Though there is evidence that the worst of the depression was over by 1787, if not in the course of 1786,[12] paper money issues and agitations for more were still ongoing when the Constitutional Convention met in Philadelphia. In any case, those who had absorbed the lessons of recent history were very much concerned to do something to restrain governments from issuing paper money and forcing it into circulation. There were those who met at Philadelphia, too, who took the long view of their task. They hoped to erect a system that would endure, and to do that they wished to guard against the kind of fiscal adventures that produced both unpleasant economic consequences and political turmoil. Paper money was reckoned to be one of these.

The question of granting power to emit bills of credit came up for discussion twice in the convention. The first time was on August 16,

1787. (The convention had begun its deliberations on May 25, 1787, so it was moving fairly rapidly toward the conclusion when the question arose.) The question was whether or not the United States government should have power to emit bills of credit. Congress had such a power under the Articles of Confederation, and most of the powers held by Congress under the Articles were introduced in the convention to be extended to the new government.

Constitutional Convention Debates

Gouverneur Morris of Pennsylvania "moved to strike out 'and emit bills on the credit of the United States.'" That is, he proposed to remove the authority for the United States to issue such paper money. "If the United States had credit," Morris said, "such bills would be unnecessary: if they had not, unjust & useless." His motion was seconded by Pierce Butler of South Carolina.

James Madison wondered if it would "not be sufficient to prohibit making them a *tender?* This will remove the temptation to emit them with unjust views. And promissory notes in that shape may in some emergencies be best." (Madison's distinction between bills of credit that may be freely circulated and those whose acceptance is forced by tender laws should remind us that paper instruments serving in some fashion as money are not at the heart of the problem. After all, private bills of exchange had for several centuries been used by tradesmen, and these sometimes changed hands much as money does. They are what we call negotiable instruments, and the variety of these is large. What Madison was getting at more directly, however, was that governments, if they are to borrow money from time to time, may issue notes, and these may be negotiable instruments which may take on some of the character of money in exchanges. But Madison's objection was overcome, as we shall see.)

Gouverneur Morris then observed that "striking out the words will leave room still for notes of a *responsible* minister which will do all the good without the mischief. The Monied interest will oppose the plan of Government, if paper emissions be not prohibited."

However, Morris had moved beyond his motion, which was for removing the power, not specifying a prohibition, and Nathaniel Gorham of Massachusetts brought him back to the point. Gorham said he "was for striking out, without inserting any prohibition. If the words stand they may suggest and lead to the measure."

Not everyone who spoke, however, favored removing the power. George Mason of Virginia "had doubts on the subject. Congress he thought would not have the power unless it were expressed. Though he had a mortal hatred to paper money, yet as he could not foresee all emergences [sic], he was unwilling to tie the hands of the legislature. He observed that the late war could not have been carried on, had such a prohibition existed."

Nathaniel Gorham tried to reassure Mason and others who might have similar doubts by declaring that "The power so far as it will be necessary or safe, is involved in that of borrowing."

Both Positions Argued

On the other hand, John Francis Mercer of Maryland announced that he "was a friend to paper money, though in the present state & temper in America, he should neither propose nor approve of such a measure. He was consequently opposed to a prohibition of it altogether. It will stamp suspicion on the Government to deny it a discretion on this point. It was impolitic also to excite the opposition of all those who were friends to paper money. The people of property would be sure to be on the side of the plan [the Constitution], and it was impolitic to purchase their further attachment with the loss of the opposite class of Citizens."

Oliver Elsworth of Connecticut pronounced himself of the opposite view. He "thought this a favorable moment to shut and bar the door against paper money. The mischiefs of the various experiments which had been made, were now fresh in the public mind and had excited the disgust of all the respectable part of America. By withholding the power from the new Government more friends of influence would be gained to it than by almost any thing else. Paper money can in no case be necessary. Give the Government credit, and other resources will offer. The power [to emit bills of credit] may do harm, never good."

Edmund Randolph of Virginia still had doubts, for he said that "notwithstanding his antipathy to paper money, [he] could not agree to strike out the words, as he could not foresee all the occasions which might arise."

James Wilson of Pennsylvania favored removing the power: "It will have a most salutary influence on the credit of the United States to remove the possibility of paper money. This expedient can never succeed whilst its mischiefs are remembered, and as long as it can be resorted to, it will be a bar to other resources."

Pierce Butler "remarked that paper was a legal tender in no country in Europe. He was urgent for disarming the Government of such a power."

George Mason, however, "was still averse to tying the hands of the Legislature *altogether*. If there was no example in Europe as just remarked, it might be observed on the other side, that there was none in which the Government was restrained on this head." His fellow delegates forebore to remind Mason that except for Britain there was hardly a government in Europe that was restrained on that or any other head by a written constitution.

In any case, the last remarks were made by men vehemently opposed to the power. George Read of Delaware "thought the words, if not struck out, would be as alarming as the mark of the Beast in Revelations." John Langdon of New Hampshire "had rather reject the whole plan [the Constitution] than retain the three words," by which he meant "and emit bills."

Denying the Power to Emit Bills of Credit

The vote was overwhelmingly in favor of removing the authority of the United States to emit bills of credit. The delegates voted by states, and nine states voted in favor of the motion while only two opposed it. (New York delegates were not in attendance, and Rhode Island, of course, sent none.) It is a reasonable inference from the discussion that the delegates believed that by voting to strike out the words they had removed the power from the government to emit bills of credit. George Mason, who opposed the motion, admitted as much. Moreover, James Madison explained in a footnote that he voted for it when he "became satisfied that striking out the words would not disable the Government from the use of public notes as far as they could be safe & proper; & would only cut off the pretext for a paper currency, and particularly for making the bills a tender for public or private debts."[13]

The other discussion of paper money took place in connection with the powers to be denied to the states in the Constitution. The committee report had called for the states to be prohibited to emit bills of credit without the consent of the United States Congress. James Wilson and Roger Sherman, who was from Connecticut, "moved to insert after the words 'coin money' the words 'nor emit bills of credit, nor make any thing but gold & silver coin a tender in payment of debts'," thus, as they said, "making these prohibitions absolute, instead of making the measures allowable (as in the XIII article) *with the consent of the Legislature of the U.S.*"

Nathaniel Gorham "thought the purpose would be as well secured by the provision of article XIII which makes the consent of the General Legislature necessary, and that in that mode, no Opposition would be excited; whereas an absolute prohibition of paper money would rouse the most desperate opposition from its partizans."

To the contrary, Roger Sherman "thought this a favorable crisis for crushing paper money. If the consent of the Legislature could authorise emissions of it, the friends of paper money, would make every exertion to get into the Legislature in order to licence it."[14]

Eight states voted for the absolution prohibition against states issuing bills of credit. One voted against it, and the other state whose delegation was present was divided. The prohibition, as voted, became a part of the Constitution.

Paper Money Rejected

Three other points may be appropriate. The first has to do with any argument that there might be an implied power for the United States government to issue paper money since it is not specifically prohibited in the Constitution. Alexander Hamilton, the man credited with advancing the broad construction doctrine, maintained the opposite view in *The Federalist*. While he was making a case against the adding of a bill of rights, his argument was meant to have general validity. He declared that such prohibitions "are not only unnecessary in the proposed Constitution but would even be dangerous. They would contain various exceptions to powers which are not granted; and, on this very account, would afford a colorable pretext to claim more than were granted. For why declare that things shall not be done which there is no power to do."[15] In short, the government does not have all powers not prohibited but only those granted.

Second, this point was driven home by the 10th Amendment when a Bill of Rights was added to the Constitution. It reads, "The powers not delegated to the United States by the Constitution, nor prohibited by it to the States, are reserved to the States respectively, or to the people." The power to emit bills of credit or issue paper money was not delegated to the United States. More, it was specifically not delegated after deliberating upon whether to or not. The power was prohibited to the states. The logical conclusion is that such power as there may be to emit bills of credit was reserved to the people in their private capacities.

And third, not one word has been added to or subtracted from the

Constitution since that time affecting the power of government to emit bills of credit or issue paper money.

Since the United States is once again in the toils of an ongoing monetary inflation, it is my hope that this summary review of the experience, words, and deeds of the Founders might shed light on some of the vexing questions surrounding it.

1. Actually this phrase, "fiat money," did not come into use until the 1880s. It might have helped the Founders to specify more precisely what they had in mind to prevent, but they had no such term.

2. E. H. Scott, ed., *Journal of the Federal Convention Kept by James Madison* (Chicago: Albert, Scott and Co., 1893), p. 47.

3. *Ibid.*, p. 60.

4. Charles E. Tansill, ed., *Formation of the Union of American States* (Washington, D.C.: Government Printing Office, 1927), p. 306.

5. Merrill Jensen, *The New Nation* (New York: Vintage Books, 1950), p. 324.

6. Andrew C. McLaughlin, *The Confederation and the Constitution* (New York: Collier Books, 1962), pp. 107–08.

7. John C. Miller, *Triumph of Freedom* (Boston: Little, Brown, and Co., 1948), p. 438.

8. *Ibid.*, p. 462.

9. Quoted in Albert S. Bolles, *The Financial History of the United States*, vol. I (New York: D. Appleton, 1896, 4th ed.), p. 132.

10. *Ibid.*, p. 139.

11. Quoted in *ibid.*, pp. 177–78.

12. See Jensen, *op. cit.*, pp. 247–48.

13. All the discussion and quotations can be found in Tansill, *op cit.*, pp. 556–57. While there is no way to know if the record of the debates on this and other matters is complete, nothing has been omitted from Madison's notes.

14. *Ibid.*, pp. 627–38. The committee on style eventually reduced the number of articles in the Constitution to seven, so there is not now an Article XIII, of course.

15. Alexander Hamilton, *et. al.*, *The Federalist Papers* (New Rochelle: N. Y.: Arlington House, n. d.), pp. 513–14.

Judicial Monopoly over the Constitution: Jefferson's View

by Clarence B. Carson

Do the Federal courts have a monopoly of the interpretation of the Constitution? Further, are the judges, in the words of Thomas Jefferson, "the ultimate arbiters of all constitutional questions ... "?[1] There is little reason to doubt that the prevailing view in the country would give a resounding affirmative answer to the first question. There are dissenters, of course, but so far as they are numerous and widely influential, their dissents are to particular decisions or opinions of the courts, not to the propriety of the courts making some decision.

The judges act as if they have a monopoly of the interpretation of the Constitution. Members of Congress usually make it clear that they believe the opinions of the Federal courts, especially the Supreme Court, are determinative. Presidents increasingly leave to the courts the questions they may have about the constitutionality of laws that come before them. The academic world generally supports this view, and many legal scholars make pronouncements that suggest they do not think it worthwhile to consider any other view.

In recent decades, the press, or the media, have mightily assisted the courts in maintaining this position. For example, when the courts began compelling states to reapportion legislative seats on the basis of population, the *Washington Post* declared that these

> rulings have unquestionably become the law of the land. It is not the function of Congress to set aside that law, or to thwart its operation. The spectacle of Congress trying to use its legislative power to deny or temporarily nullify constitutional rights which the Supreme Court had clearly upheld is such a serious encroachment upon the orderly division of powers that even extraordinary measures would be justified to defeat it.
>
> There is much controversy, to be sure, over the soundness of the Constitution's edict that both houses of the state legislature must be apportioned on the basis of population.... The

This article appeared in the October 1983 edition of *The Freeman* next Congress will be free, if it wishes, to propose a constitutional amendment . . . ; however, Congress should not seek to shortcircuit judicial decisions.[2]

The editorial assumes that the courts have a monopoly of the interpretation of the Constitution. It enjoins the Congress against intermeddling in such matters. It asserts that the decisions are "the law of the land." More, it appears to add the court decisions to the body of the Constitution itself, for it holds that these are edicts of the Constitution. If it was not commonplace to make this last identification at the time, it has become so since, for writers and speakers frequently refer to the decisions of the court as if they were an integral part of the Constitution itself. In any case, the view prevails that the Federal courts have a monopoly of the interpretation of the Constitution.

It is not equally clear, however, that the view has triumphed that the courts are the "ultimate arbiters of all constitutional questions." There is at least a shadow of doubt about this, as yet. The *Washington Post* noted that a constitutional amendment could be adopted to change the courts' rulings. If so, the courts are not the ultimate arbiters, or perhaps it would be more accurate to say that they are not the penultimate arbiters, since such amendments are extremely rare. By my reading of it, the Sixteenth Amendment, adopted in 1913, was the last amendment passed to resolve a constitutional question. More important, perhaps, there is now strenuous public resistance, at least from opinion makers, to reversing a court decision in this way. Nor is it clear, given the current mood, how the courts might respond to such a direct restraint on their powers. But for now, at least, there appears to be the remote possibility of amending the Constitution as an arbiter beyond the courts.

Questioning the Monopoly

There are several reasons for raising the question of the court's monopoly of interpreting the Constitution. The first is to make clear that in the version in which it now prevails the monopoly is of recent vintage. The second is to emphasize that the Constitution does not allot the interpretation of the Constitution to any particular branch of government, any special tribunal, or any class or order of men. The main reason, however, is to explore the view of Thomas Jefferson, both because of its contrast with the contemporary one and because it was more or less in accord with a widely held view for much of the nineteenth century. And last, I want to point up some of the incongruities, tendencies, infelicities, and dangers of the current view.

None of this is meant to suggest that the courts do not have a role in the interpretation of the Constitution, that they have not always claimed and acted upon a role, or that this was unexpected by the makers of the Constitution. On the contrary, many of the Founders anticipated that the courts would have a role in applying the laws and establishing the supremacy of laws made in pursuance of the Constitution *vis à vis* the states especially. That they would do so was mentioned a number of times in the Constitutional Convention.[3] Moreover, Hamilton argued in *The Federalist*, number 78, that it was the duty of "courts of justice . . . to declare all acts contrary to the manifest tenor of the Constitution void. Without this," he said, "all the reservations of particular rights or privileges would amount to nothing."[4]

But it should be emphasized that the Constitution grants no special powers of interpretation of it to the courts. Specifically, it grants no power of judicial review of legislation to the courts. The President is granted a power of the review of legislation, and he may veto bills on constitutional or other grounds. The Convention considered more than once the advisability of having the Supreme Court review legislation in conjunction with the executive. The proposal was rejected.

"Judicial Review"

In fact, the courts do not "review" acts of Congress to determine whether or not they are in accord with the Constitution. Any literal-minded person might suppose that is what they do, or have done, by the use of the dubious phrase, "judicial review," to describe their procedures. In the course of applying the law to particular cases, courts sometimes adjudge an act of the legislature to be in conflict with the Constitution. They may then refuse to give the force of law to the legislative act. That is the basis of the traditional claim of the courts to make decisions, binding on themselves, regarding the constitutionality of acts. The power is not mentioned in the Constitution.

Jefferson was the first President to challenge the extent of the powers of the federal courts. Indeed, he raised the challenge even before he attained the highest office in the land and continued to express various concerns in letters to individuals long after he retired to private life. Also, he was the most outstanding public figure in his day to confront directly the question of a judicial monopoly of the interpretation of the Constitution. From the confrontations he developed a coherent view of the matter.

Jefferson became embroiled in this question for both broad and general as well as particular considerations. From the outset, he was a strict constructionist of the Constitution. The first major constitutional question that came up for him was about the Bank of the United States. Jefferson was Secretary of State and President Washington asked for the opinions of his heads of departments. He wrote Washington that ours is a government of delegated powers. "The incorporaztion of a bank," he said, "and the powers assumed by this bill, have not, in my opinion, been delegated to the United States by the Constitution."[5] He went on to explain the case by an examination of the powers enumerated and to recommend that the bill be vetoed.

Jefferson's Concern for Liberty

Jefferson's insistence on the strict construction of the Constitution was based on two broad and enduring concerns which lasted the whole of his adult life. One was his commitment to individual liberty. On one occasion, he wrote: "I have sworn upon the altar of God eternal hostility against every form of tyranny over the mind of man."[6] As to a definition "of liberty," he explained, "I would say that, in the whole plenitude of its extent, it is unobstructed action according to our will, but rightful liberty is unobstructed according to our will within limits drawn around us by the equal rights of others."[7] Jefferson subscribed to the natural rights theory, holding that man has certain God-given rights. Although there are many listings of these rights, he thought those most often threatened were "the rights of thinking and publishing our thoughts by speaking or writing; the right of free commerce; the right of personal freedom."[8]

His second broad concern was to restrain and limit government so that people might enjoy their rights. "The natural progress of things," he said, "is for liberty to yield and government to gain ground."[9] It was not safe, he thought, to confide overmuch power in government. "I own," Jefferson said, "I am not a friend to a very energetic government. It is always oppressive. It places the governors indeed more at their ease, at the expense of the people."[10] It was to hold governments in their place and restrain them in their activities that he was so concerned with strict construction of the Constitution.

"In questions of power, then," Jefferson declared in his draft of the Kentucky Resolution, "let no more be heard of confidence in man but bind him down from mischief by the chains of the Constitution."[11] Further, "Our peculiar security is in the possession of a written Constitution. Let us not make it a blank paper by construction. I say the same as to the opinion of those who consider the grant of the treaty making power as boundless. If it is, then we have no Constitution. If it has bounds, they can be no others than the definitions of powers which that instrument gives."[12]

Although Jefferson wrote boldly and frequently without equivocation, it may be well to point out that he was not by temperament a controversialist. He did not like to debate, and avoided public confrontations before crowds. Though he was trained in the law, Jefferson did not like the courtroom clashes and only practiced it briefly. He relished intellectual exchanges among people of a questing disposition and much preferred the search for truth to any contest of wills for dominance.

All that is a way of saying that Jefferson did not enjoy political controversy, nor was he long a member of Washington's cabinet before he was thinking of some way to retire. He wrote James Madison that he had devoted more than 20 years to the public service and that he thought he ought to be able to leave it with a clear conscience, having paid his debt to society, so to speak. He wrote the President in 1792 that he looked forward to his early retirement "with the longing of a wave-worn mariner, who has at length the land in view, and shall count the days and hours which still lie between me and it."[13]

As he prepared to step down the next year, he wrote Madison that "The motion of my blood no longer keeps time with the tumult of the world. It leads me to seek for happiness in the lap and love of my family, in the society of my neighbors and my books, in the wholesome occupations of my farm and my affairs, in an interest or affection in every bud that opens, in every breath that blows around me...."[14] It was in this frame of mind, so far as we can know, that he left public life in 1793, hoping never to return to it.

Return to Public Office

But however strong his resolve to stay out, Jefferson was drawn, almost inevitably, back into the political maelstrom within two or three years. He was a man still in the full vigor of his middling years, among the most prominent men in America, and the concern he felt for restraining the government by strict construction and thus protecting individual liberty did not diminish out of office. A political party was abuilding in the mid-1790s, the Republican Party, Jefferson called it, which opposed Hamilton's banking and taxing policies, and Jefferson became its leader. He was elected Vice President in 1796, but this did not alter the course of the government, which was controlled by the Federalists, with John Adams at the head.

Although there were other issues, Jefferson's concern about how the Constitution was being interpreted had been increasing from the early 1790s. These concerns provided him with the particulars of the case. As already noted, Jefferson opposed Hamilton's broad construction of the Constitution to justify the chartering of the bank. Indeed, that Hamilton won Washington to his side may have precipitated Jefferson's resignation from the cabinet as early as he thought he decently could.

The manner of the imposition of the whiskey and other similar taxes in the course of the 1790s disturbed Jefferson just as much. The Constitution required that direct taxes be apportioned among the states on the basis of their populations. To Jefferson, and to many others, these were clearly direct taxes. But Hamilton and the Federalists called them excises, thus evading the constitutional requirement. That aside, however, Jefferson was bothered by the intrusion of revenue agents in the affairs of citizens in order to collect these taxes.

The Alien and Sedition Acts

But it was the Alien and Sedition Acts, passed in 1798, that really aroused Republicans in general and Jefferson in particular. It certainly appeared that the Federalists were bent on riding roughshod over constitutional limitations, to say nothing of what they were prepared to do to their Republican opponents. The Alien Acts were bad enough, particularly for their ignoring due process, required by the Fifth Amendment, in authorizing the President to deport aliens without even the semblance of a trial. Good John Adams, however, was no enemy to liberty, or even aliens, and he never exercised the authority.

The Sedition Act, however, was another matter. It prohibited people to defame or slander high government officials either in speech or in writing. Jefferson drew up what became known as the Kentucky Resolution in which he declared that these acts violated constitutional prohibitions, and he called on other states to join in opposing it. Madison followed suit in a somewhat milder Virginia Resolution.

The Sedition Act was no idle threat to Republicans and particularly newspaper publishers. Government attorneys and the courts began to bring them to trial and punish them for their alleged seditious acts. Only Republicans, it should be added, were prosecuted. The Jeffersonian suspicion of the courts dates from the late 1790s, if not before. Indeed, judges did seem to try such cases with inordinate zeal, charging juries sometimes in such a way as to assure guilty verdicts, and meting out tough sentences. Even Supreme Court justices who, in those days, rode circuit and tried cases, were high handed in conducting their courts.

By the time he became President in 1801, then, Jefferson had incentive aplenty for limiting the government by a strict construction of the Constitution. He had a theory for how it could be done and was determined to do it. Meanwhile, another development had occurred which aroused his fears about a judicial monopoly of the interpretation of the Constitution. Before leaving office, the Federalists had created new courts, new judgeships, positions for government attorneys, and the like. The outgoing President Adams filled these positions with Federalists, so that Federalists were solidly ensconced in the courts with lifetime appointments. The stage was set for a confrontation between the Jeffersonians and the courts, if ever there was to be one.

But Jefferson was not a man inclined to engage in confrontations. He was quiet and thoughtful, even philosophical, in demeanor, not given to attempting to ride roughshod over anyone. He always professed to respect the independence of the other branches in their proper spheres, and there is evidence to support his claims. He simply acted with the powers of the President and encouraged Congress to act with its powers so as to prevent any monopoly by the courts over the Constitution. He took care, generally, to see that if there were a confrontation it would be instituted by one of the other branches, not by himself. Nor did he engage in public declamations on the question, as a rule; most of what we know of his views comes from private correspondence—and what may be deduced from his acts.

First, do the courts have a monopoly of the interpretation of the Constitution? Jefferson did not equivocate on his answer. He answered the question most emphatically in a letter written in 1820, long after he had left office. "You seem to consider the judges as the ultimate arbiters of all constitutional questions," he wrote to a correspondent. But that, Jefferson said, is "a very dangerous doctrine indeed and one which would place us under the despotism of an oligarchy.... The constitution has erected no such single tribunal, knowing that, to whatever hands confided, with the corruptions of time and party its members would become despots."[15]

Who Decides?

Who, then, does decide constitutional questions? Let us leave to the side for the moment how they may be ultimately decided, so far as they ever are, in order to get to Jefferson's intermediate answer. So far as the Federal government is concerned, each of the branches—and in the Congress, each of the houses—decides for itself in matters that come before them. "The constitution has," Jefferson pointed out, "wisely made all the departments co-equal and co-sovereign within themselves."[16] He explained how it works this way: "Questions of property, of character, and of crime being ascribed to the judges through a definite course of legal proceeding, laws involving such questions belong of course to them, and as they decide on them ultimately and without appeal, they of course decide *for themselves.* The constitutional validity of the law or laws again prescribing executive action and to be administered by that branch ultimately and without appeal, the executive must decide for *themselves* also. . . . So also as to laws governing the proceedings of the legislature, that body must judge *for itself* the constitutionality of the law and equally without appeal or control from its co-ordinate branches. And, in general, that branch which is to act ultimately and without appeal on any law is the rightful expositor of the validity of the law, uncontrolled by the opinions of the other co-ordinate authorities."[17]

On first reading of the above it may appear that Jefferson has evaded the issue or begged the question. It may be given that appearance, I think, because he used the qualifying phrase, "without appeal," and that may have a legal ring to it, suggesting an appeal to the judiciary. But that was not his meaning, or not his only meaning. Of course, in a case taken and decided in a lower court there may be an appeal to a higher court. But Jefferson was referring to something much broader than this. Many of the powers of the government are jointly exercised by or intertwined with other branches. In that case, usually there is no appeal from a negative decision of one of the other branches. For example, if the Senate refuses to approve an appointment of the President, there is no appeal, and the decision is final.

Checks and Balances

In order to understand Jefferson's view it is necessary to view it in the context of the constitutional provision of checks and balances and the separation and partial independence of powers, not in the judicial framework to which we have become accustomed. The powers of government are divided among the branches, Jefferson was maintaining, and with that division goes the power of determining the constitutionality of what they do. To put it in its strongest form, none of the branches may force the others to act on its view of the Constitu-

tion. Jefferson said, "If the legislature fails to pass laws for a census ...
; if the President fails to supply the place of a judge ... , the judges
cannot force [them]. ..."[18]

How these checks and balances work, how each branch interpreting the Constitution for itself limits and restrains government, may
best be illustrated with actual examples. When Jefferson became President, he pardoned those who had been convicted under the Sedition
Act. He explained his action in letters to Abigail Adams: "I discharged
every person under punishment or prosecution under the Sedition
Law because I considered, and now consider, that law to be a nullity. ... The judges, believing the law constitutional, had a right to pass
a sentence of fine and imprisonment, because the power was placed
in their hands by the Constitution. But the executive, believing the law
to be unconstitutional, was bound to remit the execution of it, because
that power has been confided to them by the Constitution. That instrument meant that its co-ordinate branches should be checks on one
another."[19]

Marbury vs. Madison

Chief Justice John Marshall also wisely avoided a confrontation
with the President by his opinion in the celebrated case of *Marbury vs.
Madison.* William Marbury had been appointed justice of the peace by
President Adams, but the appointment was so late that the commission was not delivered. James Madison, the incoming Secretary of
State, refused to deliver it under orders from Jefferson. Marbury sued
in the Supreme Court for a writ of mandamus that would force Madison to deliver the commission.

Marshall held that Marbury was indeed entitled to a commission
and force was appropriate, but, unfortunately, by his reading of the
Constitution, he had applied to the wrong court. Thus, petition denied,
and no mandamus was issued. It was just as well, too, for the general
view has been that Jefferson would not have honored it, and the court
would have been powerless to enforce it. By Jefferson's interpretation
of the Constitution the court could no more force him to act than he
could force it to render a decision in accord with his wishes.

Marshall got his opportunity to try force on the President again
in the Burr trial for treason in 1807. He issued a subpoena, on motion
of defense, for Jefferson to appear in court. Jefferson declined, though
he did send some papers, and gave the court a lecture on the separation of powers.[20] Marshall took no further action.

But before either of these cases came before the courts, Congress had begun to move to rein in and restrain the courts. In 1802, it repealed the Judiciary Act of 1801, taking away a number of new offices. Shortly after, it passed a new act returning Supreme Court justices to riding circuit and restricting the Supreme Court to one session each year. Then, gently prodded by Jefferson, it zeroed in on the most notorious of the judges.

District judge John Pickering, ill famed for his drunken, if not insane, carrying on in court, was impeached by the House and removed from office by the Senate. Supreme Court justice Samuel Chase was impeached by the House for his intemperate behavior in court, but the Senate failed of the two-thirds majority required for conviction. Jefferson was disappointed and thereafter maintained that impeachment was very nearly an empty threat. That was surely an overly pessimistic assessment, however, for it appears that the behavior of judges improved perceptibly for quite a while after the Pickering and Chase cases.

The broader point is this. As Jefferson held, the House of Representatives, the Senate, and the President, as well as the courts, are empowered to act in ways that depend upon interpreting the Constitution. They take oaths to uphold and defend the Constitution, and if its meaning could only be divined by the courts this would amount to nothing more than oaths to obey the courts. Happily, however, the Constitution is written in English, and the other branches have powers that enable them to act upon their own interpretations and even restrain the courts if they get out of line.

All legislative power is vested in the Congress and executive power in the President. If the courts invade the legislative domain of the Congress by their constructions of the Constitution, as they have most certainly done in recent years, Congress has the power to set them straight. The Constitution authorizes Congress to define and limit (or expand) the appellate jurisdiction of the courts.

The President can refuse to enforce court orders he believes in conflict with the Constitution. (The courts have no enforcement machinery, i. e., prosecuting attorneys, police, armies, prisons, or electric chairs, of their own.) As Andrew Jackson is alleged to have said, "John Marshall has made his decision; now let him enforce it."

Judges can be impeached and removed from office, though lawyers rail impotently that they can only be removed for indictable crimes. It happens that when the Senate acts as such a high court, there is no appeal from its decisions. As a last resort, Congress can refuse to appropriate money for the operation of the courts. In short, not only can the other branches interpret the Constitution, but they are also in as good position as the courts to make their interpretations stick.

A System of Limited Government

What I have been describing is a system of checks and balances, a system in which no branch has a monopoly of interpretation, in which any branch with a will can work to restrain the others. It is a system of limited government, limited toward the branch which most strictly construes the Constitution. Jefferson hoped that clashes between the branches over the Constitution could be avoided. To that end, he recommended that each branch refrain from approaching too near to the bounds of its powers. That would tend to limit government even more and give room for the liberty of the people, which he thought was the greater end of government.

Jefferson did not believe, however, that all the branches of government together are the final arbiters of constitutionality. Not even the Federal and state governments, to whom he would certainly provide some place, are the ultimate arbiters. Government is too dangerous, too bent on aggrandizing its own powers, to leave to it or them the final decision. "I know of no safe depository of the ultimate powers of the society but the people themselves," he said.[21] In the final analysis, he thought, that was where the power of interpreting the Constitution resides. The people may turn out members of Congress who displease them on constitutional issues. They can refuse the re-election of a President. If all else fails, or if the branches of government cannot agree, the constitution can be amended by the consensual process prescribed.

There is great danger, Jefferson thought, in a court monopoly of the interpretation of the Constitution. Any monopoly would be fearsome, but that of the courts would be the most dangerous. The members of the court are appointed for life, are difficult to remove, and hold perilous power over the populace. Although Jefferson's nose was undoubtedly finely tuned to sniff the threat of despotism in every tainted breeze, he meant no exaggeration when he said that it would be an oligarchic despotism.

---

1. Edward Dumbauld, ed., *The Political Writings of Thomas Jefferson* (New York: Liberal Arts Press, 1955), p. 153.

2. Quoted in L. Brent Bozell, *The Warren Revolution* (New Rochelle, N. Y.: Arlington House, 1966), p. 111.

3. For example, see Elbridge Gerry's remarks in Charles C. Tansill, ed., *Formation of the Union of the American States* (Washington D.C.: Government Printing Office, 1927), p. 147. But there were objections to this view as well; see pp. 548–49.

4. Alexander Hamilton, James Madison, and John Jay, *The Federalist Papers* (New Rochelle, N. Y.: Arlington House, n.d.), p. 466.

5. Henry S. Commager, ed., *Documents of American History*, vol. I (New York: Appleton-Century-Crofts, 1962), p. 159.

6. Dumbauld, *op. cit.*, p. 76.

7. *Ibid.*, p. 55.

8. *Ibid.*, p. xxvi.

9. Adrienne Koch and William Peden, ed., *The Life and Selected Writings of Thomas Jefferson* (New York: Modern Library, 1944), p. 447.

10. *Ibid.*, p. 440.

11. Dumbauld, *op. cit.*, p. 161.

12. Koch and Peden, *op. cit.*, p. 573.

13. *Ibid.*, p. 520.

14. *Ibid.*, p. 523.

15. Dumbauld, *op. cit.*, p. 153.

16. *Ibid.*

17. *Ibid.*, p. 151. Emphasis by Jefferson.

18. *Ibid.*, p. 153.

19. *Ibid.*, p. 154.

20. See Claude G. Bowers, Jefferson in Power (Boston: Houghton Mifflin, 1964), p. 410.

21. Dumbauld, *op. cit.*, p. 154.

The General Welfare

by Clarence B. Carson

"I wish the Constitution was not so vague," one of my daughters said. My first reaction to that was to deny that the document is particularly vague or, for that matter, obscure. "Why," she persisted, "does it contain a clause on the general welfare?" Actually, her question was a good one, and it gave point to her observation on the vagueness of the Constitution, if, as I think, I know where she was coming from, as they say. She is a college sophomore and is taking courses in American history and government, among others. Undoubtedly, she had hoped to find that the Constitution would be a bulwark against the claims of the welfare state. Yet, after studying it in her classes, she has been struck by its ambiguity and what appears to be the slipperiness of its phrases. It is my hope that what follows may throw some light on the troublesome phrase, both for sophomores and the rest of us as well.

The phrase, "general welfare," occurs twice in the Constitution. It occurs first in the Preamble, which announces that one of the purposes of the Constitution is to "promote the general Welfare." Since this is a statement of purpose, not a grant of power, it need not detain us beyond noting that it is there. The other use of the phrase, however, is much more significant. It is contained in the first sentence of Article I, Section 8, which lists the powers of Congress. Equally important, it is used in connection with the grant of the power of taxation, which, then as now, was reckoned to be an essential power of government. The relevant clause reads, "The Congress shall have Power to lay and collect Taxes, Duties, Imposts and Excises, to pay the Debts and provide for the common Defence and general Welfare of the United States. . . ."

Clearly, Congress is empowered to levy taxes to provide for the general welfare. Viewed from the present perspective, this gives color, at least, to the idea that the welfare state has some constitutional foundation.

But that is to look at the matter wrong-end-to. What counts, in the first place, is what the words meant when they were used. "Welfare" is commonly used today to refer to or denote government programs

---

This article was originally published in the August 1983 issue of *The Freeman*.

to provide for the poor, the disabled, those without work, and those reckoned to be without sufficient means to provide for their basic wants. It is so used in such phrases as, welfare state, welfare programs, welfare worker, and welfare recipient. Until quite recently it was used in that way in the name of a cabinet rank department, namely, the Department of Health, Education and Welfare. This usage, however, was unknown to the makers of the Constitution. If they had intended to authorize what are nowadays called welfare programs, they would not have used the word, "welfare," to express that intent. It is the other way around: welfare programs bear that name to give the color of constitutionality to them. But let that wait for a bit.

What Americans began calling welfare programs in the late 1930s, or thereabouts, the Founders would have known by the name of "poor relief," so far as they were familiar with it at all. In England, tax supported relief of the poor was required under the poor laws, more specifically, the Elizabethan Poor Law, during the American colonial period. Poor laws were passed in the wake of the Reformation, the suppression of monasteries, and the confiscation of church lands. The destitute had received aid before that time from organizations within the church, but when much of the wealth of the church was taken away, the state took over last resort poor relief. Actually, Parliament simply required that local communities tax for and provide such relief.

A similar system took shape in the American colonies. In New England, relief for the poor was a charge upon the villages and towns, paid for from locally levied tax monies. Where the Anglican Church was established, poor relief was a duty of the parishes, and parishioners were taxed to pay for it.

Poor relief was hardly a sumptuous affair in the colonies, or, for that matter, in nineteenth-century America. Unless the person were totally incapacitated, more attention was given to reforming the poor, i.e., getting them to become productive and self-supporting, than helping them to fare well. For example, "The vestries in Virginia disposed of the able bodied poor, destitute orphans, and the illegitimate children of indentured servants by binding them to masters as apprentices or servants."[1] Workhouses were set up in some places for those who had no visible means of support. In New England, "The town provided materials and tools with which the inmates were required to earn a living."[2] The incapacitated were sometimes provided almshouses or otherwise given some minimal aid.

No one at the time of the writing of the Constitution would have associated the life of the poor dependent upon public relief with the word welfare. "Welfare," in common usage for centuries, stems from the roots "well" and "fare," and means basically, according to my dictionary, a "state of faring well; well-being." Synonyms are: "prosperity, success, happiness, weal." No sensible person would have confused poor relief with prosperity, success, or even faring well. Indeed, it was in every respect the opposite.

So far as my researches have revealed, the word, "welfare," began to take on a new connotation around the beginning of the twentieth century. The phrase, "welfare-manager," appeared in print in England in 1904. Some factories, it seems, were employing people to assist workers in improving their well-being. Thus, the *London Daily Express* declared in 1916 that "Welfare work tends to improve the condition of life for women and girls employed in factories."[3] However, the word still had no clear connection with relief for the poor.

That connection was made in the United States in the course of the routinization, regularization, and bureaucratization of government aid programs in the 1930s. The key piece of legislation for making this change was the Social Security Act, passed in 1935. There is reason to believe that the adoption of the word "welfare" in place of relief was a more or less deliberate action. It served a highly important political and constitutional purpose. Much of the early New Deal legislation was tied up in court tests by 1934. As it turned out, the central pieces of New Deal legislation were nullified in the next year or so. New Dealers were casting about frantically for ways to overcome the constitutional impasse.

Secretary of Labor Frances Perkins remarked to Supreme Court Justice Harlan Stone, in 1934, that she was worried that the social security system they were devising might not pass the constitutionality test. "The taxing power of the Federal Government, my dear," Stone replied; "the taxing power is sufficient for everything you want and need." This pointed clearly toward the general welfare phrase in the clause of the Constitution authorizing taxation. In the same year Professor E. S. Corwin, a recognized constitutional authority, maintained that the taxing and spending authority of Congress was unchecked by the Constitution. Another law professor declared, after the Supreme Court nullified crucial portions of the NRA: "The waters dammed by judicial restriction on the commerce power may break out in unwelcome fields of taxing and spending. What seems a great victory against national regulation may prove to be a Pyrrhic one."[4]

Indeed, it did. The Social Security Act leaned heavily upon the general welfare phrase in the Constitution. It opens with the claim that it is "An Act to provide for the *general welfare* by establishing a system of Federal old-age benefits, and by enabling the several States to make more adequate provision for aged persons, blind persons, dependent and crippled children, maternal and child welfare, public health, and the administration of their unemployment compensation laws. . . ."[5]

Social Security Involves a Bundle of Programs

Since many people may not think of Social Security as a welfare measure, it may be well to emphasize that, however old-age benefits— the phrase then used to describe Social Security payments to the retired—should be classified, there was a bundle of programs provided in the act which formed the core of the welfare programs. The bundle included such things as pensions to those who had not contributed to Social Security and aid to dependent children, among others.

Moreover, these programs were administered in the states by what generally became known as welfare departments in the 1940s and 1950s. Frequently, they were formally titled Department of Public Welfare (DPW), and those who administered the programs were referred to as welfare workers. In 1953, an assortment of these programs were moved into the new cabinet ranked Department of Health, Education and *Welfare*. In this fashion, the shift from referring to these programs as poor relief to public welfare was completed, and the claim that such government activities were sanctioned by the reference in the Constitution to general welfare was linguistically ratified after the fact.

The main point, of course, is that the Founders could not have intended to include what they knew as poor relief in their reference to the general welfare. Poor relief was the last resort of local governments to provide minimal means for survival; it was at the opposite end of the scale from faring well. Beyond that, the evidence presented here points toward the conclusion that as late as the early 1930s it took a great deal of straining to make the beginnings of an identification between relief and welfare.

But there is much more involved in this claim that the federal government is constitutionally authorized to provide for the general welfare than such programs as have been identified, however spuriously, with welfare. The whole concatenation of redistributionist and interventionist programs which comprise the welfare state find their main justification under it. Thus, we are brought back to the consideration of the claim regardless of what meanings may be attached to the word welfare.

The crucial question then becomes whether or not there is a grant of power in the Constitution to provide for the general welfare. There are at least two approaches that can be taken to answering this question. One is to try to discern the meaning of the phrase, "general welfare," in the clause in which it occurs. The other is to see the clause within the context of the whole Constitution.

The Taxing Power

First, then, let us look at the clause again, which reads: "The Congress shall have Power to lay and collect Taxes, Duties, Imposts and Excises, to pay the Debts and provide for the common Defence and general Welfare of the United States...." One thing is certain: Congress is authorized to levy taxes. Is it authorized to do anything else? My view is that it is not. What follows the word "Excises" is restrictive rather than being a grant of powers, restrictive of the taxing power. The operative words, in my reading of the relevant parts, would be that taxes are to be levied to "provide for the *common* Defence and *general* Welfare *of the United* States."

What was being guarded against by these restrictions was the levying of taxes on the whole people to pay for some benefit to some locale, state, or region of the country. For example, by this reading, taxes could not be properly levied to pay for an undertaking such as the Tennessee Valley Authority. There was a definite interest in the Constitutional Convention to restrict such practices. At one point, Benjamin Franklin proposed that the general government be given "a power to provide for cutting canals where deemed necessary." Roger Sherman "objected. The expence in such cases will fall on the U. States, and the benefit accrue to the places where the canals may be cut."[6] Franklin's motion was defeated by a vote of eight states to three.

is aut let me hasten to add that there is no way to make certain that my interpretation of the words as being restrictive is correct simply by reading the clause and selecting emphases within it. Furthermore, even if it were restrictive to the *general* welfare, there might still remain a potentially broad power to provide for the general welfare. After all, in ordinary usage the granting of the power to pay for something tacitly authorizes the buying of it. For example, if I tell my daughter that she may write checks to pay for her college expenses, it is a logical inference that I am authorizing such expenses. The same might be expected to apply to statements in the Constitution. To see that they do not it is necessary to place the clause thus far examined in the context of the whole Constitution. Phrases and clauses that may appear to be vague and general when considered in isolation take on much more precision when viewed from the angle of the whole.

A Limited Government

The Constitution of the United States is no ordinary set of statements or document. It is, if not unique, a very special case among documents. It describes the form for and grants power to a limited government. There are no omnibus grants of power in the Constitution; every power granted is limited in one or more and usually several ways (though not necessarily in the clause that grants it). It does not grant the powers of government generally to the United States government.

What makes the Constitution almost unique is that the government it authorizes has only such powers as are granted to it. Thus, what can be inferred from ordinary speech or, for that matter, the general run of legal documents, is no guide in construing the provisions of the Constitution. It is concerned with granting and limiting power in an arrangement for which there are few, if any, parallels in ordinary life situations.

It is contrary to the whole tenor of the Constitution that the power to provide for the general welfare should have been granted in the sentence authorizing taxation. The men who drew the Constitution did not assume that by granting the power to tax in order to pay debts that they had authorized indebtedness. On the contrary, the very next sentence authorizes Congress "To borrow Money on the credit of the United States." Nor did they assume that by authorizing taxation to pay for the common defense that they had granted the power to bring into being a military establishment. On the contrary, again, there is a list of powers to accomplish this purpose granted to Congress:

> To define and punish Piracies and Felonies committed on the high Seas and Offences against the Law of Nations:
> To declare War, grant letters of Marque and Reprisal, and make Rules concerning Captures on Land and Water;
> To raise and support Armies . . . ;
> To provide and maintain a Navy;
> To make Rules for the Government and Regulation of the land and naval Forces. . . .

If the power to provide for the common defense had been granted in the taxing power, each of these powers would have been implied by it. Such an enumeration of powers would have been redundant. Redundancies are commonplace, of course, in ordinary legal documents nowadays, but the Constitution is remarkably free of them. It is spare, lean, and once stated, repetition of a position is avoided.

Indeed, the powers which the Founders reckoned necessary to the general welfare of the United States are enumerated along with those mentioned above. Among them are the power of Congress to enact uniform laws on bankruptcies, to coin money, to fix standards of weights and measures, to establish post offices and post roads, to give authors and inventors exclusive right for a time to their writings and discoveries, and the like. Undoubtedly, they considered all the powers granted useful or necessary to the general welfare, including the powers of taxation and those for a military establishment. But my point is that the powers granted were enumerated, and those not so enumerated were reserved to the states or to the people.

That did not keep some from claiming or asserting that some object they wanted to achieve by government was provided for in the phrases of the taxation clause, even in the early years of the Republic. The issue came up for President Madison in 1817, when he was presented with a bill for making internal improvements such as roads and canals. He vetoed it on constitutional grounds.

Madison's Interpretation of Enumerated Powers

Madison said, in part, "The legislative powers vested in Congress are specified and enumerated in the eighth section of the first article of the Constitution, and it does not appear that the power proposed to be exercised by the bill is among the enumerated powers...." Regarding the general welfare phrase specifically, he said: "To refer the power in question to the clause 'to provide for the common defense and general welfare' would be contrary to the established and consistent rules of interpretation, as rendering the special and careful enumeration of powers which follow the clause nugatory and improper. Such a view of the Constitution would have the effect of giving to Congress a general power of legislation instead of the defined and limited one hitherto understood to belong to them...."[7]

President Monroe echoed Madison's views, and added some of his own, in vetoing a bill for maintaining the Cumberland Road in 1822. He denied that Congress had the power to do this. "If the power exist," he said, "it must be either because it has been specifically granted to the United States or that it is incidental to some power which has been granted. If we examine the specific grants of power we do not find it among them, nor is it incidental to any power which has been specifically granted." Among those from which he could not trace the power, he declared, was the clause "to pay the debts and provide for the common defense and general welfare."[8] In an addendum to his veto message, he included this thought: "Have Congress a right to raise and appropriate the money to any and to every purpose according to their will and pleasure? They certainly have not. The Government of the United States is a limited Government, instituted for great national purposes, and for those only."[9]

In sum, then, it is most unlikely that the makers of the Constitution would have chosen the phrase, "general welfare," to authorize the federal government to provide what they understood to be poor relief. It would have violated both their understanding of the meaning of words and the common practice as to what level of government should provide the relief. On the contrary, it appears that relief came to be called welfare to give it a semblance of constitutionality. Indeed, close analysis within the sentence and the context of the Constitution points to the conclusion that the reference "to provide for the general welfare" was the restriction of the taxing power rather than a separate grant of power.

In short, no powers were enumerated granting authority to the federal government either to enact relief measures or to erect what has come to be called a welfare state. Nor is the language of the Constitution especially vague or carelessly general when it is viewed within the context of the whole document. It only appears to be so when wrenched out of context and construed to cover purposes not intended.

---

1. Curtis P. Nettels, *The Roots of American Civilization* (New York: Appleton-Century-Crofts, 1963), p. 463.

2. *Ibid.*, p. 462.

3. This information comes from the *Oxford English Dictionary*.

4. See Arthur M. Schlesinger, Jr., *The Politics of Upheaval* (Boston: Houghton Mifflin, 1960), pp. 398–99.

5. Henry S. Commager, Documents of American History, vol. II (New York: Appleton-Century-Crofts, 1962), p. 326. Italics added.

6. Charles C. Tansill, ed., *Formation of the Union of American States* (Washington, D.C.: Government Printing Office, 1927), p. 724.

7. James D. Richardson, ed., *A Compilation of the Messages and Papers of the Presidents*, vol. II (New York: Bureau of National Literature, 1897), pp. 569–70.

8. *Ibid.*, p. 712.

9. *Ibid.*, p. 736.

V. THE FOLLIES OF DEMOCRACY

Not So Democratic: The Caution of the Framers

by M. E. Bradford

It has been my pleasure for the past several months to read through the written remains of the Framers of our form of government and to live by an act of will and imagination in something like the intellectual atmosphere which enveloped their deliberations in Philadelphia and in the state ratification conventions called for by the results of the Great Convention.

On two occasions in recent years I have had the opportunity to visit the City of Brotherly Love and to examine what survives there of the charming provincial Capital, known to John Dickinson, Robert Morris, and Benjamin Franklin as their home. This experience helped me a good deal in penetrating the barriers created by the two intervening centuries in our history as a people. Even so, I am in this work constantly made aware of the danger anachronism—of the size of the gulf that separates us from the serenity and reasonableness and anti-ideological caution of the Fathers. But is one respect I believe I have identified a feature of their thought visible in particular during the Constitutional Convention that is hidden from us by the accepted myth of our national beginnings: a feature which we might do well to recover and apply in restoring the Republic to its original character.

It is important for us to remember when we examine the Constitution made in Philadelphia that it was written before the French Revolution occurred and that the education of its authors was English and classical: principally an education in history, Roman literature, and law.

The upper reaches of metaphysical speculation concerning the nature of man and the possibility of creating a perfect Commonwealth for him to inhabit was not an important element in the political deliberations of the English Old Whigs or their progeny, the original American republicans. True enough, a few of them had read Hobbes and Locke and, more importantly, Montesquieu and David Hume.

M. E. Bradford was professor of English at the University of Dallas. He was author of numerous books, among them *A Better Guide Than Reason*, *Against the Barbarians*, and *Original Intentions*. This article originally appeared in the June 1981 edition of *The Freeman*.

But what they learned from these authorities was in most cases under-stood to be only a gloss upon the historic rights of Englishmen and the history of English liberty out of which they had made a Revolution. The most important evidence in support of this understanding of their habits of mind comes from the way in which they treated the hypo-thetical imperative to what James Wilson of Pennsylvania, in speaking for the radical minority in the Convention, referred to as the "inherent, indisputable, and unalienable rights of men," to a kind of equality in political rights.[1]

It is true, of course, that the Framers often conceded that men were equal in a "state of nature": equally ungoverned and equally unprotected. But some of them also maintained, as did Calhoun later, that the unpleasant and hypothetical condition thus described was a mischievous abstraction and that the truly natural state for man, as opposed to that of beasts, was social: art being, as Burke taught, man's nature. What signifies in the reaction of the Framers to the appeals by Wilson and, to a certain extent, Madison, to a doctrine specifying the political equality of citizens in the Republic they were shaping from the raw materials of the Articles of Confederation and the extant and stubborn identities of the states is that they ignored them altogether.

Departures from Equality

I invite you to consider with me the many ways in which the "rights of man" are violated in the document agreed to in Philadel-phia. The most important of these has to do with the "great compro-mise," so called: the provision that one house of the national legisla-ture should give an equal vote to each of the states, regardless of its size or population; and the attendant provision that every state should have at least one Congressman, regardless of its population. Not every delegate who opposed the insistence of the small states on this formula was a serious devotee of "natural rights." Some were interested simply in the political influence of their own states. But the delegates from the smaller commonwealths made it quite clear that they were going home if they were not given their own way in this particular.

The prudence of such compromising spirits as Benjamin Franklin, who was ideological about almost nothing, intruded at this point. The old freethinker, always ready to make it up as he went along, called upon his colleagues to invite a minister to come and pray over their deliberations. The larger states continued to grumble, but recognized necessity. Later, another violation of equal rights—in this case of the rights of posterity—was added to confirm the compromise over legislative representation. I refer here to the provision of the Constitution which precludes any amendment at some future date that would deprive any state of its equal voice in the United States Senate.

Of course, the provision for state equality in the Senate goes against the sacrosanct doctrine of majority rule. But that is precisely what the Framers wished it to do. And they followed the same principle in most of the important sections of the Constitution. The rule requiring a two-thirds vote of both Houses of Congress and a three-fourths vote of the states to amend the Constitution (the rule which has thus far prevented the adoption of the ERA, and which will, without doubt, prevent the conversion of the District of Columbia into a state by giving it seats in the Senate) gives an unequal weight to the vote of the first generation of Americans who accepted the Constitution, and to opponents of such changes in the succeeding generations.

The same holds true for the two-thirds rule with regard to the overriding of a Presidential veto, the two-thirds rule for the confirmation of ambassadors, justices of the Supreme Court and "of all other officers of the United States, whose appointments are not . . . otherwise provided for"[2]; and the two-thirds rule in cases of impeachment, expulsion of members in the House or Senate, and the validation of treaties.

Voting Power

Allowing the House of Representatives and the Senate to make their own rules concerning the limitation of debate has, as we all know, been another restriction upon the will of the simple majority in the operation of our political system—and, I might add, a good one. So was the provision in the original Constitution which allowed for the election of United States Senators by the state legislatures or in any other fashion the states thought proper.

The much abused Electoral College works to the same effect and has, we should remember, produced several minority Presidents. If New York or California decide by one vote to send electors in favor of Candidate X, and Texas and Pennsylvania decide by the margin of shall we say, a million to commit their representatives in the Electoral College to Candidate Y, the results of such disparity will not be reflected in the number of votes given in the only election that counts to the respective candidates. Our Presidents are elected by the people of the states, acting separately, but in unison. Simple plebiscitary democracy as proposed in some suggestions that we abolish the College goes against the tenor of the United States Constitution as a whole, and makes this mistake precisely because its proponents imagine that equality of individual political rights was the regnant abstraction in the political lexicon of the Fathers.

Other Departures from the Doctrine of Majority Rule

Four other examples of the indifference of the Framers to the doctrine of majority rule are (1) the provision in the Constitution for the election of the President by the House of Representatives with each state casting one vote in the case of a deadlock in the Electoral College; (2) the process by which the Constitutional Convention itself was called; (3) the manner in which the Convention voted, with each state having one vote; and (4) the way in which the Constitution was adopted, the equivalent of the way in which it may be modified today.

But there are often overlooked and more serious contradictions of the gospel of equality buried in the Constitution that go beyond mere restraints upon the will of the majority. Some of these are obvious, such as the protections for the institution of Negro slavery in the Fugitive Slave clause, the twenty-year extension of the slave trade, and the three-fifths formula for the representation of slaves in determining the voting strength of the South in the House of Representatives. It is noteworthy that no member of the Convention entertained any idea that the institution of slavery, as it stood within the various states, could be affected or threatened by the instrument of government that they hoped to create.

Slavery Condoned

A majority of the 55 members of the Constitutional Convention owned slaves. Farrand tells us that slavery was "accepted" by the Framers "as part of the established order,"[3] and that they did not provide any procedure for its eventual extinction. On the contrary, some Northern members of the Convention complained (and perhaps rightfully) that the three-fifths formula allowed the South to increase its political power by the mere expedient of purchasing slaves. Twenty years was thought enough time to facilitate the importation of all the Negroes the South could possibly need, and almost suggests that such purchases were to be encouraged.

In the specific exclusion of Indians from the calculation of the census, equality is once again contradicted. And in the provisions requiring a certain age or status as citizen as a precondition for holding office, a political onus is attached to youth and foreign birth.

But far more important are the inequalities left to the discretion of the states. Qualification for the franchise, as was agreed by the members of the Convention after much debate, was to be determined in the several commonwealths and was not to be meddled with by any component of the national power. One is fully a citizen of the United States by being a citizen of one of its member states.

No less a Federalist than James Madison developed this distinction when serving as a Congressman from Virginia during Washington's administration. The discussion concerned the right of one William L. Smith of South Carolina to hold the seat as Representative from South Carolina to which he had been elected. The dispute arose because he had been overseas during the years of the Revolution. Madison's argument was uncomplicated. Representative Smith had never ceased to be a member of the society into which he had been born. Therefore, he became a citizen of the United States when South Carolina came into the Union.

Let the States Decide

That American citizens living in territories and possessions of the Republic and in the District of Columbia do not vote in Federal elections (except, according to a recent change, for President in the District) unless they vote by absentee ballot in one of the states, is evidence to the same effect. Political citizenship for representation in Congress is not within the gift of the government of the United States, or so the Framers intended. Indeed, the states were left by the original Constitution with the authority to impose a religious test for office. The First Amendment did not alter this prerogative, as it left untouched the state-supported religious establishments surviving in such places as Massachusetts and Connecticut. All that the amendment provided was that there should be no federally established church for the entire Union. This situation was modified with the Fourteenth Amendment. But Indians were still exempted from its protection. And Professor Raoul Berger, in his *Government by Judiciary*, has taught us to read even that innovation in our fundamental law as less drastic than some of our advanced thinkers would imagine.[4]

Most of the Framers, including even such generous spirits as George Mason, expected the states to provide for a property qualification as a condition of the franchise. The one mentioned most often is drawn from English law, that of the "50 shilling freeholder." For it was their consensus that a man (and we all know the Constitution gave no political rights to women) should have a stake in the society before he was given the right to have an influence over its future.

What propertyless men might do with their votes was the nightmare before the house when the Great Convention assembled in Philadelphia. They called this nightmare by a simple name—democracy. And they connected that term of pejoration, an anathema with over half of the 55 members there gathered, with the rebellion in western Massachusetts led in the previous year by one Captain Daniel Shays. The overtly anti-democratic spirit of the Framers is to the uninitiated reader of the records of their proceedings the greatest possible surprise.

Fear of Democracy

In one sense, the fear of democracy and of the despotism that was likely to come after it is the "given" of the Great Convention. Almost as soon as the meeting convened and the Virginia delegation got control of the chair and then placed its plan of government before the house as its first order of business, Elbridge Gerry of Massachusetts (at this point in his career, as vigorous a republican as could be found) asserted that "the evils we experience flow from the excess of democracy," and urged his colleagues to be "taught by experience the danger of the leveling spirit." Governor Edmund Randolph, the spokesman for the Virginia Plan, picked up Gerry's theme and urged the adoption of his resolutions as a counter to the "turbulence and follies of democracy" in which every "evil" of government under the Articles found its "origin."[5] And more of the same is to be heard throughout these debates.

General Washington had come to the Convention expressing the hope that New England would eschew those "leveling principles" that had made her men so difficult to command. Madison said the same in his letters. We have all heard what Hamilton called the people—"that great beast." Gouverneur Morris described them as a "reptile," and had added, "he who wishes to enjoy natural Rights must establish himself where natural Rights are admitted. He must live alone."[6] And Rufus King of Massachusetts announced the opinion that "the unnatural Genius of Equality [is] the arch Enemy of the moral world."[7]

If these sayings of our political forefathers do not sound like what the myth has taught us to expect, the text of the Constitution should persuade us that the statements were in character and are reflected in the most significant kind of action, the drafting of a fundamental law.

A Religious Restraint

The Framers were, again contrary to the myth, a body of religious men, skeptical concerning human nature, particularly of its collective manifestations. Only four or five of the Framers were Deists, and even they, as for instance Franklin, were undogmatic about politics, devoted to no vast, *a priori* scheme. The caution of David Hume and the pessimism of St. Paul can have the same political results. Experience, as gathered in history and prescription, was, in the eyes of the Framers, the proper guide in political questions, as in most others. At the end of the Convention with the finished document on the table before them, the venerable Franklin bespoke the caution of the entire Assembly when he asked each of his colleagues to "doubt a little of his own infallibility."[8]

It was a fine thing to tinker with a stove or even to invent a city, and especially so if the stove and the city were what people wanted, and what circumstances either required or allowed. But the secular religion of an ideology, the mindset which we associate with a Robespierre or a Marx, would not have been well received in Independence Hall during those hot late spring and summer months of 1787. The very physical appearance of the place and of the buildings surviving from the community which then surrounded it should tell us that. What they say iconically is that extremists are not in the proper style.

No Sudden Shifts of Power

The culture of the English Enlightenment shared by the authors of our Constitution was essentially anti-rationalistic, anti-metaphysical. "Enthusiasm" was the opposite of what they meant by philosophy. And large-scale theories of human rights are "enthusiastic." They threaten property and the going social order, opening the way to a situation in which men like Captain Shays might replace the natural leaders, the men of virtue; confiscate and distribute everything in sight. Such a prospect frightened the Framers into altering the form of government established in the Articles, providing for an authority to check all such rebellions, even if they were peaceful and political. And certainly if they offered violence.

However, since our country crossed the Great Divide of the War Between the States, it has been more and more the habit of our historians, jurists, and political scientists to read the Continental Enlightenment, and the Age of Revolution that was its political consequence, back into the record of our national beginnings by way of an anachronistic gloss upon the Declaration of Independence.

I will not here belabor the vexed question of how we might best interpret the Declaration, as I have already said enough on that subject in another context.[9] But my argument on this occasion does demonstrate that whatever the Declaration meant to Thomas Jefferson or later to Abraham Lincoln, the "political religion" of equality got short shrift from the men who wrote our Constitution. And the Constitution, not the Declaration, is law. It provides that our government follow the deliberate sense of the American people. As the South has always recognized, concern for minority rights is not the major explanation for its anti-egalitarian features, but rather a determination that the majorities with power to change the law be very large indeed.

The Constitution makes it difficult or even impossible for us to alter our political identity on whim or when momentarily carried away by the adjuration of demagogues. But it allows, indeed requires, that we hammer out a consensus on the important things affecting a very limited public sphere, working under the shadow and from the example of those judicious men who first set the great engine of our government in motion. To keep it running, we must remember how and why it was made.

---

1. James Madison, *Notes of Debates in the Federal Convention of 1787* (Athens: Ohio University Press, 1966), p. 221.

2. U. S. Constitution, Article I, Section 2.

3. Max Farrand, The Fathers of the Constitution: A Chronicle of the Establishment of the Union (New Haven: Yale University Press, 1912), p. 130.

4. Suffrage for the freedmen is not contemplated in the Fourteenth Amendment, which explains subsequent Republican enthusiasm for the Fifteenth Amendment—once the party began to lose its white support.

5. Madison, *Notes*, pp. 39 and 42. See also p. 658, where Gerry calls democracy "the worst . . . of all political evils."

6. Max M. Mintz, *Gouverneur Morris and the American Revolution* (Norman: University of Oklahoma Press, 1970), p. 73.

7. Robert Ernst, *Rufus King: American Federalist* (Chapel Hill: University of North Carolina Press, 1968), p. 299.

8. Madison, *Notes*, p. 654.

9. M. E. Bradford, "The Heresy of Equality: A Reply to Harry Jaffa," on pp. 29–57 of *A Better Guide Than Reason* (La Salle, Ill.: Sherwood Sugden & Co., 1979).

The Meaning of Federalism

by Clarence B. Carson

Several developments have contributed to making the meaning of federalism obscure. Some are old, some recent. Some may be more or less innocent; others are destructive of federalism itself. One of these that may be more or less innocent is the habit of referring to the United States government as the "federal government." Whether it is innocent or not, it does tend to confuse the unwary. These United States have a federal system of government. The system embraces both the general government and those of the states. Thus, both the United States government and the state government are correctly alluded to as "federal" governments.

When Felix Morley called attention some years ago "to the illogical practice of referring to the central government as the 'federal government'," he declared that the confusion was "due to historical accident." What he had in mind was that the supporters of the Constitution, when it was being considered for ratification, called themselves "federalists," and the government under examination "federal." From that beginning, he thinks, the idea of the general or central government being the federal government began to take hold.[1]

That much is correct, but there is an additional reason: the Founders devised what was essentially a new system of government. It has come to be called federalism. But they were so intent upon promoting or preventing its ratification and acceptance that they neglected to devise logical appellations for it in general discourse. Before the devising of a federal structure, leagues or unions of more or less independent states were usually referred to as confederations. The organizations over these leagues could be referred to as confederation governments. There is a comparable word—"federation"—in use. But it would be inaccurate and misleading to refer to the United States government as the federation government. Such terminology would imply that the central government is over the states rather than over the people. Whereas, it has a jurisdiction over the people primarily.

This article was first published in the January 1983 edition of *The Freeman*.

People Are Governed

The distinctive feature of the federal system of government is that the general government acts directly upon the people. For example, the government is financed by taxes on persons, not by levies upon states. The government in question can be described with sufficient precision by calling it the United States, general, central, or national government. However, my purpose is not so much to reform the use of the language as to remove the confusion engendered by referring to it as the federal government. More on this point later.

Another source of confusion about federalism is the doctrine of states' rights, as it is commonly called. In the first place, states have powers (as do all governments), not rights. In the second place, what is being disputed within the federal system of government when so-called states' rights are asserted is the jurisdiction of the national government to act in some field. It is important that states act to restrain the national government to the exercise of its powers within its allotted jurisdiction. They are most apt to do so in defense of their jurisdiction. But what is ultimately important in this is the rights of persons and the liberties of the people. It is easy to lose sight of this when the dispute is conducted in the name of "states' rights."

Rights belong to individuals in the American constitutional system. Any government (whether state or national) may misuse its powers so as to violate the rights of persons. It is exceedingly important, then, that the rights of persons not become identified with the powers of government, either national or state. That can easily become the means for the enlargement of the powers of government (one or the other, or both) at the expense of the rights of persons. That can result from confusing either states' powers with rights or treating jurisdictions as if any power that can be conceived falls in one or the other. These are confusions of the federal system that have become implicit in the states' rights doctrine.

A Mistaken Use of the States' Rights Arguments

How easy it is to fall into this trap is illustrated in the opinion accompanying a Supreme Court decision announced in 1936. The case was *The United States v. Butler* in which the main provisions of the Agricultural Adjustment Act were nullified. The majority opinion was written by Justice Owen Roberts. (It should be noted that Justice Roberts did not linguistically confuse jurisdiction with rights, but he did rely on the states' rights argument in such a way as to ascribe powers to the states which they neither claimed nor possessed.)

Justice Roberts based his decision upon the fact that the act provided for taxing food processors in order to purchase the compliance of farmers with the programs it outlined. His main conclusion was stated in these words: "Congress has no power to enforce its commands on the farmer to the ends sought by the Agricultural Adjustment Act. It must follow that it may not indirectly accomplish these ends by taxing and spending to purchase compliance. The Constitution and the entire plan of government negative any such use of the power to tax and to spend as the act undertakes to authorize...." Then, as if it were an afterthought, he appended this dictum: "A possible result of sustaining the claimed federal power would be that every business group which thought itself under-privileged might demand that a tax be laid on its vendors or vendees the proceeds to be appropriated to the redress of its deficiency of income.... "[2] This last is about as close as he came to dealing with the violation of the rights of individuals involved.

Even so, he was within shouting distance of the issue in the points he made that are quoted above. But then he dragged in the dubious issue of the alleged intrusion of the provisions of the act upon the jurisdiction of the states. He went on at length about the dangers to the states of such action. At one point, Justice Roberts concluded that the "Congress cannot invade state jurisdiction to compel individual action; no more can it purchase such action." At another point, he declared that if the principle of the act were accepted, Congress could invade the reserved jurisdiction of the states and accomplish the "total subversion of the governmental powers reserved to the individual states." The proponents of the act, Justice Roberts said, were trying to claim that the Constitution "gave power to the Congress to tear down the barriers, to invade the states' jurisdiction, and to become a parliament of the whole people...."[3]

This claim flew in the face of the 10th Amendment, he charged.[4]

In short, Justice Roberts did his best to bring the whole weight of federalism to bear on his position with what were spurious arguments about the jurisdiction of the states. If the act was not authorized by the Constitution, it was irrelevant whether or not it violated the jurisdiction of the states. That any or all states had power to pass any such act is nowhere proved.

The 10th Amendment does not disclose a single power possessed by the states. Rather, it disposes of the question as to whether the general government has some reservoir of powers not otherwise enumerated. (It doesn't.) And, if a state does not have the power to pass such an act, it would be no trespass upon its jurisdiction for the general government to pass one. He does not even explore the possibility that the states might be prohibited from passing such acts by the United States Constitution, for which an excellent case could be made. The most that can be said for the argument is that Justice Roberts grabbed the states' rights ball when it came floating by and ran with it with all his might.

None of this is said in derogation of jurisdictional claims of the states, of the decision the Supreme Court reached, nor of the powers of reasoning of the court. Rather, it is to illustrate the results of the confusion of federalism inherent in the states' rights doctrine and some of its corollaries.

Subordinating the States

But the greatest confusion about federalism and threat to its survival has come from the concerted effort for more than half a century to turn the states and their dependent organizations into administrative units of the national government. The way was eased for this by the habit of referring to the national government as *the* "federal government." Off-the-mark talk about states' rights has had little more impact than dogs have upon the moon by barking at it. State organizations have been most effectively turned into administrative units in connection with the development of the welfare state.

More precisely, as the national government became more and more involved with redistributing wealth, state organizations, particularly counties, became instruments of much of the distribution. For example, state welfare agencies (called by a multiplicity of names nowadays) administer a great variety of programs funded by the national government. Over the past three decades, too, the courts of the United States have asserted increasing and widespread authority over agencies funded primarily by the states, such as schools, prisons, mental institutions, colleges, and what have you. There should be no doubt that there have been large scale intrusions upon the jurisdictions of the states.

The confusion has been further compounded in recent years by what has been called the "New Federalism." Currently, the phrase is being used by the Reagan Administration to designate the plan to turn over some welfare programs to the states, to disentangle some state-national joint efforts by having the national government take over the funding of them entirely, and to reduce national controls over grants made to states by the government. But the idea of a New Federalism had been around for several years before Reagan became President.

The late Nelson Rockefeller proposed doing something to revive federalism in a book published in 1962, entitled *The Future of Federalism*. At the beginning of his second term, President Richard Nixon advanced the idea of having the national government aid in the recovery of federalism. About all that came out of that was the practice of providing large grants from the central government under the rubric of revenue sharing. What these various proposals and plans have in common is the notion that federalism can be restored to its full vitality by action of the national government. That may well be the problem rather than the solution. At any rate, it has succeeded thus far more in confusing than in clarifying the meaning and function of federalism.

The main point I wish to make about the function of federalism is that it is a system for the protection of the liberties of people and the rights of individuals. The freedom of a people consists in the voluntary use of their property and faculties to their chosen ends. The Founders of the United States generally understood well something that is universally the case: that government is ever the greatest potential threat to freedom of action. The liberties that prevail consist of those acts not prohibited by law and those rights of individuals that governments are forbidden to violate and are enjoined to protect from all intruders. In short, the precondition of extensive liberty for a people is limited government. It is, then, as a device for limiting government that a federal system of government performs its most valuable function. But to grasp the full implications of this, the meaning of federalism needs to be clearly stated as free of confusion and complications as possible.

Two Governments in Power

A federal system of government is one in which two governments have jurisdiction over the inhabitants. In this country, the two governments are those of the states and of the United States. Both governments have sanctions, that is, may use force upon the inhabitants. Both have enforcement officers and courts. This system is sometimes referred to as one of dual sovereignty. The phrase is, however, misleading, and when carried very far leads to conflicts for which there is no resolution short of the destruction of such independence as one or the other governments may have.

The term sovereignty came into currency in the modern world in the sixteenth century. Monarchs came to be referred to as sovereigns. The concept was used to buttress absolute monarchy. It means the supreme, or ultimate authority, over a land, state, or country. The United States does not have a monarch, or king; literally, it does not have a sovereign. It goes deeper than that, however. Neither the Constitution of the United States nor the constitutions of the states vest supreme authority in any man, any group of men, or the people as a whole.

It is the genius of American federalism that government is limited, not supreme. Sovereignty is a mischievous notion, an improper analytical tool for describing government in this country. It sends people in quest for an authority which can only exist in defiance of the constitutions of the states and of the Constitution of the United States.

Federalism is best understood, not as a political concept, but as a legal concept, which is what it is. Sovereignty is a political concept (an absolutist authoritarian one, at that); jurisdiction is a legal concept. Thus, the conclusion that in the United States the states have a jurisdiction, and the United States has a jurisdiction.

Defining the Jurisdiction

The Constitution of the United States, aside from describing the method of selection of its officers and the inner workings of the government, is mainly concerned with defining the jurisdiction of the government that it authorizes. Also, it denies jurisdiction to the states in certain areas, prohibits states to act in certain ways, and reserves powers to the states, and rights to the people. Before offering some proof for this and delineating the jurisdictions, however, there are two basic points that need to be nailed down.

The first is to show why state governments are federal governments as well as the United States. These United States have a federal system of divided jurisdiction in government. Severally, the states exercise authority over persons in one of these jurisdictions. The United States government exercises authority in the other. Both, therefore, are federal governments. To acclaim one as the federal government to the exclusion of the other is to deny, implicitly, that we have a federal system of government.

The other point has to do with the independence of the state governments of the central government and the powers of action independent of state governments by the United States government. That is not to say that each does not rely on the other in important ways—they do—but to affirm that their operations as governments are independent. Indeed, the independence of the states stands on more solid historical ground than does that of the national government.

James Madison noted that in this and several other matters, "The State governments will have the advantage of the federal government." As proof, he pointed out that "The State governments may be regarded as constituent and essential parts of the federal government; whilst the latter is nowise essential to the operation or organization of the former." His meaning was that elections occur within states, and that the general government depends upon the states to come into being. "On the other side," he continued, "the component parts of the State governments will in no instance be indebted for their appointment to the direct agency of the federal government...."[5] Moreover, some of the states existed before the United States. True, after the adoption of the Constitution, states are admitted to the union by act of Congress. But they come into being at their own instance, draw up their own constitutions, and select their own officers. Their independence of the general government, then, is antecedent to it.

The important point, however, is that both the government of the union and the states are distinct and separate entities. They are governments in their own right, neither being the creation of the other. Devotees of the states have sometimes argued that the United States was created by the states.[6] Not so, however. The states did send delegates to the Constitutional Convention, and they did hold elections for the consideration of ratification of the Constitution. But the latter delegates were chosen by the electorate, and the preamble to the Constitution refers to "We the people" as the origin of the government. In any case, both governments possess the essentials of separateness, distinctness, powers, and independence to be considered governments in their own rights.

Local Governments

By contrast, local governments are not independent governments. Except for the District of Columbia, all local governments are creatures of the states. They come into being by authority of the states, and derive such powers of governments as they exercise from the states. They are not, then, a part of the federal system of government, but rather a part of state government. Or, to be absolutely precise, they are linked to federalism only by their ties to state governments.

If the independence of the state and United States governments were all that could be said about federalism, however, it would be a fearful and monstrous system of government. To have one independent government over the inhabitants is bad enough, but to have two would be intolerable, if each or either could exercise its power without restraint. That is not the case, however. Both governments are restrained, restrained by each other by the delineation of their separate jurisdictions, the denial of powers to one or the other or both, and by the specified manner in which they are to exercise their powers. Their independence of each other is important, because it provides a safeguard against intrusion by either into the jurisdiction of the other. But it is of even greater importance—that in the assignment of jurisdictions both governments are limited and restrained. It is these restraints that protect the liberties of the people.

The bulk of these restraints are found in the United States Constitution. In the first place, the United States government was never granted all the powers that it might be claimed are inherent in government itself. It was granted only a limited jurisdiction to deal with certain objects of government. These powers were described in general terms in the following ways at the time of the debate over the ratification of the Constitution. John Jay, speaking in the New York state convention, maintained that the powers were largely restricted to the following objects: "They comprehend the interests of the states in relation to each other, and in relation to foreign powers."[7] James Madison observed that "the powers of the general government relate to external objects and are but few."[8] Again, he emphasized that "The powers delegated by the proposed Constitution to the federal government are but few and defined."[9] In the Virginia convention, Edmund Pendleton argued that the general government was to act "in great national concerns, in which we are interested in common with other members of the Union.... At another point, and more heatedly, he insisted that the government authorized was not clothed with all powers of government. "It only extends," he said, "to the general purposes of the Union. It does not intermeddle with the local, particular affairs of the states."[10]

Specified Limited Powers

It is not necessary, however, to rely solely upon the comments and descriptions of contents by the Founders to learn that the Constitution granted only limited powers to the general government. The document speaks for itself in this regard. The powers of the government were enumerated in several places in the Constitution, above all, in Article I, Section 8. For example, such powers as these are granted:

To define and punish Piracies and Felonies committed on the high Seas and Offences against the Law of Nations,

To declare War, grant Letters of Marque and Reprisal, and make Rules concerning Captures on Land and Water.

To raise and support Armies. . . .

To provide and maintain a Navy.

To establish an uniform Rule of Naturalization, and uniform Laws on the subject of Bankruptcies throughout the United States.

In the most general terms, then, the Constitution provided for a general government to conduct foreign relations, to settle disputes among the states, and to facilitate trade and intercourse among the peoples of the states.

Further, the United States government is prohibited to do some things. For example, "No Bill of Attainder or ex post facto Law shall be passed." "No Tax or Duty shall be laid on Articles exported from any State." "No Title of Nobility shall be granted by the United States . . . ," and so on. The government is further restricted by amendments, such as the Fourth, which reads: "The right of the people to be secure in their persons, houses, papers, and effects, against unreasonable searches and seizures, shall not be violated, and no Warrants shall issue, but upon probable cause, supported by Oath or affirmation, and particularly describing the place to be searched and the persons or things to be seized." Beyond all these, there is a blanket limitation contained in the 10th Amendment: "The powers not delegated to the United States by the Constitution, nor prohibited by it to the States, are reserved to the States respectively, or to the people."

Limits to State Powers

The jurisdiction of the states was conceived as being much more comprehensive than that of the United States at the time of the drawing of the Constitution. The Constitution does prohibit certain powers to the states. For example, "No State shall enter into any Treaty, Alliance, or Confederation; grant Letters of Marque and Reprisal; coin money, emit Bills of Credit; make any Thing but gold and silver Coin a Tender in Payment of Debts; pass any Bill of Attainder, ex post facto Law, or Law impairing the Obligation of Contracts, or grant any Title of Nobility."

There are further prohibitions on the states in amendments, the most general of which are to be found in the Fourteenth, and the central ones are embodied in these words: "No State shall make or enforce any law which shall abridge the privileges or immunities of citizens of the United States; nor shall any State deprive any person of life, liberty, or property, without due process of law; nor deny to any person within its jurisdiction the equal protection of the laws." Beyond such prohibitions, however, the main powers of government over the lives of persons were reserved to the states.

James Madison stated the case for the residual powers of the states this way. "Those which are to remain in the State governments are numerous and indefinite. . . . The powers reserved to the several States will extend to all the objects which, in the ordinary course of affairs, concern the lives, liberties, and properties of the people, and the internal order, improvement, and prosperity of the State."[11]

State Constitutions also Limit

It should be noted, however, that the states are further restrained by their own constitutions, and most of these have much more extensive restrictions than are contained in the United States Constitution. Moreover, as already noted, since the time of Madison, further extensive prohibitions on the states have been added to the Constitution. Thus, it is correct to say that both the United States and state governments are limited and that neither possesses all those powers which may be conceived as inherent in government itself.

The object of this limitation, indeed, the highest object of federalism itself, was the rights of individuals and the liberties of the people. Alexander Hamilton put it this way: "This balance between the nation and state governments ought to be dwelt on with peculiar attention, as it is of the utmost importance. It forms a double security to the people. If one encroaches on their rights, they will find a powerful protection in the other. Indeed, they will both be prevented from overpassing their constitutional limits, by a certain rivalship, which will ever subsist between them."[12]

From our perspective, it is easy to conclude that Hamilton was wrong, at least in part, in his prediction. He was right, of course, in holding that the national government would defend its jurisdiction from intrusion by the states. He was right, too, in maintaining that this would provide security against states' encroaching upon the rights of the individual. It has worked that way historically, and it is still working that way. But what of that "rivalship" of the states over their jurisdiction and the security that was supposed to afford against concentration of power in the central government and its violation of the rights of the people?

Aside from clamors about "states' rights" and an occasional suit by some state in the courts of the United States, the states appear to be paper tigers. They are largely unable either to protect their own jurisdiction or the rights of their inhabitants from the central government. Either Hamilton was wrong or something has happened in the interval.

An Important Balance

It will be my position that Hamilton was right about the Constitution as it then stood. To understand why, it is necessary to look at the structure of the government and how it has been changed so as to effect the power of the states to defend their jurisdiction. The answers to two questions should lay open to view the crucial structure of the government. First, what branch or organization in the central government was crucial to the defense of the jurisdiction of the United States? While all the branches play a role in it, the ultimate power for the defense lies in the Supreme Court. By its power of review of legislation, both national and state, where a constitutional question is raised, it can vigorously and effectively assert and defend the jurisdiction of the United States.

Second, in what branch of what government is there an organization with the power and under the control of the states to defend the jurisdiction of the states? There is no such organization today. There has not been one in the United States since 1913. Until 1913, the United States Senate had power to do it (and it still does), and state legislatures had crucial leverage over the Senate. That leverage was removed in that year by the 17th Amendment. The amendment provided for the direct election of Senators.

In the original Constitution, Senators were elected by the legislatures of the states. In effect, the state governments had representatives in Congress; they were the members of the Senate. The Senate is well placed in the government to defend the jurisdiction of the states, if it will and must. It can refuse to pass any bill which intrudes upon the jurisdiction of the states. Moreover, Supreme Court, indeed, all court, appointees of the United States government, have to be approved by the Senate. Presidents, too, have large incentives to get along well with the Senate, for all their major appointees and all treaties must be approved by the Senate. Further, trials of impeachment, including judges, are conducted before the Senate.

Since 1913, state legislatures have had little or no effective control over Senators. No longer do they have to please the state legislatures to be reelected. State governments are no longer represented in the central government. It is not surprising, then, that the great growth and expansion of power of the national government have occurred since 1913. The main balance wheel for the states in the Senate no longer operates to restrain it. The courts have ever more vigorously asserted and expanded the jurisdiction of the United States, and the presidents and Congress have not been far behind.

That is not to say that federalism is meaningless today. It is still used to restrain the states. Moreover, the states still retain much jurisdiction, or portions of it, thanks largely, I suspect, to the voters. But the central government is no longer restrained significantly by federalism. It has become *the* government, indeed, *the* federal government, as we acknowledge in our references to it.

If the above analysis is correct, federalism can hardly be restored by redistributing welfare programs. It will hardly be revitalized, in any case, by federal aid or revenue sharing. It will only be able to perform its salutary function of protecting its jurisdiction so as to defend the rights of its inhabitants when it has a means for doing so within the general government itself. Looked at that way, the election of Senators by state legislatures was a good idea.

---

1. Felix Morley, *Freedom and Federalism* (Chicago: Henry Regnery, a Gateway edition, 1959), p. 21.

2. Henry S. Commager, *Documents of American History*, vol. II (New York: Appleton-Century-Crofts, 1963), p. 251.

3. *Ibid.*, pp. 251–52.

4. *Ibid.*, p. 249.

5. *The Federalist Papers*, Willmoore Kendall and George W. Carey, intro. (New Rochelle, N. Y.: Arlington House, n. d.), pp. 290–91.

6. See, for example, James J. Kilpatrick, *The Sovereign States* (Chicago: Henry Regnery, 1957), p. 4.

7. Elliot's *Debates*, Bk. I, vol. 2, p. 283.

8. *Ibid.*, vol. 3, p. 259.

9. *The Federalist Papers*, p. 292.

10. Elliot's *Debates*, Bk. I, vol. 3, pp. 40, 301.

11. *The Federalist Papers*, pp. 292–93.

12. Elliot's *Debates*, Bk. I, vol. 2, pp. 257–58.

Freedom and Democracy

by John Hospers

The very word "democracy" in our time has become a term of commendation. Every system of government wants to call itself a democracy, even if it is actually a dictatorship. "Democracy" has become such a term of approval that to call something democracy is implicitly to commend it. Even Communist nations whose governments are tyrannical to the core pride themselves on being "people's democracies." In non-Communist nations such as the United States this tendency is equally evident: we hear of wars to defend democracy, and the need to "preserve the tradition of liberal democracy."

Whether one is talking about the right to vote or the "need to share our resources," people will use the word "democracy" to praise whatever political system or ideal they favor. The harshest criticism of any procedure is that it is "anti-democratic." And yet it was not always so: even a hundred years ago in this country, to call a nation a democracy could be construed simply as a description, not an evaluation—sometimes even as a criticism. Almost nowhere is this any longer true.

Majority Rule

Democracy is rule by the majority. In a direct democracy, such as that of ancient Athens, or like the New England town meetings, every citizen can vote on every measure. In an indirect, or representative, democracy, each citizen can vote to elect representatives (Congress, Parliament) who then do the voting, and it is the majority of the representatives rather than the majority of the citizens themselves who determine the outcome.

Let us consider representative democracy, the only kind that is feasible in large nations. Several conditions have first to be spelled out before our description is complete.

First, in a democracy there are elections. But how often? Suppose there were an election only once in a hundred years. In such a "democ-

Dr. Hospers is professor emeritus in the Department of Philosophy at the University of Southern California, Los Angeles. This article was originally published in the June 1984 edition of *The Freeman*.

racy" voters could not vote to change governments more than once in a lifetime. Clearly, elections must be fairly frequent, enough to give voters a chance to vote for new candidates.

Second, the vote must be rather widely distributed. If only one percent of the population could vote, or only persons whose initials were R. Z., no election would represent the will of the majority of the people, no matter how often they were held. There are almost always certain restrictions on voting—e.g., minors cannot vote, convicted felons cannot vote while in prison, persons in mental institutions cannot vote, and non-citizens cannot vote—but in the twentieth century at least there are many times more residents who can vote than cannot. Only after World War I could women vote in the United States, and for many decades no blacks could vote, as they still [1984] cannot in South Africa.

Third, even if everyone could vote, and at frequent intervals, it would be to no purpose if there were no diversity of positions available to vote for (or against). In the Soviet Union people can vote, at least for some offices, but only for one Communist candidate or another—non-Communists are not permitted to be on the ballot. In other Eastern bloc nations, numerous political parties are permitted, but no one is permitted to be a candidate who is not officially approved by the government in power. Such a restriction on candidacy can have the same effect as permitting only Communists to be candidates. In both cases, a wide diversity of preferences is ignored. If a democracy is to function at all, it must be possible for persons of whatever opinion to sponsor candidates for office and there must be means for getting them on the ballot.

Nor is even this sufficient. No choice by voters is meaningful unless that choice has at least the opportunity to be an informed choice; and this is not possible if all the channels of *publicity* are reserved for the officially sponsored parties. Electors must be able to find out all they need to know about the alternative candidates. If the government owns all the television and radio stations, and owns or controls the content of newspapers and magazines, the voter will not be able to receive an accurate impression of the choices available.

Even if the press is not owned by the government, if newspapers are censored or prohibited from expressing opinions contrary to those of the party in power, voting citizens will not be able to make choices on the basis of reliable information. If newspapers and the media are monopolized by one group or party, it is not possible for the groups which are denied access to the media to receive a fair hearing. And thus a controlled press is incompatible with democracy, and a free press essential to it.

There may well be other conditions, but these at least are indispensable if any system of government is to be called a functioning democracy.[1]

Self-Government

Democracy is often spoken of as "self-government." But if we treat this term with any care at all, it is clear that democracy is no such thing. I can govern myself, determine to a large extent the course of my life, curb my desire for immediate satisfactions in order to achieve long-range goals, and so on. And you can do the same with yourself. If ten people do this, each is governing himself or herself. But when people speak of democracy as self-government, they are not speaking about each person governing himself; they are speaking of a process in which a majority of voters, or a majority of members of a legislature, make decisions which have the force of law for everyone, including those who are opposed to what is enacted. It is true that each adult individual in a democracy can *participate* in determining who shall sit in the seats of political power—but only in a very small way, seldom enough to change the outcome of an election.

In any case, self-government means governing oneself; it is a mistake to extend this from an individual to a collection of individuals and say that via democracy the collection is "governing itself." Democracy is simply government by the majority of a collective (or the majority of the representatives the voters have voted for). Their decisions may not accord with the needs or wishes of you as an individual at all. To the extent that they exert coercive power over your life, you are being governed *by others.*

An individual, of course, may govern himself badly: he may make constant mistakes, may ruin his own life, may waste his years on useless projects or alcohol; but at least he is doing it to himself. A democratic government may also govern others badly. When inhabitants of a nation freed from colonial rule say, "At least we're governing ourselves," what they are saying is that instead of people from outside the nation ruling them, there are now people from inside the nation ruling them—and sometimes doing so far worse than their colonial masters did.

Objections to Democracy

The most usual, and most easily understood, objection to democracy as a form of government is that it enables the majority to ride roughshod over the rights of a minority—to persecute them, to censor their activities, even to kill them. A majority might vote to kill certain minority racial elements, or to make life difficult for them in many ways. If feelings run high and a majority knows it can get by with it, there is every temptation to vote into law whatever prejudices a majority may have. Is it inconceivable that a majority of Germans, had they voted on it, would have voted to do something (not necessarily death) to Jews? Certainly a majority of Americans for generations used the political means to keep blacks "in their place." When there is no criterion but majority rule, anything can become law, depending on what the whims of the majority are; it is like a ship without a rudder.

But a second, and even more telling, criticism of democracy is that the majority of voters will often vote for policies which turn out to be ruinous to *themselves*, though they do not see this at the time. Legislatures, responding to the voters who elected them, may vote billions of dollars for various schemes of welfare. Even though only a small part of the money ultimately reaches the poor for whom it was intended, the legislators continue to vote for more of these measures. If they don't, they are branded as "cold" and "unhumanitarian" (as if it were somehow humanitarian for A to take B's money and give it to C) and they won't get re-elected. But the voters rebel at the resulting high taxes, so the government resorts to increasing quantities of printing-press money, and the result of course is inflation. The consumer's dollars will no longer buy what they did before, and almost everyone is worse off than before. But they didn't see the causal connection between the measures they voted for and their resultant poverty. They didn't realize that if 40 percent of their income went to finance the government, that was 40 percent they couldn't use themselves, and yet that 40 percent wasn't enough to finance the government projects which they themselves favored.

When they said "It's government money," they didn't realize that it was *their* money that was being taken from them to finance the projects they wanted. They didn't realize that money isn't like manna from heaven—that the government has no way of financing anything except by taking it from the people themselves. They didn't see that for every person who gets something for nothing there must be at least one other person who gets nothing for something. Even a superficial knowledge of elementary economics should have told them this much; but they didn't have even that elementary knowledge, so they voted themselves into disaster. Thus, beginning in relative independence of government, they voted themselves into utter dependence on government, a result they had completely failed to foresee.

One may say, "Well, then they deserve it. They brought it on themselves." Perhaps so—but who is the "they"? The "they" is the majority. The minority, who warned against these consequences, and were only ridiculed for their efforts, certainly did not deserve such a fate; they knew well enough what would happen. But in a democracy they must suffer consequences along with the ignorant majority that favored the disastrous policies.

When Benito Juarez, the first president of Mexico, said, "Since people do not vote themselves into slavery, freedom flows from democracy as water flows from the hills," his words were doubtless eloquent and inspiring. But unfortunately they were not true; people do vote themselves into slavery.

Plato on Democracy

What, after all, is so great about a majority view? Does a majority's taste in art determine which art is best? Does a majority vote on Newton vs. Einstein determine which of their theories was right? Are the masses of mankind so imbued with political wisdom that the majority can always be trusted to make the right choices? On the contrary: the majority of people appear to be influenced more by a candidate's image than by his argument, and to become bored and uncomprehending when even moderately difficult points are discussed (such as the need for capital investment to bring about prosperity). Ignorance and confusion multiplied 100 million times are still ignorance and confusion. That is why Louis Napoleon characterized democracy cynically as "government of the cattle, for the cattle, by the cattle." And that is why Plato more than two thousand years ago spoke of democracy in the following manner:

> Imagine this state of affairs on board a ship or a number of ships. The master is bigger and burlier than any of the crew, but a little deaf and short-sighted and no less deficient in seamanship. The sailors are quarrelling over the control of the helm; each thinks he ought to be steering the vessel, though he has never learnt navigation and cannot point to any teacher

under whom he has served his apprenticeship; what is more, they assert that navigation is a thing that cannot be taught at all, and are ready to tear in pieces anyone who says it can.

Meanwhile they besiege the master himself, begging him urgently to trust them with the helm; and sometimes, when others have been more successful in gaining his ear, they kill them or throw them overboard, and, after somehow stupefying the worthy master with strong drink or an opiate, take control of the ship, make free with its stores, and turn the voyage, as might be expected of such a crew, into a drunken carousal.

Besides all this, they cry up as a skilled navigator and master of seamanship anyone clever enough to lend a hand in persuading or forcing the master to set them in command. Every other kind of man they condemn as useless. They do not understand that the genuine navigator can only make himself fit to command a ship by studying the seasons of the year, sky, stars, and winds, and all that belongs to his craft; and they have no idea that along with the science of navigation, it is possible for them to gain, by instruction or practice, the skill to keep control of the helm whether some of them like it or not.

If a ship were managed in that way, would not those on board be likely to call the expert in navigation a mere stargazer, who spent his time in idle talk and was useless to them? ... But our present rulers may fairly be compared to the sailors in our parable, and the useless visionaries, as the politicians call them, to the real masters of navigation.... Democracy will promote to honor anyone who merely calls himself the people's friend.[2]

A Republic

The government of the United States is not a democracy, and the Founding Fathers never thought of it as such. It is, rather, a *republic*.

A republic may be democratic in many of its procedures, but there are certain things it cannot do. In the constitution of a republic are contained certain *limitations* on what the majority may do. Thus, the First Amendment declares that Congress shall pass no law abridging freedom of speech or of the press. Even if a law banning freedom of speech were passed by Congress, it would be unconstitutional and presumably would be struck down by the courts.

In the same way, the Constitution provides for "due process of law," protects citizens against search and seizure of property, entitles them to protect themselves against aggressors, and so on—and having these protections embedded in the Constitution gives all of us protection against measures that an ignorant or whimsical majority might enact. In short, the Constitution recognizes and protects *individual rights*—against their violation by other individuals, and by the government itself—whereas unlimited democracy may flout them with abandon, and with nothing between them and us to protect us against the ever-changing whims of the majority.

As James Madison wrote in *The Federalist Papers,* "A pure democracy can admit no cure for the mischiefs of faction. A common passion or interest will be felt by a majority, and there is nothing to check the inducements to sacrifice the weaker party. Hence it is, that democracies have ever been found incompatible with personal security or the rights of property; and have, in general, been as short in their lives as they have been violent in their deaths."

What Kind of Republic?

What whims we are protected against depends, of course, on what kind of republic it is. It depends on what kinds of protection are written into the constitution; it also depends on whether the constitution is actually followed in practice or is simply there for self-advertisement or window-dressing, like the constitution of the Soviet Union.

The best constitution is one which provides maximum freedom under a rule of law. Maximum freedom means freedom to live by one's own choices and not to live by the choices forced on one by others. But some choices that people make interfere with the freedom of others; some people choose to murder, to plunder, to steal the fruits of others' labor. Such errant behavior is the reason why law is required. The first maxim of the law is: Do not harm others—whether those inflicting the harm are other individuals or the government itself. Law is required so that people may live in freedom, not having that freedom forcibly interfered with by the choices of others.

All this was certainly the intent of the Founding Fathers of the American republic. Such freedoms include, certainly, the *political* freedoms, such as the freedom of speech and press, freedom of peaceable assembly, and freedom from harm to one's person or property; they also include *economic* freedom, such as the freedom to start a new enterprise, freedom to sustain it by one's efforts (not to have it confiscated), and freedom to employ others or be employed by others on terms voluntarily agreed to by both; in short, the freedom of the market.

The Founding Fathers saw no reason to assume that a majority of citizens should have the final and deciding word on what bills should be enacted into law; decisions of such depth and complexity could not be left to the ever-changing whims of a majority. "No one imagines that a majority of passengers should control a plane. No one assumes that, by majority vote, the patients, nurses, elevator boys and cooks and ambulance drivers and internes and telephone operators and students and scrubwomen in a hospital should control the hospital. Would you ever ride on a train if all the passengers stepped into booths and elected the train crews by majority vote, as intelligently as you elect the men whose names appear in lists before you in a voting booth? Then why is it taken for granted that every person is endowed on his 21st birthday with a God-given right and ability to elect the men who decide questions of political philosophy and international diplomacy?

"This fantastic belief is no part of the American Revolution. Thomas Paine, Madison, Monroe, Jefferson, Washington, Franklin, did not entertain it for a moment. When this belief first affected American government, it broke John Quincy Adams' heart; to him it meant the end of freedom on earth."[3]

And yet, things haven't quite turned out that way. As one observes the United States today, it often seems as if very little of the original republic remains, and that it has been gradually, sometimes imperceptibly, but nevertheless surely been transformed into the democracy that the Founding Fathers feared. How has this happened?

Election to Federal Offices

One important straw in the wind is the gradual transformation of the manner in which individuals are elected or appointed to high office in the federal government. Most people seem to assume that congressmen and presidents always came into office as the result of democratic elections. But the founders of our republic carefully framed it otherwise. Consider how it was when the republic was founded, and for many years thereafter, based on the original (unamended) Constitution:

1. The only exercise of majority rule in the federal government was the House of Representatives. The majority of voters were empowered to elect—and to recall in two years—the members of the House, the only body having the authority to spend the money col-

lected from the people in taxes. (Voting was also much more restricted during those years.)

2. The Senate was not elected by the citizens. Its members—two from each state—were appointed by the legislatures of their respective states, according to rules determined by the states and not the federal government. The popular election of senators did not come about until the 17th Amendment, in 1913.

3. The president was not elected by popular vote at all. Article 2 of the Constitution reads, in part: "Each state shall appoint, in such manner as the legislature thereof may direct, a number of electors, equal to the whole number of senators and representatives to which the state may be entitled in the Congress. . . . The electors shall meet in their respective states, and vote by ballot for two persons. . . . They shall make a list of all the persons voted for, and of the number of votes for each, which list they shall sign and certify, and transmit sealed to the seat of the government of the United States, directed to the president of the Senate. The president of the Senate shall, in the presence of the Senate and House of Representatives, open all the certificates, and the votes shall then be counted. The person having the greatest number of votes shall be the president, if such number be a majority of the whole number of electors appointed. . . ." It was done this way so that the president would not be subject to the whims of any section of the nation, but would represent the entire republic.

Today, of course, the president is elected by popular vote, and the Electoral College is an empty charade. This is yet another step toward emasculating the republic and instituting democracy. "And many a president in a time of crisis, since that right [freedom from popular election, hence from special interest groups] was taken away from his high office, must have silently cursed the amendment that plunges him to the neck in a mob of short-sighted, local-minded, clamoring men, clutching and pulling at him with a thousand hands. Today that Amendment does not let the captain of this ship of State make one clear decision unhampered by the ignorance and prejudices and fears of all the passengers on all the decks and all the men playing poker in the ship's bar. An ocean liner could not be navigated for a day under such conditions."[4]

The Courts and the Republic

But that is only the tip of the iceberg. What has occurred in this nation, and only partly because of changes in the method of electing presidents and Congressmen, is an enormous *expansion of governmental powers.* When this republic was founded, the main purpose of the federal government was defense against aggression: police to defend citizens against internal aggression, and armed forces to defend them against external aggression. But since government, to discharge these functions, requires a monopoly on the use of physical force—or at least a monopoly on the power to say who will be entitled to wield that force—it is tempting for a government, once installed, to use that coercive force in ways that were no part of the original plan. "Give them an inch and they'll take a mile" was never more applicable than to the powers usurped by governments: power to regulate industry and agriculture, power to control and inflate the currency, power to seize the earnings of those who work and give them to those who do not—and so on endlessly.

"But the United States is a republic; and the republic's powers are limited by its constitution. The Constitution does not mention any of these powers as being among those delegated to the federal government. The federal government is not constitutionally empowered to do any of these things."

This is quite true. But the Constitution is interpreted by the courts, and the courts—particularly during and since Roosevelt's "New Deal"—have conspicuously failed to prevent the expansion of Federal powers. The result has been to sanction Federal interference in virtually every branch of economic activity, in which, as a republic, it has no place.

Interstate Commerce

For example, the Constitution empowers the federal government to handle "interstate commerce." But the interstate commerce clause has been construed by the courts so as to permit all manner of activities never envisaged by the framers of the Constitution, such as "taxing North Dakota farmers to build flood control dams on a dry creek rising in the mountains of Los Angeles County, flowing through Los Angeles County, and discharging into the Pacific Ocean in Los Angeles County."[5] Interstate commerce has been construed to include the wages of men who wash the windows of buildings in which interstate trade is conducted. It has been construed to permit all manner of regulation of agriculture, such as regulating the kind and amounts of crops a farmer may grow. (The federal government has the authority to regulate that which it subsidizes, said the Court; but what gave it the authority to subsidize in the first place?) It has been construed so as to permit the government to set the price of natural gas at the well-head (the Phillips Petroleum Case of 1954), thus discouraging the search for new sources of natural gas and meanwhile encouraging consumers to be wasteful of gas because of the government-set low price. Indeed, it has enabled the government to create an energy shortage where in nature no energy shortage exists.[6] These and thousands of other intrusions into the free market have been brought about by these court decisions, giving to the federal government tremendous regulatory powers never granted in the Constitution of this republic.[7]

And yet, in numerous polls throughout the last decade, a majority of Americans appear to believe that what is needed are *more* controls, not fewer. The majority have no idea of the cost of these controls: the tremendously expensive and wasteful regulatory apparatus, the ball and chain it places on production, the countless men and women who *would* have helped to create a prosperous economy, who would (for example) have found natural gas and sold it at market price (and with greater abundance, the price would have come down). The majority see only that "we think the price is too high," and vote to control the producers. And thus they kill the goose that lays the golden egg. The minority who see clearly enough what is happening are outvoted at the polls. Such is the course of democracy.

The General Welfare

The federal government has also assumed enormous powers through a distortion of the phrase "the general welfare." In the first Congress, in 1789, a bill was introduced to pay a bounty to fishermen at Cape Cod, as well as a subsidy to certain farmers. James Madison said: "If Congress can employ money indefinitely to the general welfare, they may take the care of religion into their own hands; they may appoint teachers in every state, county, and parish, and pay them out of the public treasury: they may take into their own hands the education of children, establishing in like manner schools throughout the Union: they may seek the provision of the poor . . . [all of which] would subvert the very foundations, and transmute the very nature of the limited government established by the people of America."

And so Congress rejected the bill, and Thomas Jefferson said with relief, "This will settle forever the meaning of the phrase 'general welfare,' which, by a mere grammatical quibble, has countenanced the general government in a claim of universal power." It is an irony of history that the Hydra that Jefferson thought he had laid to rest has within our own century grown a hundred new heads, each of them aimed at our liberty.

The Constitution read: "Congress shall have the power to lay and collect taxes, duties, imposts and excises, to pay the debts and provide for the defense and general welfare of the United States." This meant that the national government could raise money *only* and spend money *only* to carry out its enumerated powers. They thought it ridiculous to construe two words "general welfare" as if they superseded the detailed enumeration of specific powers, rather than as merely summarizing them. The two words were always interpreted in the latter way by the Supreme Court during the first century and a half of American history. Their meaning, they held, could be changed only by amendment to the Constitution.

Yet today the amount of transfer payments—to promote "the general welfare"—takes up almost half the budget; more than that, if one includes all the entitlement programs. Moreover, the majority of Americans apparently consider all these things as their *right*. Those receiving money from the federal government now outnumber those who labor to sustain it. The resulting level of taxation, as well as national indebtedness, is causing the republic to hemorrhage to death in the name of the democracy.

Market Alternatives

Without the vast bureaucracy created through the regulatory agencies, free-market alternatives could be devised. For example, "Building codes and fire codes could presumably be replaced quite easily by privately enforced codes drafted by insurance companies. Few developers would construct hazardous firetraps if they knew beforehand that they could not acquire insurance for their buildings. And as Bernard Siegan brilliantly demonstrated in his 'Non-zoning in Houston,'[8] egregious, incompatible property uses will not often cohabit if land use regulations were summarily abolished. Restrictive covenants that run with the land, renewable at intervals of several decades, could very expeditiously insure that a slaughterhouse will not locate in the middle of Shaker Heights, Beverly Hills, or Boca Raton. If one were so unfortunate as to find one's house suddenly within proximity of a noisome chemical plant a remedy would lie in nuisance law, for no one has a right to use his property in such a way as to adversely affect another's enjoyment of his property."[9]

Democracy vs. the Market

The only thing that can increase a nation's standard of living is greater *production.* And anything that inhibits that production makes the nation poorer. If a farmer or manufacturer has part of his output taken away from him for distribution to others, he will be less motivated to produce in the future. If he is regulated by men from the Department of Agriculture who trample over his fields to determine how much corn he has planted, if the factory owner is regularly fined for trivial offenses that shouldn't be offenses at all (but are only contrary to rules set up by the government regulatory agency), he will sooner or later be forced into bankruptcy or to continue production under great difficulties (and higher prices). And if the government pays the farmer money to grow or not to grow crops, this increases the burden of every taxpayer in the land without any increase of production.

In a democracy, all such processes are easily sanctioned by popular outcries: "He's a profiteer—take it away from him." "He's getting too much—give it to us." People who haven't succeeded, or weren't willing to make the sacrifices he made, will do all they can to take it away from him after he has succeeded. A democracy easily becomes dominated by the morality of *envy.* A fickle mob, unaware of the facts of basic economics, but easily swayed by demagogues demanding as their right the fruits of the labor of others, can easily bring about the passage of laws which will inhibit production, destroy the free market, and in the end lead to such shortages and bottlenecks in production that they result, just as Plato said, in riots, calls for "law and order," and dictatorship.

Only a republic, in which the powers of the government are constitutionally limited, can avoid this fate. That is why the Founding Fathers were careful to create this nation as a republic, so that each person could determine his own destiny and not have it determined by others, whether by the tyranny of one (dictatorship) or of a few (oligarchy), or of many (democracy). "It is the blessing of a free people, not that they live under democratic government, but that they do not."[10]

If the return to a republic is not achieved, Alexis de Tocqueville's prediction of a century and a half ago may yet come true: that the American government will become for its citizens "an immense and tutelary power, which takes upon itself alone to secure their gratifications, and to watch over their fate.... For their happiness such a government willingly labors, but it chooses to be the sole agent and the only arbiter of that happiness: it provides for their security, foresees and supplies their necessities, facilitates their pleasures, manages their principal concerns, directs their industry, regulates the descent of property, and subdivides their inheritances—what remains, but to spare them all the care of thinking and all the trouble of living? . . . The will of man is not shattered, but softened, bent, and guided; men are seldom forced by it to act, but they are constantly restrained from acting; such a power does not destroy, but it prevents existence; it does not tyrannize, but it compresses, enervates, extinguishes, and stupefies a people, till each nation is reduced to nothing better than a flock of timid and industrious animals, of which the government is the shepherd."[11]

Indeed, it is not difficult to make a case for the view that what Tocqueville predicted has already come to pass.

---

1. See S. I. Benn and Richard Peters, *Social Principles and the Democratic State* (London: Allen & Unwin, 1959), Chapter 15. Also published as Collier-Macmillan paperback entitled *Principles of Political Thought*.

2. Plato, *The Republic*, translation by Francis M. Cornford (London: Oxford University Press, 1941), pp. 195–6.

3. Rose Wilder Lane, *The Discovery of Freedom* (New York: Arno Press, 1943), pp. 207–8.

4. Rose Wilder Lane, *op. cit.*, p. 203.

5. Newton Garber, *Of Men and Not of Law* (Greenwich, Conn.: Devin-Adair, 1962), pp. 13 ff. See also Philip Kurland, ed., *The Supreme Court and the Constitution* (Chicago: University of Chicago Press, 1960), and the recent book by Henry M. Holzer, *Sweet Land of Liberty?* (Costa Mesa, Calif.: Common Sense Press, 1983), for many other examples.

6. On the so-called energy crisis, see for example C. V. Myers, *Money and Energy* (Darien Conn.: Soundview Books, 1980), and Lindsey Williams, *The Energy Non-Crisis* (Wheatridge, Colo.: Worth Publishing Co., 1980).

7. Dan Smoot, *The Business End of Government* (Belmont, Mass.: Western Islands, 1973), p. 83. See also Alan Stang, *The Oshacrats* (from the same publisher).

8. Bernard Siegan, "Non-Zoning in Houston," *Journal of Law and Economics*, Vol. 13 (1970); and *Land Use without Zoning* (Lexington Books, 1972), Chapter 2.

9. Ellen Frankel Paul, "On Three 'Inherent Powers of Government,'" *The Monist*, Vol. 66, No. 4 (Oct. 1983), pp. 539–40.

10. Richard Taylor, "The Basis of Political Authority," *The Monist*, Vol. 66, No. 4 (Oct. 1983), p. 471. See also Richard Taylor, *Freedom, Anarchy, and the Law* (Prentice-Hall, 1973).

11. Alexis de Toqueville, *Democracy in America*, pp. 579–80 of the edition edited by Henry Steele Commager, 1946.

Reasserting the Spirit of '76

by W. H. Hillendahl

A fresh spirit of change is in the air. It has swept into the Office of President a man who, as the Governor of California, has shown his dedication to the principles of limited government. It has carried into ascendancy in the halls of Congress men who by their records have demonstrated their commitment to support constitutional principles which were designed to protect individual liberty.

Let us seek the roots of that spirit. Perhaps we may find the key to curing what the late Dean Clarence Manion termed "Cancer in the Constitution."[1]

An examination of the Declaration of Independence will produce several important clues: "(Men) are endowed by their Creator with certain unalienable rights ... among these are life, liberty and the pursuit of happiness. ... [T]o secure these rights governments are instituted ... deriving their just powers from the consent of the governed." Government is to be founded on principles and its powers organized in such form "most likely to effect safety and happiness."

Men capable of expressing thoughts such as these had of necessity developed an inbred sense of self-reliance. They were God-fearing, Bible-reading people who were accustomed to taking responsibility for their own actions. Whence would they likely receive guidance for these ideas of liberty? We know they invariably looked to the Bible as the source of inspiration and direction. So let us follow their steps.

James, the President of the church at Jerusalem, was eloquent in translating the spirit of the Old Testament law into Christianity. In Chapter 1:25 he wrote: "But whoever looks into the perfect law of liberty and abides in it is not merely a hearer of the word which can be forgotten, but a doer of the work, and this man shall be blessed in his labor."[2] In Chapter 2:11, James admonished those who have broken the commandments: "You have become a transgressor of the law ... so speak and act as men who are to be judged by the law of liberty."[3] This clearly denotes that individuals are to be held respon-

Mr. Hillendahl, a retired bank officer, was a long-time member of FEE's Board of Trustees. This article was originally published in the March 1981 edition of *The Freeman*.

sible for their choices and actions. Irresponsible actions are to be judged accordingly.

Paul wrote from Corinth encouraging the Galatians to maintain Christian liberty. Chapter 5:1, "Stand firm therefore in the liberty with which Christ has made us free, and be not harnessed again under the yoke of servitude." In Romans 8:21 we find that servitude is the bondage of corruption. Then in Galatians, Chapter 5:13 and 14, "For my brethren you have been called to liberty, only do not use your liberty for an occasion to the things of the flesh, but by love serve one another. For the whole law is fulfilled in one saying that is: You shall love your neighbor as yourself." Underlying liberty is freedom of choice. We are admonished to make only responsible choices. Our actions should focus on service rather than on the accumulation of wealth as an end in itself. To live within the laws of the Commandments also includes the prohibition of making laws which institutionalize greed, envy, lust, or coveting of property. So herein is the spirit of the law.

The Purpose of Law

As to the purpose of law, we may turn to the great English judge, Sir William Blackstone, who said "The principal aim of society is to protect individuals in the enjoyment of those absolute rights which were vested in them by the immutable laws of nature.... The first and primary end of human laws is to maintain and regulate those 'absolute' rights of individuals."[4] Frederic Bastiat, a Frenchman, wrote in *The Law:* "We hold from God the gift which includes all others. This gift is life—physical, intellectual and moral life.... Life, faculties, production—in other words, individuality, liberty, property—this is man. And in spite of the cunning of artful political leaders, those three gifts from God precede all human legislation, and are superior to it.

"Life, liberty and property do not exist because men have made laws. On the contrary, it was the fact that life, liberty, and property existed beforehand that caused men to make laws in the first place.... The law is the organization of the natural right of lawful defense. It is the substitution of a common force for individual forces. And this common force is to do only what the individual forces have a natural and lawful right to do; to protect persons, liberties, and properties; and to maintain the right of each, and to cause justice to reign over us all."[5]

Constitutional Law—Power to the People

In the United States Constitution we find a codification of the Biblical laws. It provided for the protection of life, liberty, property, and the pursuit of happiness. It provided for the freedom of choice of individuals with implied self-responsibility for their actions, and the protection of individuals against those who would abridge or infringe those rights. A society wherein individuals are free to choose requires a government supported willingly by the consent of the governed. Individuals who choose to be free must be willing to support laws which protect the rights of all others who choose to be free. This constitutes a free and open society wherein each can choose to serve God and mankind in the ways of his own choice, free from the will of others.

At the same time, the men who drafted the Constitution accepted the fact that individuals are corruptible. They are subject to temptation; they can be envious, and greedy; they may steal, or covet property. As someone has said, each man has his price, and it is indeed a rare individual who is totally incorruptible, given the opportunity to gain power. So the principal concern of the Framers was how to develop a legal framework that would prevent corruptible individuals or groups from acquiring power to infringe on the rights of other individuals. The key word is power. The division of power, fragmentation of power, and the checks and balances of power extend through the entire fabric of the Constitution. A horizontal division of power was provided in the form of legislative, executive, and judicial separation. A vertical division of power appears in the form of the federal, state, and local governments. The goal was to limit opportunities to concentrate powers taken from the people.

Limiting the Government

The Bill of Rights includes a set of specific "thou shalt nots" which were designed to constrain the federal government from infringing on specific individual rights. In substance, the Constitution is a document which was designed to hold in chains the powers and authority of the federal government along with those who would use government to further their own ends.

For such a system to survive requires a continual effort toward maintaining the distribution and balance of power at all times. During a speech in Ireland on July 10, 1790, John Curran warned, "The condition upon which God hath given liberty to man is eternal vigilance."

The guarantees of "freedom to"—to choose, to try and to fail—can only be made under a government which is restricted from interfering with individual choices. In contrast, the constitution of the Soviet Union and the United Nations charter are vehicles of unlimited power.

Their goals of "freedom from"—from war, disease, want, unemployment, and the like—can only be enforced by an unlimited central authority and bureaucracy.

Being aware that neither the Constitution nor statutory law can ever change the nature of man, nor force him to be what he cannot or will not be, we may ask how successful were the framers of the Constitution. We live in an imperfect world. It is an imperfect Constitution and we are imperfect individuals. Yet for nearly two centuries with freedom of opportunity the people of the United States increased their standard of living more rapidly than did those of any other nation in the world. Given the choice, the acid test is whether one would rather live in the United States or somewhere else in the world. The vast influx of legal and illegal aliens speaks for itself.

The Problems of Government—Man Was Made Vain

Yet we are troubled today; inflation, unemployment, economic instability, housing shortages, high taxes, high interest rates, are but a few of our problems. How do the conditions underlying the problems of today compare with the concerns and grievances of the Founding Fathers? Let's look again at the Declaration of Independence. The signers were concerned about "relinquishing the rights of representation in the legislature." Today we are concerned about centralized government and administrative law.

In 1776 they were concerned about being "exposed to dangers of invasion from without and convulsions from within." Increasing numbers today are concerned about our defense posture today and the problems of internal unrest.

They complained that "judges were dependent on the will (of the King) for tenure of their offices." Today's judges are political appointees who, to a significant extent, legislate according to their ideologies rather than seek precedent for decisions.

The Founders were concerned about "a multitude of new offices," and we are concerned about burgeoning bureaucracy.

They were concerned about "imposing taxes without our consent." Who isn't concerned today about high taxes, with our consent or otherwise?

They were concerned about "deprived . . . benefits of trial by jury." Today administrative law has gone a long way to the same end, and has altered fundamentally the forms of government.

They complained about exciting "domestic insurrections among us." Today who is not concerned about crime and personal safety?

The very survival of our system is threatened by the encroachment of a totalitarian ideology.

Are we not faced again today with the problems of 200 years ago? We are in fact encountering an ageless collision with a destructive ideology. Paul wrote in his letter to the Romans 8:20, 21, "For man was made subject to vanity...." (Definitions of vanity include "inflated pride of one's self" or "emptiness, worthlessness." We may ponder the significance of this polarity of meaning.) "For man was made subject to vanity, not willingly, but by reason of him who gave him free will in the hope that he would choose rightly. Because man himself shall be delivered from the bondage of corruption into the glorious liberty of the Children of God."

Or perhaps more clearly, man (of) himself shall be delivered.... Man only by his own choice of responsible thoughts and actions can achieve the soul growth that is required to achieve grace, and entrance into the Kingdom of God.

But in fact, has he chosen "rightly"? In spite of the commandment "Thou shalt not covet thy neighbor's property," we have permitted laws to be passed which, taken all together, confiscate almost half of our neighbor's property via taxes in the vain concept of doing good. These vain thoughts manifest in a number of syndromes:

- The "welfare" syndrome which enforces the privilege of the few at the expense of the rights of the individuals who constitute the body politic.
- The "free lunch" syndrome which looks on dollars sent from Washington as free. If we don't get them, someone else will.
- The "meddling in the affairs of others" syndrome in which individuals feel compelled to attempt to solve the problems of others rather than minding their own business and concentrating on solving their own problems.
- Similarly, the "let George do it" syndrome considers today's problems to be too complex to be solved equitably at the state or local level—they must be sent to Washington.
- The "exploitation" syndrome in which the producers in society are held to have victimized those less stationed. Therefore the producers must be chained with regulations and their ill-gotten profits must be taxed away.
- The "victims of society" syndrome maintains that criminals are the innocent victims of society—they cannot be held responsible for their crimes or misdeeds; therefore they

must be pampered and "rehabilitated" rather than punished, while many live in fear that they may be the next victims.

• Finally, the "homogenized milk" syndrome which is destroying all natural affinity groups and is forcing all people to live and work together on the basis of a "social adjustment" formula of equality based on race, color, creed, or whether one fancies dogs, cats, horses or, white rats.

These syndromes are all manifestations of an ideology that is anathema to liberty. They reflect the attitude of those who lack faith in the ability of each individual to solve his or her own problems; hence, a forced redistribution of society is necessary to overcome maladjustments.

The thermometer of a redistributive society is what? Inflation. Inflation is a measure of the maldistribution of wealth via government—no more, no less. The underlying motivating forces and the mechanics of inflation are complex and widely misunderstood. Yet no one in good conscience can deny the necessity to help those who are in a condition of misfortune. However, today much redistributed wealth is going to those who have established vested positions of privilege. The consequence is that regardless of how legitimate a given cause may be, the total burden of aggregate causes on the nation has exceeded the carrying capacity of its productive resources to the point where inflation is an unavoidable condition. The problem goes far deeper than any transient federal administration, its roots extend back through decades. Inflation is the manifestation of vain thoughts and ideas applied cumulatively since the Civil War. It represents the misapplication of free will and an accumulation of a vast number of wrong choices.

The Redistribution of Power

What have been the mechanics of change wherein these false doctrines have gained ascendancy?

Dr. Cornelius Cotter, Professor of Political Science at the University of Wisconsin, appeared before a special Senate committee in April, 1973.[6] He remarked: "You know, Senator Mathias, it has been said—and, I think wisely so—that if the United States ever developed into a totalitarian state we would not know it. We would not know that it had happened. It would be all so gradual, the ritualism would all be retained as a facade to disguise what had happened. Most people in the United States, in official position, would continue to do the sorts of things that they are doing now. The changes would have all been so subtle although so fundamental that people generally would be unaware."

Senator Church responded, "That is the way it happened in Rome, is it not?"

Dr. Cotter: "Indeed."

Senator Mathias: "No Roman was more deferential than Augustus."

Dr. Cotter: "Exactly."

Senator Church: "And kept the Senate happy, although the Senate had lost its power."

So this age-old collision of ideas is producing very subtle changes in the power structure of the United States. The mechanism of change involves power, its balance and the concentration. Four simultaneous flows have been underway for a century: (1) Power from the Congress to the Executive Branch, (2) power from the Congress to the Supreme Court, (3) power from the states to the federal government, and (4) power from individuals to the government.

Judicial Abuses

Let's examine some of these flows of power. First, the Supreme Court. The Bill of Rights expressly forbids the federal government to interfere with the fundamental personal liberties of individuals in this society. That's clear enough. As an outfall of the Civil War, the Fourteenth Amendment was adopted in 1868. This amendment forbids the states to interfere with the rights of the people. However, it had a devious intent, namely to give Congress control over the people of the South. But in 1873 the Supreme Court thwarted that intent in the "Slaughterhouse Cases." For half a century an ideal situation prevailed in which both the federal government and the states were constrained by the Constitution and its amendments from interfering with the liberties of the people.

However, in more recent years a subtle but profound change has been effected by the Supreme Court. Dean Clarence Manion wrote, "For the 32 years of service together on the Supreme Court, Justices Black and Douglas have been repetitiously citing each other as authority for a gross and gratuitous misconstruction of the First and 14th Amendments."[7]

"The accumulation of these malignant constitutional misconstructions of the first eight amendments with the 14th has placed a cancer near the heart of our constitutional system which is proliferated with each successive term of the United States Supreme Court."[8] Essentially, today the Court has legislated its jurisdiction over the rights of people by effectively merging the Bill of Rights into the Fourteenth Amendment and reversing its position in 1873.

The specific consequences of the Black and Douglas decision were highlighted in an editorial which appeared in the *San Diego Union:* "The United States Supreme Court has returned three more decisions drastically altering the pattern of American life.

"For more than 15 years now the Court has been steadily rewriting the laws and reinterpreting the Constitution to suit the ideological bias or judicial whims of its members. . . .

"In recent days the Supreme Court has ridden over states' rights abolishing residency requirement for relief, sidestepped a ruling in a case of burning the American Flag, and placed further restrictions on law enforcement by freeing a convicted rapist because the police took his fingerprints in some legal hocus-pocus. . . .

" . . . Court majorities in those 15 years have returned more than 30 decisions . . . have brought about basic and often demoralizing changes in the fields of politics, criminal procedure, religion, race relations, subversion and communism, antitrust laws and obscenity.

"The Court has told the states how they are to portion their legislatures, granted avowed Communists the run of defense plants; made a criminal's confession almost impossible to use; approved even secondary school demonstrations against the South Vietnam war; banned prayers or reading of the Bible in public classrooms; ruled that passports cannot be withheld from Communists just because they are Communists; and held that deserters from the armed forces, even in wartime, cannot be stripped of citizenship. . . .

"In the notorious Keylishian case, a majority opinion held that a college professor may not be dismissed for teaching and advocating, in college, or anywhere, the overthrow of our government by force and violence. . . .[9] The Court, once the ultimate in both prudence and jurisprudence, is now the darling of the liberal radicals; it has done for them what the Congress has refused to do."[10]

This is a most concise summary of the consequences of the Court's abrogation of states' rights and the jurisdiction of Congress.

Courts Take Charge as Congress Forfeits Control

At this point, the more perceptive will grasp the real issue which underlies the polarization of the nation concerning the Equal Rights Amendment. Under the facade of women's rights, the real objective is to deliver the jurisdiction for defining the rights of all individuals into the hand of a congress which has already defaulted its jurisdiction to the legislative whims of the Supreme Court. At the heart of the opposition to ERA are those who recognize its passage would give validity to the Supreme Court's abridgement of the Bill of Rights, and encourage further intrusions into the private affairs of individuals.

As a curtain over these actions, a myth has been erected which holds that Supreme Court decisions are the "Law of the Land." It presumes that once the Court takes a position on a case, every similar case would be adjudged that way. In actuality, each ruling is the "law of the case." It is possible for a court, made up of the same or different justices, to arrive at a different interpretation if it were to rule on a similar case.

Under a second myth, the prevailing belief is that Congress has no control over the Supreme Court, hence, Congress has no way to redress the sorties of the Court into the legislative arena. Such an alleged lack of control is far from fact. Congress enacted the first Federal Judiciary Act in 1789 and this act has been employed to apply its unquestioned constitutional power over the jurisdiction of all Federal courts.

The Congress by a wide margin recently voted to deny the Supreme Court the right to spend appropriated funds to conduct hearings into school busing cases, in effect, denying the court jurisdiction.

Dean Clarence Manion of Notre Dame held that a major step will be taken toward rectifying the consequences of the Court's unconstitutional decisions when the Congress restricts, abolishes or controls selected types of appellate jurisdiction of both the Supreme Court and all other Federal Courts.[11] A federal court system comprised mainly of judges and justices who are committed to upholding the original tenets underlying the Constitution, can do a great deal to curb the judicial misuses and excesses which have prevailed in recent years.

Legislative Abuses

For many decades the Supreme Court routinely struck down as unconstitutional various acts passed by Congress which infringed on the Bill of Rights. However, over the last two decades the Congress, taking its cue from the Black-Douglas Supreme Court decisions, has enacted a number of bills which have intruded ever-increasingly into those rights which were originally held to be out of bounds. These intrusions are being felt by the public in their opportunities for employment, work environment, on the highway, in the air, while shopping and banking, in schools, among family relations and in the home. While obviously accomplishing some benefits, the bulk of this legislation has been undertaken in response to the highly vocal, sometimes rowdy, pressure of special-interest groups. In the main, these intrusions have caused vast numbers of people to become outraged, resentful, and rebellious.

In its attempts to legislate social justice and equality, the Congress has cut to the core of the mores of the incredibly complex but generally balanced and tolerant American society.

The wisdom of those who insisted on including the Bill of Rights in the Constitution is gradually seeping into the subconscience of all but the most hardheaded advocates of reform by coercion. It would be a wise Congress indeed that undertook to reverse or modify these unconstitutional intrusions which prior congresses have made over the years.

Executive Abuses

The scope of the powers of the executive branch has been expanded enormously, particularly in recent years. Authority of the office of the President has increased while departments, commissions, boards and agencies have proliferated.

Professor Cotter and Professor J.M. Smith determined that the powers entrusted by Congress to the Executive Branch can be grouped in four categories: (1) Powers over persons, (2) powers to acquire property, (3) powers to regulate property, and (4) control of communications.[12]

Executive Orders: The President normally employs Executive Orders to implement the efficient conduct of the daily routines of the office.[13] However, several presidents have employed Executive Orders to conduct international relations and to effect legislation.

For example, President Roosevelt used an Executive Order in 1933 to establish diplomatic relationships with the Communist regime in Russia at a time when it was unlikely that such action by Congress would have been supported by a consensus of the people.

Under the pressure of time, the President has employed emergency orders properly in the declaration of national emergencies.

However, one would believe that matters as basic as the legal frame-work for the conduct of government under such national emergencies would be given extensive examination by the Congress in the process of passing suitable laws. Such is not the case.

President John F. Kennedy issued a series of Executive Orders in 1962 which established a comprehensive legal framework to deal with any national emergency as defined by the President or the Congress.[14] On its face, this would appear to have constituted an unwarranted intrusion into the legislative process.

On October 11, 1966, President Lyndon Johnson issued Executive Order 11310 which continued the process by transferring the authority granted under the emergency orders from the Office of Emergency Planning to the Department of Justice.

President Richard Nixon also gave attention to updating the emergency orders while in office.

Early in the 1970s Congress became sufficiently concerned about the existence of national emergencies that the Senate established a Special Committee on the Termination of the National Emergency.[15] This led in 1976 to the passage of the National Emergencies Act.[16] This act terminated all existing declared emergencies and established procedures and limits for the declaration of future national emergencies.

The matter took on new impetus when, on July 20, 1979, President Jimmy Carter issued two new Executive Orders:

(1) E.O. 12148 Federal Emergency Management, which authorized a thorough overhaul of both civil and war emergency procedures and placed them under a newly created Federal Emergency Management Council.

(2) E.O. 12149 Federal Regional Councils, which established councils for ten standard federal regions, their principal function being to implement federal programs.

Taken separately or together these Executive Orders provide wide-ranging ramifications when analyzed from the point of view of the powers delegated to these Councils. While these structures may be thought of as logical provisions for the implementation of federal policy, increasing numbers of states are taking the position that Regional Councils constitute a major intrusion into their autonomy.[17]

Such widespread reaction would lead one to conclude that a deep rift has developed in the power structure as a consequence of the thrust underlying these Executive Orders. As a consequence of these and other Executive Orders, a broad review by Congress of their use and abuses should lead to establishing guidelines which define appropriate uses of Executive Orders by the Executive Branch.

Administrative Law: The myriad of statutes, regulations, and codes by which the various departments and bureaus of government administer their operations under the Executive Branch constitute administrative law. In large part they are established to implement details of the broad language of the acts of Congress. These regulations are essential to the smooth and orderly functioning of government.

Nevertheless, the structure of departments which combines executive, legislative, and enforcement or judicial functions, provides a concentration of power and authority which lends itself to potential bureaucratic abuses. Among many possible examples, congressional hearings have revealed that the detailed statutes developed in administering the Occupational Safety and Health Act (OSHA) went far beyond the intent of the act, and provided the basis for executive abuses and deliberate harassment, in particular of small business. Many are aware of instances in which the Antitrust Division of the Justice Department, using the charge of conspiracy and restraint of trade, has imposed fines and/or jail sentences though the accused firms and their officers were innocent. These firms chose to make payment under a plea of *nolo contendre* because the legal fees required to establish their innocence would exceed the fine.

Administered properly, government agencies should facilitate trade and commerce, and protect the various interests of the people. At best, administrative law can only regulate, prohibit, or constrain individuals or groups from imposing on the rights of others. However, in increasing numbers of cases the bureaucracy has gone far beyond its legitimate functions. One may find dozens of magazine and newspaper articles reciting wasteful or counterproductive bureaucratic activities, and arrogant abuses of power.

Today the friction and costs to society of the bureaucracy have reached destructive proportions. These excesses must be brought again under control. The implementation of reforms is too broad a subject to address here. A comprehensive report by the Heritage Foundation[18] has recommended a broad platform of reforms to President-Elect Reagan "to roll back big government." Included are specific recommendations concerning Executive Orders and administrative law. Implementation of these recommendations should go a long way in restoring a proper balance of power.

Revitalizing the American Dream

The foregoing are but a few examples of the restructuring of power which has been achieved during the last century. They have been selected to illustrate the vast departure from the spirit in which the Constitution was written some 200 years ago. As a consequence, people in all walks of life—both the providers and the recipients of government aid—are hurting as they have never hurt before. The thermometer—inflation—shows that the waters of our economic and political environment are approaching the boiling point. Not one amongst us is immune to the heat.

In the face of these adversities, a new spirit is emerging in the land. The new religious revival extending from neighborhoods to nation-wide television is a new expression of the old Spirit of '76. People are going back to basics. They are thinking, questioning, and organizing.[19]

The overwhelming choice by the electorate of a new administration dedicated to redressing these abuses of power is a manifestation of the revival of the spirit.

The retirement of many congressmen who have aided and abetted this misdirection of power, together with the election of other congressmen who affirm the original precepts of the Constitution are further manifestations of the spirit.

Yet this is only a beginning. We must not expect miracles from any administration, nor can any of us escape the painful process of readjustment. We are presently in a position to achieve a victory in this battle. But the foes in the ageless war for the minds of men are not to be easily vanquished. It will require years of unrelenting effort to overcome the damages which have been incurred by the Republic.

We know in our hearts that cold, impersonal welfare will never succeed loving charity. Government can never provide security to replace self-reliance. No government can accomplish those things we must do for ourselves if our souls and spirits are to expand. If we are to restore the American dream we must never again become complacent and allow ourselves to be overridden by those who are in a vain quest for false goals.

Let us again restore the balance between spiritual and material values. The institutions of church and state are inseparable, they are as inseparable as two ends of a rope, each is a manifestation of the spirit and substance of society.[20] We may recall that the spirit of liberty was heralded from every pulpit during our Revolutionary War. I maintain that Spirit of '76 has never really disappeared, we have simply allowed it to become encrusted with false doctrine.

Paul offered words of encouragement: "Stand firm therefore in liberty with which Christ has made us free. Be not harnessed again under the yoke of servitude ... the bondage of corruption." James urged us: "So speak and so act as men and women who are to be

judged by the law of liberty." Let freedom-loving individuals prevail
by reasserting the Spirit of '76.

1. Clarence E. Manion, *Cancer in the Constitution* (Shepherdsville, Ky.: Victor Publishing Company, 1972).

2. *Holy Bible*, trans., George M. Lamsa (Philadelphia: A. J. Holman, 1957). This version is translated into English form the Aramaic, the language of Jesus and is recognized for accuracy and clarity of expression.

3. The Law of Liberty within the context of Bible usage expresses freedom of choice with consequence. All thoughts and actions cause reactions for which we are to be held accountable. The Law of Liberty is the Christian counterpart of the Sanscrit term, Karma.

4. James Mussatti, *The Constitution of the United States, Our Charter of Liberties* (Princeton: D. Van Nostrand Co., Inc., 1960), p. 9.

5. Frederic Bastiat, *The Law*, trans. Dean Russell (Irvington-on-Hudson N.Y.: The Foundation for Economic Education, Inc., 1950), pp. 5, 6, 7. (*The Law* was first published as a pamphlet in June 1850.)

6. U. S. Congress, Senate Special Committee on the Termination of the National Emergency, *National Emergency, Part 1 Constitutional Questions Concerning Emergency Powers*, Hearings before the Special Committee of the Senate, 93rd Cong., 1st sess., April 11, 12, 1973, p. 29.

7. Manion, p. 33.

8. *Ibid.*, p. 35.

9. As a consequence of this Supreme Court decision, by 1975 an estimated 2,000 campus "radical economists" who "respect the point of view of Mao" and who believe in "a socialism of affluence" were members of the Union of Radical Political Economists. (*Los Angeles Times*, December 21, 1975).

10. *San Diego Union*, April 28, 1969.

11. Manion, p. 27.

12. C. P. Cotter and J. M. Smith, *Powers of the President During Crises* (Washington, D. C.: Public Affairs Press, 1960).

13. Executive Orders are issued by the President, reviewed by the Office of Legal Counsel, and published in the Federal Register. They become law unless rescinded by Congress within a specified period of time.

14. Executive Orders including numbers 10995, 10997, 10998, 10999, 11000, 11001, 11002, 11003, 11004, 11005, and 11051 define procedures during war, attacks, or other emergencies for executive control of communications, energy, food and farming, all modes of transportation, civilian work brigades, health, education and welfare functions, housing, public storage, and so on.

15. U.S. Congress, Senate, *National Emergency*.

16. *National Emergencies Act*, U.S. Code, vol. 50, sec. 1601–51 (1976).

17. Extensive hearings on regional governance have been conducted by legislative committees in a score of states. The proceedings of these hearings appear in bulletins published by the Committee to Restore the Constitution, Inc., Fort Collins, Colorado.

18. Charles Heatherly, ed. *Mandate for Leadership* (Washington, D.C.: Heritage Foundation, 1980).

19. For an example of grass roots organization see "The Pro-Family Movement: A Special Report" in *Conservative Digest* 6 (May/June 1980).

20. Into the artfully contrived rift between church and state has been driven the wedge of Humanism. According to the book *The Assault on the Family*, "As a religion,

Humanism demands the end of all religions that are God oriented, and the abolition of the profit-motivated society, so that a world utopian state may be established which will dictate the distribution of the means of life for everyone." See "Our Last Opportunity" in *Don Bell Reports*, November 13, 1980.

VI. EPILOGUE

On the Destiny of Liberty

by Jackson Pemberton

The Creator endowed man with the power to perceive and to understand his world, the ability and the will to act upon it, and the liberty to choose his actions. His discernment and freedom stretches from the center of his secret heart to the outermost stars of his celestial world, and his decisions determine his destiny.

Man is a mighty being, capable of unthinkable feats, and that wondrous capacity coupled as it is with freedom of his will, favors him with the most awesome potentialities. A man may, by learning and energy, make himself a god or a devil, to build or to destroy, to experience exquisite joys or perverted pleasures. The choice is left to each to decide from which cup he shall drink. To make the wise choice is to make him more powerful and more free, for that places him in harmony with the laws of all Nature and releases his capacity to create, which together provide an enduring happiness; but to make the choice elicited by the sirens of pleasure and pride is to bind him down with the chains of enslaving habit, an afflicted mind, and a weakened body. Thus he reaps the just reward of the use of his liberty.

Every man bears in his breast a spark struck from the soul of Almighty God, and in that spark glows the light of love and liberty. Every man yearns to be good and to be great, to be a blessing to all within the circle of his society; yet there are those who, intoxicated with the lust for power and wealth, turn from that divine inheritance for the corrupt pleasure of control over their fellows, and gain by their loss. Thus has the vanity of kings and despots devoured the lives of their poor subjects, and thus began the King of England to feed upon our toils and treasures. We repulsed his intrusions and gave you the Constitution to protect you from such, for we knew the history of man to he overflowing with the tyranny of bad governments.

In our day the tyrant came to us in open defiance of our rights, with hostility and violence, with sword and cannon. Through tears, prayer, and blood we threw him off and drove him out.

Now he is among you again, but not in open war upon your houses and lands, but in subtle disguise, bearing gifts of free money,

---

This article originally appeared in the December 1976 issue of *The Freeman*.

free food, free houses, and free security; trading them to you in the name of equality, rights, and liberty: offering the goods he took from you by heavy taxes and a deliberate inflation. With flattering words he coddles your vanity, legalizes your selfishness, and leads you through a political mirage into his fool's paradise where he has appointed himself the Grand Regulator. Yet, your greatest danger lies in none of those things, but in your failure to recognize the pattern he follows, for it is ancient; what he cannot accomplish by force and violence he will attempt by lure and deceit.

You are now engaged in a mighty conflict: a contest between freedom and "free-loading," between liberty and license, and between government by the people and government by the government: a struggle testing whether you can stand tall enough amidst the turmoil to see above the trappings of your proud affluence and catch the vision of your own sons of liberty a hundred years hence, moving as free beings in a world where free men can labor and draw to themselves a portion of this world's blessings and work and live in the safety and liberty of their own self-discipline; or whether your appetite and passion for the transitory pleasures of your opulence will propel you on into the enslaving security of the oppressive government you are allowing to grow up around you as an angry bramble about the feet of the last free people on the planet.

But for all this, you must be careful to understand me, for I have not come to discourage you or to prepare the grave of liberty, but to warn and encourage you to be about the work which is to be done before all mankind may enjoy the fullness of the rights with which the Creator endowed them. For the perfection of human governments was conceived in this nation and has been carried in its womb these many years, and you now enter into the time of the last travail before it is brought forth to all the world; a time in which conspiring men seek to destroy it that they might own the glory and riches of the world for themselves.

I have come to you in humility, and I speak from my heart. I have raised the cry of freedom and the alarm of oppression in your minds. Do not be troubled that I think your lot is destruction, or that you will not awake in time to save yourselves. Nay, not that, for I know you, and I know you will act in time. The cause of my great concern is my love for my children and the knowledge that the slower you act the more you will pay for your liberty: a lesson we learned in fear.

Contrary to your many doubts, it is not inevitable that you must go down. Was it inevitable that we should have won our struggle for freedom? Nay, 'twas the natural consequence of the pouring out of our purses and our blood, and the intervention of Divine Providence in the affairs of His children. You may act in the same faith, with the same courage, with the same determination, and with the same assurance of the same glorious result.

And I am consoled, for even now the nation is stirring, the desire for liberty wells up in the nation's bosom, and the cry of freedom whispers in its mind. Nay, I have no fear for your destiny, but I fear the price you may pay for it if you hesitate another decade.

I challenge you to set a noble cause: to set your face, your hand, and your heart to the restoration of the Constitution. If you harbor any doubt as to the correctness or worthiness of that aim, then search for a better goal until you are convinced. Study my words, for I have brought you the fundamentals of good government and laid them before you in earnestness and simplicity. Then set about to apply those principles; first in your own lives, then in your towns and cities, then your counties and states. Thus you will gain by experience the wisdom necessary to fully restore the most effective protector of human rights, and the most skilled artisan of noble human progress ever given to man for his general government.

More than any other institute of governments, the Constitution has guided the virtue of man, discouraged his baseness, and given full release to the productive capacity of his talents and energies. When you have restored those three functions to your government, you will have set the stage for the fulfillment of the manifest destiny of the nation. You will have displayed the proper example before the world, you will have gone back into an era of social and technical progress far beyond your fondest dreams, and thus you will be empowered by wealth and wisdom to instruct a jealous planet in the way of true progress.

But you live in a day when selfishness is glorified, benevolence belittled, and the government enthroned as the patriarchal source of all blessings, the healer of all wounds, the savior of society, a singular entity to which one prays for his share of his neighbor's goods. And there are many who promote the deception, unwittingly moved by a lazy conscience and a selfish habit. And all are partakers in the delusion; all are tainted by the hypocrisy of public distribution of private production.

Those who seek to rule you promise to make you happy by capturing you in their private utopia; and while their desires may sometimes be honorable, their theory is dross; and while they know it unjust for one to thrust his will upon another or to revel in the fruits of another's toil, yet they refuse to confess the immorality of their politics. Yet, notwithstanding their false theories, they will succeed in your capture if you allow them to spoil you with promises of wealth without labor and security without honor.

You stand now as at the wye of time. Your mind feels the two alternatives before you; you may trade your respect and your freedom for a short-lived security and sell your children to the aristocracy, or you may work and strive for liberty with honor. In your heart you know the right, while the comforts of government welfare and the narcotic of a lazy morality woo you to carelessness in the choice.

How long my children will you halt between? For decades you have stood, hoping you might be spared the price of liberty, hoping all would be well with you while the ambitious and the vain have framed the laws to enforce your happiness. Now as their work nears completion, the urgency of their success strikes fear in your hearts while their soft promises urge you to sleep.

How long will you halt between? How high must the cost of freedom ascend ere you appreciate its worth and determine to pay its price? Can you not perceive that we once made the self-same error: Must each generation stumble in the same road? Must the cycles of history ever turn full round?

Nay, my children! Not so! This time you may break the ancient pattern, for this is the first time and the last time the cycles in the nations have all been brought together in step and in time, for now the whole world lies in bondage, save a few. But the seeds of liberty germinate quickly under the tyrant's heel, and the embers of freedom glow brightest in the dark winds of oppression. Now those seeds grow and those embers glow, and the people of the earth peer out of darkness and look for *your light!* Now you, being free, may lead yourselves and them also into the full light of liberty.

Oh, America! America! May the Almighty look upon you with the tenderness of a loving Father. May you look to Him with the faith of a chosen child. If you will reach for Him, He will touch you. If you will serve Him, He will lift you up. Can you hear my voice? This is the message I have come to deliver: I challenge you, each and every one of you, to listen to the humility of your own heart, for it will guide you back to the glorious liberty which is your rightful inheritance if you will but qualify yourself by obedience to the voice of your own conscience. If you will listen and follow, the light of liberty will shine again in your face, and the nation will shine forth in a world darkened by the tyranny of despots and evil politicians. Rise up my people! Take your proper place in the progress of freedom!

If you will be faithful to your own hearts and the blood of your fathers, you may have the privilege of being the political saviors of the world, not by coercion or conspiracy but by example and precept. That is your challenge and your duty, your opportunity and your blessing. And that is the true destiny of liberty. I know it; and there is not one of you who does not in his own heart know it also. Then—my Sons of Liberty—be true to it! Farewell!

APPENDIX

The Virginia Declaration of Rights
1776

A declaration of rights made by the representatives of the good people of Virginia, assembled in full and free convention; which rights do pertain to them and their posterity, as the basis and foundation of government.

1. That all men are by nature equally free and independent, and have certain inherent rights, of which, when they enter into a state of society, they cannot, by any compact, deprive or divest their posterity; namely the enjoyment of life and liberty, with the means of acquiring and possessing property, and pursuing and obtaining happiness and safety.

2. That all power is vested in, and consequently derived from, the people; that magistrates are their trustees and servants, and at all times amenable to them.

3. That government is, or ought to be, instituted for the common benefit, protection, and security of the people, nation, or community; of all the various modes and forms of government, that is best which is capable of producing the greatest degree of happiness and safety, and is most effectually secured against the danger of maladministration; and that when any government shall be found inadequate or contrary to these purposes, a majority of the community hath an indubitable, unalienable, and indefeasible right to reform, alter, or abolish it, in such manner as shall be judged most conducive to the public weal.

4. That no man, or set of men, are entitled to exclusive or separate emoluments or privileges from the community, but in consideration of publick services; which, not being descendible, neither ought the offices of magistrate, legislator, or judge to be hereditary.

5. That the legislative and executive powers of the state should be separate and distinct from the judiciary; and that the members of the two first may be restrained from oppression, by feeling and participating the burthens of the people, they should, at fixed periods, be reduced to a private station, return into that body from which they were originally taken, and the vacancies be supplied by frequent, certain, and regular elections, in which all or any part of the former members to be again eligible or ineligible, as the laws shall direct.

6. That elections of members to serve as representatives of the

people in assembly ought to be free; and that all men having sufficient evidence of permanent common interest with, and attachment to the community, have the right of suffrage, and cannot be taxed or deprived of their property for publick uses, without their own consent, or that of their representatives so elected, nor bound by any law to which they have not, in like manner, assented for the public good.

7. That all power of suspending laws or the execution of laws by any authority, without consent of the representatives of the people, is injurious to their rights, and ought not to be exercised.

8. That in all capital or criminal prosecutions a man hath a right to demand the cause and nature of his accusation, to be confronted with the accusers and witnesses, to call for evidence in his favor, and to a speedy trial by an impartial jury, of his vicinage, without whose unanimous consent he cannot be found guilty; nor can he be compelled to give evidence against himself; that no man be deprived of his liberty, except by the law of the land or the judgment of his peers.

9. That excessive bail ought not to be required, nor excessive fines imposed, nor cruel and unusual punishments inflicted.

10. That general warrants, whereby an officer or messenger may be commanded to search suspected places without evidence of a fact committed, or to seize any person or persons not named, or whose offence is not particularly described and supported by evidence, are grievous and oppressive, and ought not be granted.

11. That in controversies respecting property, and in suits between man and man, the ancient trial by jury is preferable to any other, and ought to be held sacred.

12. That the freedom of the press is one of the great bulwarks of liberty, and can never be restrained but by despotic governments.

13. That a well-regulated militia, composed of the body of the people trained to arms, is the proper, natural, and safe defence of a free State; that standing armies in time of peace should be avoided as dangerous to liberty; and that in all cases the military should be under strict subordination to and governed by the civil power.

14. That the people have a right to uniform government; and, therefore, that no government separate from, or independent of the government of Virginia, ought to be erected or established within the limits thereof.

15. That no free government, or the blessings of liberty, can be preserved to any people but by a firm adherence to justice, moderation, temperance, frugality and virtue, and by frequent recurrence to fundamental principles.

16. That religion, or the duty which we owe to our Creator, and

the manner of discharging it, can be directed only by reason and conviction, not by force or violence; and therefore all men are equally entitled to the free exercise of religion, according to the dictates of conscience; and that it is the mutual duty of all to practise Christian forbearance, love, and charity towards each other.

The Declaration of Independence
In Congress, July 4, 1776

The unanimous Declaration
of the thirteen united States of America,

When in the Course of human events, it becomes necessary for one people to dissolve the political bands which have connected them with another, and to assume among the Powers of the earth, the separate and equal station to which the Laws of Nature and of Nature's God entitle them, a decent respect to the opinions of mankind requires that they should declare the causes which impel them to the separation.

We hold these truths to be self-evident, that all men are created equal, that they are endowed by their Creator with certain unalienable Rights, that among these are Life, Liberty and the pursuit of Happiness. That to secure these rights, Governments an instituted among Men, deriving their just powers from the consent of the governed, That whenever any Form of Government becomes destructive of these ends, it is the Right of the People to alter or to abolish it, and to institute new Government, laying its foundation on such principles and organizing its powers in such form, as to them shall seem most likely to effect their Safety and Happiness. Prudence, indeed, will dictate that Governments long established should not be changed for light and transient causes; and accordingly all experience hath shown, that mankind are more disposed to suffer, while evils are sufferable, than to right themselves by abolishing the forms to which they are accustomed. But when a long train of abuses and usurpations, pursuing invariably the same Object evinces a design to reduce them under absolute Despotism, it is their right, it is their duty, to throw off such Government, and to provide new Guards for their future security. Such has been the patient sufferance of these Colonies; and such is now the necessity which constrains them to alter their former Systems of Government. The history of the present King of Great Britain is a history of repeated injuries and usurpations, all having in direct object the establishment of an absolute Tyranny over these States. To prove this, let Facts be submitted to a candid world.

He has refused his Assent to Laws, the most wholesome and necessary for the public good.

He has forbidden his Governors to pass Laws of immediate and pressing importance, unless suspended in their operation till his Assent should be obtained; and when so suspended, he has utterly neglected to attend to them.

He has refused to pass other Laws for the accommodation of large districts of people, unless those people would relinquish the right of Representation in the Legislature, a right inestimable to them and formidable to tyrants only.

He has called together legislative bodies at places unusual, uncomfortable, and distant from the depository of their Public Records, for the sole purpose of fatiguing them into compliance with his measures.

He has dissolved Representative Houses repeatedly, for opposing with manly firmness his invasions on the rights of the people.

He has refused for a long time, after such dissolutions, to cause others to be elected; whereby the Legislative Powers, incapable of Annihilation, have returned to the People at large for their exercise; the State remaining in the mean time exposed to all the dangers of invasion from without, and convulsions within.

He has endeavoured to prevent the population of these States; for that purpose obstructing the Laws for Naturalization of Foreigners; refusing to pass others to encourage their migration hither, and raising the conditions of new Appropriations of Lands.

He has obstructed the Administration of Justice, by refusing his Assent to Laws for establishing Judiciary Powers.

He has made Judges dependent on his Will alone, for the tenure of their offices, and the amount and payment of their salaries.

He has erected a multitude of New Offices, and sent hither swarms of Officers to harrass our People, and eat out their substance.

He has kept among us, in times of peace, Standing Armies without the Consent of our legislature.

He has affected to render the Military independent of and superior to the Civil Power.

He has combined with others to subject us to a jurisdiction foreign to our constitution, and unacknowledged by our laws; giving his Assent to their Acts of pretended Legislation:

For quartering large bodies of armed troops among us:

For protecting them, by a mock Trial, from Punishment for any Murders which they should commit on the Inhabitants of these States:

For cutting off our Trade with all parts of the world:

For imposing taxes on us without our Consent:

For depriving us in many cases, of the benefits of Trial by Jury:

For transporting us beyond Seas to be tried for pretended offences:

For abolishing the free System of English Laws in a neighbouring Province, establishing therein an Arbitrary government, and enlarging its Boundaries so as to render it at once an example and fit instrument for introducing the same absolute rule into these Colonies:

For taking away our Charters, abolishing our most valuable Laws, and altering fundamentally the Forms of our Governments:

For suspending our own Legislatures, and declaring themselves invested with Power to legislate for us in all cases whatsoever.

He has abdicated Government here, by declaring us out of his Protection and waging War against us.

He has plundered our seas, ravaged our Coasts, burnt our towns, and destroyed the lives of our people.

He is at this time transporting large Armies of foreign Mercenaries to compleat the works of death, desolation and tyranny, already begun with circumstances of Cruelty & perfidy scarcely paralleled in the most barbarous ages, and totally unworthy the Head of a civilized nation.

He has constrained our fellow Citizens taken Captive on the high Seas to bear Arms against their Country, to become the executioners of their friends and Brethren, or to fall themselves by their Hands.

He has excited domestic insurrections amongst us, and has endeavoured to bring on the inhabitants of our frontiers, the merciless Indian Savages, whose known rule of warfare, is an undistinguished destruction of all ages, sexes and conditions.

In every stage of these Oppressions We have Petitioned for Redress in the most humble terms: Our repeated Petitions have been answered only by repeated injury. A Prince, whose character is thus marked by every act which may define a Tyrant, is unfit to be the ruler of a free People.

Nor have We been wanting in attention to our British brethren. We have warned them from time to time of attempts by their legislature to extend an unwarrantable jurisdiction over us. We have reminded them of the circumstances of our emigration and settlement here. We have appealed to their native justice and magnanimity, and we have conjured them by the ties of our common kindred to disavow these usurpations, which would inevitably interrupt our connections and correspondence. They too have been deaf to the voice of justice and of consanguinity. We must, therefore, acquiesce in the necessity, which denounces our Separation, and hold them, as we hold the rest of mankind, Enemies in War, in Peace Friends.

We, therefore, the Representatives of the united States of America, in General Congress, Assembled, appealing to the Supreme Judge of the world for the rectitude of our intentions, do, in the Name, and by Authority of the good people of these Colonies, solemnly publish and declare, That these United Colonies are, and of Right ought to be Free and Independent States; that they are Absolved from all Allegiance to the British Crown, and that all political connection between them and the State of Great Britain, is and ought to be totally dissolved; and that as Free and Independent States, they have full Power to levy War, conclude Peace, contract Alliances, establish Commerce, and to do all other Acts and Things which Independent States may of right do. And for the support of this Declaration, with a firm reliance on the Protection of Divine Providence, we mutually pledge to each other our Lives, our Fortunes and our sacred Honor.

The CONSTITUTION OF THE UNITED STATES
(1787)

[Preamble]

We the People of the United States, in Order to form a more perfect Union, establish Justice, insure domestic Tranquility, provide for the common defence, promote the general Welfare, and secure the Blessings of Liberty to ourselves and our Posterity, do ordain and establish this *Constitution* for the United States of America.

Article I

Section 1. All legislative Powers herein granted shall be vested in a Congress of the United States, which shall consist of a Senate and House of Representatives.

Section 2. The House of Representatives shall be composed of Members chosen every second Year, by the People of the several States, and the Electors in each State shall have the Qualifications requisite for Electors of the most numerous Branch of the State Legislature.

No person shall be a Representative who shall not have attained to the Age of twenty five Years and been seven Years a Citizen of the United States, and who shall not, when elected, be an Inhabitant of that State in which he shall be chosen.

Representatives and direct Taxes shall be apportioned among the several States which may be included within this Union, according to their respective Numbers, which shall be determined by adding to the whole Number of Free persons, including those bound to Service for a Term of Years, and excluding Indians not taxed, three fifths of all other Persons. The actual Enumeration shall be made within three Years after the first Meeting of the Congress of the United States, and within every subsequent Term of ten Years, in such Manner as they shall by Law direct. The Number of Representatives shall not exceed one for every thirty Thousand, but each State shall have at Least one Representative; and until such enumeration shall be made, the State of New Hampshire shall be entitled to chuse three, Massachusetts eight, Rhode-Island and Providence Plantations one, Connecticut five, New-York six, New Jersey four, Pennsylvania eight, Delaware one, Maryland six, Virginia ten, North Carolina five, South Carolina five, and Georgia three.

When vacancies happen in the Representation from any State, the Executive Authority thereof shall issue Writs of Election to fill such Vacancies.

The House of Representatives shall chuse their Speaker and other Officers; and shall have the sole Power of Impeachment.

Section 3. The Senate of the United States shall be composed of two Senators from each State, chosen by the Legislature thereof, for six Years; and each Senator shall have one Vote.

Immediately after they shall be assembled in Consequence of the first Election, they shall be divided as equally as may be into three Classes. The seats of the Senators of the first Class shall be vacated at the Expiration of the second Year, of the second Class at the Expiration of the fourth Year, and of the third Class at the Expiration of the sixth Year, so that one third may be chosen every second Year; and if Vacancies happen by Resignation, or otherwise, during the Recess of the Legislature of any State, the Executive thereof may make temporary Appointments until the next Meeting of the Legislature, which shall then fill such Vacancies.

No Person shall be a Senator who shall not have attained to the Age of thirty Years, and been nine Years a Citizen of the United States, and who shall not, when elected, be an Inhabitant of that State for which he shall be chosen.

The Vice President of the United States shall be President of the Senate, but shall have no Vote, unless they be equally divided.

The Senate shall chuse their other Officers, and also a President pro tempore, in the Absence of the Vice President, or when he shall exercise the Office of President of the United States.

The Senate shall have the sole Power to try all impeachments. When sitting for that Purpose, they shall be on Oath or Affirmation. When the President of the United States is tried, the Chief Justice shall preside: And no Person shall be convicted without the Concurrence of two thirds of the Members present.

Judgment in Cases of Impeachment shall not extend further than to removal from Office, and disqualification to hold and enjoy any Office of honor, Trust or Profit under the United States: but the Party convicted shall nevertheless be liable and subject to Indictment, Trial, Judgement and Punishment, according to Law.

Section 4. The Times, Places and Manner of holding Elections for Senators and Representatives, shall be prescribed in each State by the Legislature thereof; but the Congress may at any time by Law make or alter such Regulations, except as to the Places of chusing Senators.

The Congress shall assemble at least once in every Year, and such Meeting shall be on the first Monday in December, unless they shall by Law appoint a different Day.

Section 5. Each House shall be the Judge of the Elections, Returns and Qualifications of its own Members, and a Majority of each shall constitute a Quorum to do Business; but a smaller Number may adjourn from day to day, and may be authorized to compel the Attendance of absent Members, in such Manner, and under such Penalties as each House may provide.

Each House may determine the Rules of its Proceedings, punish its Members for disorderly Behaviour, and, with the Concurrence of two thirds, expel a Member.

Each House shall keep a Journal of its Proceedings, and from time to time publish the same, excepting such Parts as may in their judgment require Secrecy; and the Yeas and Nays of the Members of either House on any question shall, at the Desire of one fifth of those Present, be entered on the Journal.

Neither House, during the Session of Congress, shall, without the Consent of the other, adjourn for more than three days, nor to any other Place than that in which the two Houses shall be sitting.

Section 6. The Senators and Representatives shall receive a Compensation for their Services, to be ascertained by Law, and paid out of the Treasury of the United States. They shall in all Cases, except Treason, Felony and Breach of the Peace, be privileged from Arrest during their Attendance at the Session of their respective Houses, and in going to and returning from the same; and for any Speech or Debate in either House, they shall not be questioned in any other place.

No Senator or Representative shall, during the Time for which he was elected, be appointed to any civil Office under the Authority of the United States, which shall have been created, or the Emoluments whereof shall have been encreased during such time; and no Person holding any Office under the United States, shall be a Member of either House during his Continuance in Office.

Section 7. All Bills for raising Revenue shall originate in the House of Representatives; but the Senate may propose or concur with Amendments as on other Bills.

Every Bill which shall have passed the House of Representatives and the Senate, shall, before it become a Law, be presented to the President of the United States; If he approve he shall sign it, but if not he shall return it, with his Objections to that House in which it shall have originated, who shall enter the Objections at large on their Journal, and proceed to reconsider it. If after such Reconsideration two thirds of that House shall agree to pass the Bill, it shall be sent, together with the Objections, to the other House, by which it shall likewise be reconsidered, and if approved by two thirds of that House, it shall become a Law. But in all such Cases the Votes of both Houses shall be determined by Yeas and Nays, and the Names of the Persons voting for and against the Bill shall be entered on the Journal of each House respectively. If any Bill shall not be returned by the President within ten Days (Sundays excepted) after it shall have been presented to him, the Same shall be a Law, in like Manner as if he had signed it, unless the Congress by their Adjournment prevent its Return, in which Case it shall not be a Law.

Every Order, Resolution, or Vote to which the Concurrence of the Senate and House of Representatives may be necessary (except on a question of Adjournment) shall be presented to the President of the United States; and before the Same shall take Effect, shall be approved by him, or being disapproved by him, shall be repassed by two thirds of the Senate and House of Representatives, according to the Rules and Limitations prescribed in the Case of a Bill.

Section 8. The Congress shall have Power to lay and collect Taxes, Duties, Imposts and Excises, to pay the Debts and provide for the common Defence and general Welfare of the United States; but all Duties, Imposts and Excises shall be uniform throughout the United States;

To borrow Money on the credit of the United States;

To regulate Commerce with foreign Nations, and among the several States, and with the Indian Tribes;

To establish an uniform Rule of Naturalization, and uniform Laws on the subject of Bankruptcies throughout the United States;

To coin Money, regulate the Value thereof, and of foreign Coin, and fix the Standard of Weights and Measures;

To provide for the Punishment of counterfeiting the Securities and current Coin of the United States;

To establish Post Offices and post Roads;

To promote the Progress of Science and useful Arts, by securing for limited Times to Authors and Inventors the exclusive Right to their respective Writings and Discoveries;

To constitute Tribunals inferior to the supreme Court;

To define and punish Piracies and Felonies committed on the high Seas, and Offences against the Law of Nations;

To declare War, grant Letters of Marque and Reprisal, and make Rules concerning Captures on Land and Water;

To raise and support Armies, but no Appropriation of Money to that Use shall be for a longer Term than two Years;

To provide and maintain a Navy;

To make Rules for the Government and Regulation of the land and naval Forces;

To provide for calling forth the Militia to execute the Laws of the Union, suppress Insurrections and repel Invasions;

To provide for organizing, arming, and disciplining, the Militia, and for governing such Part of them as may be employed in the Service of the United States, reserving to the States respectively, the Appointment of the Officers, and the Authority of training the Militia according to the discipline prescribed by Congress;

To exercise exclusive Legislation in all Cases whatsoever, over such District (not exceeding ten Miles square) as may, by Cession of particular States, and the Acceptance of Congress, become the Seat of the Government of the United States, and to exercise like Authority over all Places purchased by the Consent of the Legislature of the State in which the Same shall be, for the Erection of Forts, Magazines, Arsenals, dock-Yards, and other needful Buildings;—And

To make all Laws which shall be necessary and proper for carrying into Execution the foregoing Powers, and all other Powers vested by this Constitution in the Government of the United States, or in any Department or Officer thereof.

Section 9. The Migration or Importation of such Persons as any of the States now existing shall think proper to admit, shall not be prohibited by the Congress prior to the Year one thousand eight hundred and eight, but a Tax or duty may be imposed on such Importation, not exceeding ten dollars for each Person.

The Privilege of the Writ of Habeas Corpus shall not be suspended, unless when in Cases of Rebellion or Invasion the public Safety may require it.

No Bill of Attainder or ex post facto Law shall be passed.

No Capitation, or other direct, tax shall be laid, unless in Proportion to the Census or Enumeration herein before directed to be taken.

No Tax or Duty shall be laid on Articles exported from any State.

No Preference shall be given by any Regulation of Commerce or Revenue to the Ports of one State over those of another: nor shall Vessels bound to, or from, one State, be obliged to enter, clear, or pay Duties in another.

No Money shall be drawn from the Treasury, but in Consequence of Appropriations made by Law; and a regular Statement and Account of the Receipts and Expenditures of all public Money shall be published from time to time.

No Title of Nobility shall be granted by the United States: And no Person holding any Office of Profit or Trust under them, shall, without the Consent of the Congress, accept of any present, Emolument, Office, or Title, of any kind whatever, from any King, Prince, or foreign State.

Section 10. No State shall enter into any Treaty, Alliance, or Confederation; grant Letters of Marque and Reprisal; coin Money; emit Bills of Credit; make any Thing but gold and silver Coin a Tender in Payment of Debts; pass any Bill of Attainder, ex post facto Law, or Law impairing the Obligation of Contracts, or grant any Title of Nobility.

No State shall, without the Consent of the Congress, lay any Imposts or Duties on Imports or Exports, except what may be absolutely necessary for executing its inspection Laws: and the net Produce of all Duties and Imposts, laid by any State on Imports or Exports, shall be for the Use of the Treasury of the United States; and all such Laws shall be subject to the Revision and Control of the Congress.

No State shall, without the Consent of Congress, lay any Duty of Tonnage, keep Troops, or Ships of War in time of Peace, enter into any Agreement or Compact with another State, or with a foreign Power, or engage in War, unless actually invaded, or in such imminent Danger as will not admit of delay.

Article II

Section 1. The executive Power shall be vested in a President of the United States of America. He shall hold his Office during the Term of four Years, and, together with the Vice President, chosen for the same Term, be elected, as follows:

Each State shall appoint, in such Manner as the Legislature thereof may direct, a Number of Electors, equal to the whole Number of Senators and Representatives to which the State may be entitled in the Congress: but no Senator or Representative, or Person holding an

Office of Trust or Profit under the United States, shall be appointed an Elector.

The Electors shall meet in their respective States, and vote by Ballot for two persons, of whom one at least shall not be an Inhabitant of the same State with themselves. And they shall make a List of all the Persons voted for, and of the Number of Votes for each; which List they shall sign and certify, and transmit sealed to the Seat of the Government of the United States, directed to the President of the Senate. The President of the Senate shall, in the Presence of the Senate and House of Representatives, open all the Certificates, and the Votes shall then be counted. The Person having the greatest Number of Votes shall be the President, if such Number be a Majority of the whole Number of Electors appointed; and if there be more than one who have such Majority, and have an equal Number of Votes, then the House of Representatives shall immediately chuse, by Ballot one of them for President; and if no Person have a Majority, then from the five highest on the list, the said House shall in like manner chuse the President. But in chusing the President, the Votes shall be taken by States, the Representation from each State having one vote; A quorum for this Purpose shall consist of a Member or Members from two thirds of the States, and a Majority of all the States shall be necessary to a Choice. In every Case, after the Choice of the President, the Person having the greatest Number of Votes of the Electors shall be the Vice President. But if there should remain two or more who have equal Votes, the Senate shall chuse from them by Ballot the Vice President.

The Congress may determine the Time of chusing the Electors, and the Day on which they shall give their Votes; which Day shall be the same throughout the United States.

No person except a natural born Citizen, or a Citizen of the United States, at the time of the Adoption of this Constitution, shall be eligible to the Office of President; neither shall any Person be eligible to that office who shall not have attained to the Age of thirty five Years, and been fourteen Years a Resident within the United States.

In Case of the Removal of the President from Office, or of his Death, Resignation or Inability to discharge the Powers and Duties of the said Office, the Same shall devolve on the Vice President, and the Congress may by Law provide for the Case of Removal, Death, Resignation or Inability, both of the President and Vice President, declaring what Officer shall then act as President, and such Officer shall act accordingly, until the Disability be removed, or a President shall be elected.

The President shall, at stated Times, receive for his Services, a Compensation, which shall neither be encreased nor diminished during the Period for which he shall have been elected, and he shall not receive within that Period any other Emolument from the United States, or any of them.

Before he enter on the Execution of his Office, he shall take the following Oath or Affirmation:—"I do solemnly swear (or affirm) that I will faithfully execute the Office of President of the United States, and will to the best of my Ability, preserve, protect and defend the Constitution of the United States."

Section 2. The President shall be Commander in Chief of the Army and Navy of the United States, and of the Militia of the several States, when called into the actual Service of the United States; he may require the Opinion, in writing, of the principal Officer in each of the executive Departments upon any Subject relating to the Duties of their respective Offices, and he shall have Power to grant Reprieves and Pardons for offences against the United States, except in Cases of Impeachment.

He shall have Power, by and with the Advice and Consent of the Senate, to make Treaties, provided two thirds of the Senators present concur; and he shall nominate, and by and with the Advice and Consent of the Senate, shall appoint Ambassadors, other public Ministers and Consuls, Judges of the supreme Court, and all other Officers of the United States, whose Appointments are not herein otherwise provided for, and which shall be established by Law: but the Congress may by Law vest the Appointment of such inferior Officers, as they think proper, in the President alone, in the Courts of Law, or in the Heads of Departments.

The President shall have Power to fill up all Vacancies that may happen during the Recess of the Senate, by granting Commissions which shall expire at the End of their next session.

Section 3. He shall from time to time give to the Congress Information of the State of the Union, and recommend to their Consideration such Measures as he shall judge necessary and expedient; he may, on extraordinary Occasions, convene both Houses, or either of them, and in Case of Disagreement between them, with Respect to the time of Adjournment, he may adjourn them to such Time as he shall think proper; he shall receive Ambassadors and other public Ministers; he shall take Care that the Laws be faithfully executed, and shall Commission all the Officers of the United States.

Section 4. The President, Vice President and all civil Officers of the United States, shall be removed from Office on Impeachment for, and Conviction of, Treason, Bribery, or other high Crimes and Misdemeanors.

Article III

Section 1. The Judicial Power of the United States, shall be vested in one supreme Court, and in such inferior Courts as the Congress may from time to time ordain and establish. The Judges, both of the supreme and inferior Courts, shall hold their Offices during good Behaviour, and shall, at stated Times, receive for their Services, a Compensation, which shall not be diminished during their Continuance in Office.

Section 2. The judicial Power shall extend to all Cases, in Law and Equity, arising under this Constitution, the Laws of the United States, and Treaties made, or which shall be made, under their Authority;—to all Cases affecting Ambassadors, other public Ministers and Consuls;—to all Cases of admiralty and maritime Jurisdiction;—to Controversies to which the United States shall be a Party;—to Controversies between two or more States;—between a State and Citizens of another State;—between Citizens of different States,—between Citizens of the same State claiming Lands under Grants of different States, and between a State, or the Citizens thereof, and foreign States, Citizens or Subjects.

In all Cases affecting Ambassadors, other public Ministers and Consuls, and those in which a State shall be Party, the supreme Court shall have original Jurisdiction. In all the other Cases before mentioned, the supreme Court shall have appellate Jurisdiction, both as to Law and Fact, with such Exceptions, and under such Regulations as the Congress shall make.

The Trial of all Crimes, except in Cases of Impeachment, shall be by Jury; and such Trial shall be held in the State where the said Crimes shall have been committed; but when not committed within any State, the Trial shall be at such Place or Places as the Congress may by Law have directed.

Section 3. Treason against the United States, shall consist only in levying War against them, or in adhering to their Enemies, giving them Aid and Comfort. No Person shall be convicted of Treason unless on the Testimony of two Witnesses to the same overt Act, or on Confession in open Court.

The Congress shall have Power to, declare the Punishment of Treason, but no Attainder of Treason shall work Corruption of Blood, or Forfeiture except during the Life of the Person attainted.

Article IV

Section 1. Full, Faith and Credit shall be given in each State to the public Acts, Records, and judicial Proceedings of every other State. And the Congress may by general Laws prescribe the Manner in which such Acts, Records and Proceedings shall be proved, and the Effect thereof.

Section 2. The Citizens of each State shall be entitled to all Privileges and Immunities of Citizens in the several States.

A person charged in any State with Treason, Felony, or other Crime, who shall flee from Justice, and be found in another State shall on Demand of the executive Authority of the State from which he fled, be delivered up to be removed to the State having Jurisdiction of the Crime.

No person held to Service or Labour in one State, under the Laws thereof, escaping into another, shall, in Consequence of any Law or Regulation therein, be discharged from such Service or Labour, but shall be delivered up on Claim of the Party to whom such Service or Labour may be due.

Section 3. New States may be admitted by the Congress into this Union; but no new State shall be formed or erected within the Jurisdiction of any other State; nor any State be formed by the Junction of two or more States, or Parts of States, without the Consent of the Legislatures of the States concerned as well as of the Congress.

The Congress shall have Power to dispose of and make all needful Rules and Regulations respecting the Territory or other Property belonging to the United States; and nothing in this Constitution shall be so construed as to Prejudice any Claims of the United States, or of any particular State.

Section 4. The United States shall guarantee to every State in this Union a Republican Form of Government, and shall protect each of them against Invasion; and on Application of the Legislature, or of the Executive (when the Legislature cannot be convened) against domestic Violence.

Article V

The Congress, whenever two thirds of both Houses shall deem it necessary, shall propose amendments to this Constitution, or, on the Application of the Legislatures of two thirds of the several States, shall call a Convention for proposing Amendments, which, in either Case, shall be valid to all Intents and Purposes, as Part of this Constitution, when ratified by the Legislatures of three fourths of the several States, or by Conventions in three fourths thereof, as the one or the other Mode of Ratification may be proposed by the Congress; Provided that no Amendment which may be made prior to the Year One thousand eight hundred and eight shall in any Manner affect the first and fourth Clauses in the Ninth Section of the first Article; and that no State, without its Consent, shall be deprived of its equal Suffrage in the Senate.

Article VI

All Debts contracted and Engagements entered into, before the Adoption of this Constitution, shall be as valid against the United States under this Constitution, as under the Confederation.

This Constitution, and the Laws of the United States which shall be made in Pursuance thereof; and all Treaties made, or which shall be made, under the Authority of the United States, shall be the supreme Law of the Land; and the Judges in every State shall be bound thereby, any Thing in the Constitution or Laws of any State to the Contrary notwithstanding.

The Senators and Representatives before mentioned, and the Members of the several State Legislatures, and all executive and judicial Officers, both of the United States and of the several States, shall be bound by Oath or Affirmation, to support this Constitution; but no religious Test shall ever be required as a Qualification to any Office or public Trust under the United States.

Article VII

The Ratification of the Conventions of nine States, shall be sufficient for the Establishment of this Constitution between the States so ratifying the Same.

Done in Convention by the Unanimous Consent of the States present the Seventeenth Day of September in the Year of our Lord one thousand seven hundred and Eighty seven and of the Independence of the United States of America the Twelfth. IN WITNESS whereof We have hereunto subscribed our Names,

George Washington—President and Deputy from Virginia

The Bill of Rights

Article I

Congress shall make no law respecting an establishment of religion, or prohibiting the free exercise thereof; or abridging the freedom of speech, or of the press; or the right of the people to peaceably assemble, and to petition the Government for redress of grievances

Article II

A well regulated Militia, being necessary to the security of a free State, the right of the people to keep and bear Arms, shall not be infringed.

Article III

No Soldier shall, in time of peace, be quartered in any house, without the consent of the Owner, nor in time of war, but in a manner to be prescribed by law.

Article IV

The right of the people to be secure in their persons, houses, papers, and effects, against unreasonable searches and seizures, shall not be violated, and no Warrants shall issue, but upon probable cause, supported by Oath or affirmation, and particularly describing the place to be searched, and the persons or things to be seized.

Article V

No person shall be held to answer for a capital, or otherwise infamous crime, unless on a presentment or indictment of a Grand Jury, except in cases arising in the land or naval forces, or in the Militia, when in actual service in time of War or public danger; nor shall any person be subject for the same offence to be twice put in jeopardy of life or limb; nor shall be compelled in any Criminal Case to be a witness against himself, nor be deprived of life, liberty, or property, without due process of law; nor shall private property be taken for public use, without just compensation.

Article VI

In all criminal prosecutions, the accused shall enjoy the right to a speedy and public trial, by an impartial jury of the State and district wherein the crime shall have been committed, which district shall have been previously ascertained by law, and to be informed of the nature and cause of the accusation; to be confronted with the witnesses against him; to have compulsory process for obtaining witnesses in his favor, and to have the Assistance of Counsel for his defence.

Article VII

In suits at common law, where the value in controversy shall exceed twenty dollars, the right of trial by jury shall be preserved, and no fact tried by a jury shall be otherwise reexamined in any Court of the United States, than according to the rules of the common law.

Article VIII

Excessive bail shall not be required, nor excessive fines imposed, nor cruel and unusual punishments inflicted.

Article IX

The enumeration in the Constitution, of certain rights, shall not be construed to deny or disparage others retained by the people.

Article X

The powers not delegated to the United States by the Constitution, nor prohibited by it to the States, are reserved to the States respectively, or to the people.

—Adopted December 15, 1791

Washington's Farewell Address

Friends and Fellow-Citizens:

The period for a new election of a citizen to administer the Executive Government of the United States being not far distant, and the time actually arrived when your thoughts must be employed in designating the person who is to be clothed with that important trust, it appears to me proper, especially as it may conduce to a more distinct expression of the public voice, that I should now apprise you of the resolution I have formed to decline being considered among the number of those out of whom a choice is to be made.

I beg you at the same time to do me the justice to be assured that this resolution has not been taken without a strict regard to all the considerations appertaining to the relation which binds a dutiful citizen to country; and that in withdrawing the tender of service, which silence in my situation might imply, I am influenced by no diminution of zeal for your future interest, no deficiency of grateful respect for your past kindness, but am supported by a full conviction that the step is compatible with both.

The acceptance of and continuance hitherto in the office to which your suffrages have twice called me have been a uniform sacrifice of inclination to the opinion of duty and to a deference for what appeared to be your desire. I constantly hoped that it would have been much earlier in my power, consistently with motives which I was not at liberty to disregard, to return to that retirement from which I had been reluctantly drawn. The strength of my inclination to do this previous to the last election had even led to the preparation of an address to declare it to you; but mature reflection on the then perplexed and critical posture of our affairs with foreign nations and the unanimous advice of persons entitled to my confidence impelled me to abandon the idea. I rejoice that the state of your concerns, external as well as internal, no longer renders the pursuit of inclination incompatible with the sentiment of duty or propriety, and am persuaded, whatever partiality may be retained for my services, that in the present circumstances of our country you will not disapprove my determination to retire.

The impressions with which I first undertook the arduous trust were explained on the proper occasion. In the discharge of this trust I will only say that I have, with good intentions, contributed toward the organization and administration of the Government the best exertions of which a very fallible judgment was capable. Not unconscious in the outset of the inferiority of my qualifications, experience in my own eyes, perhaps still more in the eyes of others, has strengthened the motives to diffidence of myself; and every day the increasing weight of years admonishes me more and more that the shade of retirement is as necessary to me as it will be welcome. Satisfied that if any circumstances have given peculiar value to my services they were temporary, I have the consolation to believe that, while choice and prudence invite me to quit the political scene, patriotism does not forbid it.

A Prayer of Gratitude

In looking forward to the moment which is intended to terminate the career of my political life my feelings do not permit me to suspend the deep acknowledgment of that debt of gratitude which I owe to my beloved country for the many honors it has conferred upon me; still more for the steadfast confidence with which it has supported me, and for the opportunities I have thence enjoyed of manifesting my inviolable attachment by services faithful and persevering, though in usefulness unequal to my zeal. If benefits have resulted to our country from these services, let it always be remembered to your praise and as an instructive example in our annals that under circumstances in which the passions, agitated in every direction, were liable to mislead; amidst appearances sometimes dubious; vicissitudes of fortune often discouraging; in situations in which not unfrequently want of success has countenanced the spirit of the constancy of your support was the essential prop of the efforts and a guaranty of the plans by which they were effected. Profoundly penetrated with this idea, I shall carry it with me to my grave as a strong incitement to unceasing vows that Heaven may continue to you the choicest tokens of its beneficence; that your union and brotherly affection may be perpetual; that the free Constitution which is the work of your hands may be sacredly maintained; that its administration in every department may be stamped with wisdom and virtue; that, in fine, the happiness of the people of these States, under the auspices of liberty, may be made complete by so careful a preservation and so prudent a use of this blessing as will acquire to them the glory of recommending it to the applause, the affection, and adoption of every nation which is yet a stranger to it.

Here, perhaps, I ought to stop. But a solicitude for your welfare which can not end but with my life, and the apprehension of danger natural to that solicitude, urge me on an occasion like the present to offer to your solemn contemplation and to recommend to your frequent review some sentiments which are the result of much reflection, of no inconsiderable observation, and which appear to me all important to the permanency of your felicity as a people. These will be offered to you with the more freedom as you can only see in them the disinterested warnings of a parting friend, who can possibly have no personal motive to bias his counsel. Nor can I forget as an encouragement to it your indulgent reception of my sentiments on a former and not dissimilar occasion.

Interwoven as is the love of liberty with every ligament of your hearts, no recommendation of mine is necessary to fortify or confirm the attachment.

In Union Lies Strength

The unity of government which constitutes you one people is also now dear to you. It is justly so, for it is a main pillar in the edifice of your real independence, the support of your tranquility at home, your peace abroad, of your safety, of your prosperity, of that very liberty which you so highly prize. But as it is easy to foresee that from different causes and from different quarters much pains will be taken, many artifices employed, to weaken in your minds the conviction of this truth, as this is the point in your political fortress against which the batteries of internal and external enemies will be most constantly and actively (though often covertly and insidiously) directed, it is of infinite moment that you should properly estimate the immense value of your national union to your collective and individual happiness; that you should cherish a cordial, habitual, and immovable attachment to it; accustoming yourselves to think and speak of it as of the palladium of your political safety and prosperity; watching for its preservation with jealous anxiety; discountenancing whatever may suggest even a suspicion that it can in any event be abandoned, and indignantly frowning upon the first dawning of every attempt to alienate any portion of our country from the rest or to enfeeble the sacred ties which now link together the various parts.

For this you have every inducement of sympathy and interest. Citizens by birth or choice of a common country, that country has a right to concentrate your affections. The name of American, which belongs to you in your national capacity, must always exalt the just pride of patriotism more than any appellation derived from local discriminations. With slight shades of difference, you have the same religion, manners, habits, and political principles. You have in a common cause fought and triumphed together. The independence and liberty you possess are the work of joint councils and joint efforts, of common dangers, sufferings, and successes.

But these considerations, however powerfully they address themselves to your sensibility, are greatly outweighed by those which apply more immediately to your interest. Here every portion of our country finds the most commanding motives for carefully guarding and preserving the union of the whole.

The *North*, in an unrestrained intercourse with the *South*, protected by the equal laws of a common government, finds in the productions of the latter great additional resources of maritime and commercial enterprise and precious materials of manufacturing industry. The *South*, in the same intercourse, benefiting by the same agency of the *North*, sees its agriculture grow and its commerce expand. Turning partly into its own channels the seamen of the *North*, it finds its particular navigation invigorated; and while it contributes in different ways to nourish and increase the general mass of the national navigation, it looks forward to the protection of a maritime strength to which itself is unequally adapted. The *East*, in a like intercourse with the *West*, already finds, and in the progressive improvement of interior communications by land and water will more and more find, a valuable vent for the commodities which it brings from abroad or manufactures at home. The *West* derives from the *East* supplies requisite to its growth and comfort, and what is perhaps of still greater consequence, it must of necessity owe the secure enjoyment of indispensable *outlets* for its own productions to the weight, influence, and the future maritime strength of the Atlantic side of the Union, directed by an indissoluble community of interest as *one nation*. Any other tenure by which the *West* can hold this essential advantage, whether derived from its own separate strength or from an apostate and unnatural connection with any foreign power, must be intrinsically precarious.

Harmonious Interests

While, then, every part of our country thus feels an immediate and particular interest in union, all the parts combined can not fail to find in the united mass of means and efforts greater strength, greater resource, proportionably greater security from external danger, a less frequent interruption of their peace by foreign nations, and what is of inestimable value, they must derive from union an exemption from those broils and wars between themselves which so frequently afflict neighboring countries not tied together by the same governments, which their own rivalships alone would be sufficient to produce, but which opposite foreign alliances, attachments, and intrigues would stimulate and imbitter. Hence, likewise, they will avoid the necessity of those overgrown military establishments which, under any form of government, are inauspicious to liberty, and which are to be regarded as particularly hostile to republican liberty. In this sense it is that your union ought to be considered as a main prop of your liberty, and that the love of the one ought to endear to you the preservation of the other.

These considerations speak a persuasive language to every reflecting and virtuous mind, and exhibit the continuance of the union as a primary object of patriotic desire. Is there a doubt whether a common government can embrace so large a sphere? Let experience solve it. To listen to mere speculation in such a case were criminal. We are authorized to hope that a proper organization of the whole, with the auxiliary agency of governments for the respective subdivisions, will afford a happy issue to the experiment. It is well worth a fair and full experiment. With such powerful and obvious motives to union affecting all parts of our country, while experience shall not have demonstrated its impracticability, there will always be reason to distrust the patriotism of those who in any quarter may endeavor to weaken its bands.

Divisive Issues Avoided

In contemplating the causes which may disturb our union it occurs as matter of serious concern that any ground should have been furnished for characterizing parties by *geographical* discriminations— *Northern* and *Southern, Atlantic* and *Western*—whence designing men may endeavor to excite a belief that there is a real difference of local interests and views. One of the expedients of party to acquire influence within particular districts is to misrepresent the opinions and aims of other districts. You can not shield yourselves too much against the jealousies and heartburnings which spring from these misrepresentations; they tend to render alien to each other those who ought to be bound together by fraternal affection. The inhabitants of our Western country have lately had a useful lesson on this head. They have seen in the negotiation by the Executive and in the unanimous ratification by the Senate of the treaty with Spain, and in the universal satisfaction at that event throughout the United States, a decisive proof how unfounded were the suspicions propagated among them of a policy in the General Government and in the Atlantic States unfriendly to their interests in regard to the Mississippi. They have been witnesses to the formation of two treaties—that with Great Britain and that with Spain—which secure to them everything they could desire in respect to our foreign relations toward confirming their prosperity. Will it not be their wisdom to rely for the preservation of these advantages on the union by which they were procured? Will they not hence forth be deaf to those advisers, if such there are, who would sever them from their brethren and connect them with aliens?

To the efficacy and permanency of your union a government for the whole is indispensable. No alliances, however strict, between the parts can be an adequate substitute. They must inevitably experience the infractions and interruptions which all alliances in all times have experienced. Sensible of this momentous truth, you have improved upon your first essay by the adoption of a Constitution of Government better calculated than your former for an intimate union and for the efficacious management of your common concerns. This Government, the offspring of our own choice, uninfluenced and unawed, adopted upon full investigation and mature deliberation, completely free in its principles, in the distribution of its powers, uniting security with energy, and containing within itself a provision for its own amendment, has a just claim to your confidence and your support. Respect for its authority, compliance with its laws, acquiescence in its measures, are duties enjoined by the fundamental maxims of true liberty. The basis of our political systems is the right of the people to make and to alter their constitutions of government. But the constitution which at any time exists till changed by an explicit and authentic act of the whole people is sacredly obligatory upon all. The very idea of the power and the right of the people to establish government presupposes the duty of every individual to obey the established government.

Special Interests and Factions

All obstructions to the execution of the laws, all combinations and associations, under whatever plausible character, with the real design to direct, control, counteract, or awe the regular deliberation and action of the constituted authorities, are destructive of this fundamental principle and of fatal tendency. They serve to organize faction; to give it an artificial and extraordinary force; to put in the place of the delegated will of the nation the will of a party, often a small but artful and enterprising minority of the community, and, according to the alternate triumphs of different parties, to make the public administration the mirror of the ill-concerted and incongruous projects of faction rather than the organ of consistent and wholesome plans, digested by common counsels and modified by mutual interests.

However combinations or associations of the above description may now and then answer popular ends, they are likely in the course of time and things to become potent engines by which cunning, ambitious, and unprincipled men will be enabled to subvert the power of the people, and to usurp for themselves the reins of government, destroying afterwards the very engines which have lifted them to unjust dominion.

Toward the preservation of your Government and the permanency of your present happy state, it is requisite not only that you steadily discountenance irregular opposition to its acknowledged authority, but also that you resist with care the spirit of innovation upon its principles, however specious the pretexts. One method of assault may be to effect in the forms of the Constitution alterations which will impair the energy of the system, and thus to undermine what can not be directly overthrown. In all the changes to which you may be invited remember that time and habit are at least as necessary to fix the true character of governments as of other human institutions; that experience is the surest standard by which to test the real tendency of the existing constitution of a country; that facility in changes upon the credit of mere hypothesis and opinion exposes to perpetual change, from the endless variety of hypothesis and opinion; and remember especially that for the efficient management of your common interests in a country so extensive as ours a government of as much vigor as is consistent with the perfect security of liberty is indispensable. Liberty itself will find in such a government, with powers properly distributed and adjusted, its surest guardian. It is, indeed, little else than a name where the government is too feeble to withstand the enterprises of faction, to confine each member of the society within the limits prescribed by the laws, and to maintain all in the secure and tranquil enjoyment of the rights of person and property.

The Spirit of Party

I have already intimated to you the danger of parties in the State, with particular reference to the founding of them on geographical discriminations. Let me now take a more comprehensive view, and warn you in the most solemn manner against the baneful effects of the spirit of party generally.

This spirit, unfortunately, is inseparable from our nature, having its root in the strongest passions of the human mind. It exists under different shapes in all governments, more or less stifled, controlled, or repressed; but in those of the popular form it is seen in its greatest rankness and is truly their worst enemy.

The alternate domination of one faction over another, sharpened by the spirit of revenge natural to party dissension, which in different ages and countries has perpetrated the most horrid enormities, is itself a frightful despotism. But this leads at length to a more formal and permanent despotism. The disorders and miseries which result gradually incline the minds of men to seek security and repose in the absolute power of an individual, and sooner or later the chief of some prevailing faction, more able or more fortunate than his competitors, turns this disposition to the purposes of his own elevation on the ruins of public liberty.

Without looking forward to an extremity of this kind (which nevertheless ought not to be entirely out of sight), the common and continual mischiefs of the spirit of party are sufficient to make it the interest and duty of a wise people to discourage and restrain it.

It serves always to distract the public councils and enfeeble the public administration. It agitates the community with ill-founded jealousies and false alarms; kindles the animosity of one part against another; foments occasionally riot and insurrection. It opens the door to foreign influence and corruption, which find a facilitated access to the government itself through the channels of party passion. Thus the policy and the will of one country are subjected to the policy and will of another.

Dangerous in a Free Country

There is an opinion that parties in free countries are useful checks upon the administration of the government, and serve to keep alive the spirit of liberty. This within certain limits is probably true; and in governments of a monarchical cast patriotism may look with indulgence, if not with favor, upon the spirit of party. But in those of the popular character, in governments purely elective, it is a spirit not to be encouraged. From their natural tendency it is certain there will always be enough of that spirit for every salutary purpose; and there being constant danger of excess, the effort ought to be by force of public opinion to mitigate and assuage it. A fire not to be quenched, it demands a uniform vigilance to prevent its bursting into a flame, lest, instead of warming, it should consume.

It is important, likewise, that the habits of thinking in a free country should inspire caution in those intrusted with its administration to confine themselves within their respective constitutional spheres, avoiding in the exercise of the powers of one department to encroach upon another. The spirit of encroachment tends to consolidate the powers of all the departments in one, and thus to create, whatever the form of government, a real despotism. A just estimate of that love of power and proneness to abuse it which predominates in the human heart is sufficient to satisfy us of the truth of this position. The necessity of reciprocal checks in the exercise of political power, by dividing and distributing it into different depositories, and constituting each the guardian of the public weal against invasions by the others, has been evinced by experiments ancient and modern, some of them in our country and under our own eyes. To preserve them must be as necessary as to institute them. If in the opinion of the people the distribution or modification of the constitutional powers be in any particular wrong, let it be corrected by an amendment in the way which the Constitution designates. But let there be no change by usurpation; for though this in one instance may be the instrument of good, it is the customary weapon by which free governments are destroyed. The precedent must always greatly overbalance in permanent evil any partial or transient benefit which the use can at any time yield.

Religion and Morality

Of all the dispositions and habits which lead to political prosperity, religion and morality are indispensable supports. In vain would that man claim the tribute of patriotism who should labor to subvert these great pillars of human happiness—these firmest props of the duties of men and citizens. The mere politician, equally with the pious man, ought to respect and to cherish them. A volume could not trace all their connections with private and public felicity. Let it simply be asked, Where is the security for property, for reputation, for life, if the sense of religious obligation *desert* the oaths which are the instruments of investigation in courts of justice? And let us with caution indulge the supposition that morality can be maintained without religion. Whatever may be conceded to the influence of refined education on minds of peculiar structure, reason and experience both forbid us to expect that national morality can prevail in exclusion of religious principle.

It is substantially true that virtue or morality is a necessary spring of popular government. The rule indeed extends with more or less force to every species of free government. Who that is a sincere friend to it can look with indifference upon attempts to shake the foundation of the fabric? Promote, then, as an object of primary importance, institutions for the general diffusion of knowledge. In proportion as the structure of a government gives force to public opinion, it is essential that public opinion should be enlightened.

As a very important source of strength and security, cherish public credit. One method of preserving it is to use it as sparingly as possible, avoiding occasions of expense by cultivating peace, but remembering also that timely disbursements to prepare for danger frequently prevent much greater disbursements to repel it; avoiding likewise the accumulation of debt, not only by shunning occasions of expense, but by vigorous exertions in time of peace to discharge the debts which unavoidable wars have occasioned, not ungenerously throwing upon posterity the burthen which we ourselves ought to bear. The execution of these maxims belongs to your representatives; but it is necessary that public opinion should cooperate. To facilitate to them the performance of their duty it is essential that you should practically bear in mind that toward the payment of debts there must be revenue; that to have revenue there must be taxes; that no taxes can be devised which are not more or less inconvenient and unpleasant; that the intrinsic embarrassment inseparable from the selection of the proper objects (which is always a choice of difficulties), ought to be a decisive motive for a candid construction of the conduct of the Government in making it, and for a spirit of acquiescence in the measures for obtaining revenue which the public exigencies may at any time dictate.

Observe good faith and justice toward all nations. Cultivate peace and harmony with all. Religion and morality enjoin this conduct. And can it be that good policy does not equally enjoin it? It will be worthy of a free, enlightened, and at no distant period a great nation to give to mankind the magnanimous and too novel example of a people always guided by an exalted justice and benevolence. Who can doubt that in the course of time and things the fruits of such a plan would richly repay any temporary advantages which might be lost by a steady adherence to it? Can it be that Providence has not connected the permanent felicity of a nation with its virtue? The experiment, at least, is recommended by every sentiment which ennobles human nature. Alas! is it rendered impossible by its vices?

International Policy

In the execution of such a plan nothing is more essential than that permanent, inveterate antipathies against particular nations and passionate attachments for others should be excluded, and that in place of them just and amicable feelings toward all should be cultivated. The nation which indulges toward another an habitual hatred or an habitual fondness is in some degree a slave. It is a slave to its animosity or to its affection, either of which is sufficient to lead it astray from its duty and its interest. Antipathy in one nation against another disposes each more readily to offer insult and injury, to lay hold of slight causes of umbrage, and to be haughty and intractable when accidental or trifling occasions of dispute occur.

Hence frequent collisions, obstinate, envenomed, and bloody contests. The nation prompted by ill will and resentment sometimes impels to war the government contrary to the best calculations of policy. The government sometimes participates in the national propensity, and adopts through passion what reason would reject. At other times it makes the animosity of the nation subservient to projects of hostility, instigated by pride, ambition, and other sinister and pernicious motives. The peace often, sometimes perhaps the liberty, of nations has been the victim.

So, likewise, a passionate attachment of one nation for another produces a variety of evils. Sympathy for the favorite nation, facilitating the illusion of an imaginary common interest in cases where no real common interest exists, and infusing into one the enmities of the other, betrays the former into a participation in the quarrels and wars of the latter without adequate inducement or justification. It leads also to concessions to the favorite nation of privileges denied to others, which is apt doubly to injure the nation making the concessions by unnecessarily parting with what ought to have been retained, and by exciting jealousy, ill will, and a disposition to retaliate in the parties from whom equal privileges are withheld; and it gives to ambitious, corrupted, or deluded citizens (who devote themselves to the favorite nation) facility to betray or sacrifice the interests of their own country without odium, sometimes even with popularity, gilding with the appearances of a virtuous sense of obligation, a commendable deference for public opinion, or a laudable zeal for public good the base or foolish compliances of ambition, corruption, or infatuation.

As avenues to foreign influence in innumerable ways, such attachments are particularly alarming to the truly enlightened and independent patriot. How many opportunities do they afford to tamper with domestic factions, to practice the arts of seduction, to mislead public opinion, to influence or awe the public councils! Such an attachment of a small or weak toward a great and powerful nation dooms the former to be the satellite of the latter. Against the insidious wiles of foreign influence (I conjure you to believe me, fellow-citizens) the jealousy of a free people ought to be *constantly* awake, since history and experience prove that foreign influence is one of the most baneful foes of republican government. But that jealousy, to be useful, must be impartial, else it becomes the instrument of the very influence to be avoided, instead of a defense against it. Excessive partiality for one foreign nation and excessive dislike of another cause those whom they actuate to see danger only on one side, and serve to veil and even second the arts of influence on the other. Real patriots who may resist the intrigues of the favorite are liable to become suspected and odious, while its tools and dupes usurp the applause and confidence of the people to surrender their interests.

The great rule of conduct for us in regard to foreign nations is, in extending our commercial relations to have with them as little *political* connection as possible. So far as we have already formed engagements let them be fulfilled with perfect good faith. Here let us stop.

Avoid Political Alliance

Europe has a set of primary interests which to us have none or a very remote relation. Hence she must be engaged in frequent controversies, the causes of which are essentially foreign to our concerns. Hence, therefore, it must be unwise in us to implicate ourselves by artificial ties in the ordinary vicissitudes of her politics or the ordinary combinations and collisions of her friendships or enmities.

Our detached and distant situation invites and enables us to pursue a different course. If we remain one people, under an efficient government, the period is not far off when we may defy material injury from external annoyance; when we may take such an attitude as will cause the neutrality we may at any time resolve upon to be scrupulously respected; when belligerent nations, under the impossibility of making acquisitions upon us, will not lightly hazard the giving us provocation; when we may choose peace or war, as our interest, guided by justice, shall counsel.

Why forego the advantages of so peculiar a situation? Why quit our own to stand upon foreign ground? Why, by interweaving our destiny with that of any part of Europe, entangle our peace and prosperity in the toils of European ambition, rivalship, interest, humor, or caprice?

The Simple Rules of Trade

It is our true policy to steer clear of permanent alliances with any portion of the foreign world, so far, I mean, as we are now at liberty to do it; for let me not be understood as capable of patronizing infidelity to existing engagements. I hold the maxim no less applicable to public than to private affairs that honesty is always the best policy. I repeat, therefore, let those engagements be observed in their genuine sense. But in my opinion it is unnecessary and would be unwise to extend them.

Taking care always to keep ourselves by suitable establishments on a respectable defensive posture, we may safely trust to temporary alliances for extraordinary emergencies.

Harmony, liberal intercourse with all nations are recommended by policy, humanity, and interest. But even our commercial policy should hold an equal and impartial hand, neither seeking nor granting exclusive favors or preferences; consulting the natural course of things; diffusing and diversifying by gentle means the streams of commerce, but forcing nothing; establishing with powers so disposed, in order to give trade a stable course, to define the rights of our merchants, and to enable the Government to support them, conventional rules of intercourse, the best that present circumstances and mutual opinion will permit, but temporary and liable to be from time to time abandoned or varied as experience and circumstances shall dictate; constantly keeping in view that it is folly in one nation to look for disinterested favors from another; that it must pay with a portion of its independence for whatever it may accept under that character; that by such acceptance it may place itself in the condition of having given equivalents for nominal favors, and yet of being reproached with ingratitude for not giving more. There can be no greater error than to expect or calculate upon real favors from nation to nation. It is an illusion which experience must cure, which a just pride ought to discard.

Suggestions to Guide Peaceful National Affairs

In offering to you, my countrymen, these counsels of an old and affectionate friend I dare not hope they will make the strong and lasting impression I could wish—that they will control the usual current of the passions or prevent our nation from running the course which has hitherto marked the destiny of nations. But if I may even flatter myself that they may be productive of some partial benefit, some occasional good—that they may now and then recur to moderate the fury of party spirit, to warn against the mischiefs of foreign intrigue, to guard against the impostures of pretended patriotism—this hope will be a full recompense for the solicitude for your welfare by which they have been dictated.

How far in the discharge of my official duties I have been guided by the principles which have been delineated the public records and other evidences of my conduct must witness to you and to the world. To myself, the assurance of my own conscience is that I have at least believed myself to be guided by them.

In relation to the still subsisting war in Europe my proclamation of the 22nd of April, 1793, is the index to my plan. Sanctioned by your approving voice and by that of your representatives in both Houses of Congress, the spirit of that measure has continually governed me, uninfluenced by any attempts to deter or divert me from it.

After deliberate examination, with the aid of the best lights I could obtain, I was well satisfied that our country, under all the circumstances of the case, had a right to take, and was bound in duty and interest to take, a neutral position. Having taken it, I determined as far as should depend upon me to maintain it with moderation, perseverance, and firmness.

The considerations which respect the right to hold this conduct it is not necessary on this occasion to detail. I will only observe that, according to my understanding of the matter, that right, so far from being denied by any of the belligerent powers, has been virtually admitted by all.

The duty of holding a neutral conduct may be inferred, without anything more, from the obligation which justice and humanity impose on every nation, in cases in which it is free to act, to maintain inviolate the relations of peace and amity toward other nations.

An Independent Nation

The inducements of interest for that conduct will best be to your own reflections and experience. With me a predominant motive has been to endeavor to gain time to our country to settle and mature its yet recent institutions, and to progress without interruption to that degree of strength and consistency which is necessary to give it, humanly speaking, the command of its own fortunes.

Though in reviewing the incidents of my Administration I am unconscious of intentional error, I am nevertheless too sensible of my defects not to think it probable that I may have committed many errors. Whatever they may be, I fervently beseech the Almighty to avert or mitigate the evils to which they may tend. I shall also carry with me the hope that my country will never cease to view them with indulgence, and that, after forty-five years of my life dedicated to its service with an upright zeal, the faults of incompetent abilities will be consigned to oblivion, as myself must soon be to the mansions of rest.

Relying on its kindness in this as in other things, and actuated by that fervent love toward it which is so natural to a man who views in it the native soil of himself and his progenitors for several generations, I anticipate with pleasing expectation that retreat in which I promise myself to realize without alloy the sweet enjoyment of partaking in the midst of my fellow-citizens the benign influence of good laws under a free government—the ever-favorite object of my heart, and the happy reward, as I trust, of our mutual cares, labors, and dangers.

—September 17, 1796

Index

About the Publisher

The Foundation for Economic Education Inc., was established in 1946 by Leonard E. Read to study and advance the moral and intellectual rationale for a free society.

The Foundation publishes *The Freeman,* an award-winning monthly journal of ideas in the fields of economics, history, and moral philosophy. FEE also publishes books, conducts seminars, and sponsors a network of discussion clubs to improve understanding of the principles of a free and prosperous society.

FEE is a non-political, non-profit 501 (c)(3) tax-exempt organization, supported solely by private contributions and sales of its literature.

For further information, please contact: The Foundation for Economic Education, Inc., 30 South Broadway, Irvington-on-Hudson, New York 10533. Telephone (914) 591-7230; fax (914) 591-8910.

If You Liked This Book, You'll Like The Freeman

The Freeman is the source of the chapters in this book. Since 1956, it has been published monthly by The Foundation for Economic Education (FEE).

FEE's founder, Leonard E. Read, always defended anything that's peaceful. *The Freeman* has, too. For this reason, it has been at the center of an intellectual battlefield. If you're now committed to this battle, you need intellectual ammunition. You also need moral support.

The Freeman offers serious readers a unique source of free-market information. No other magazine, newspaper, or scholarly journal introduces readers to so many implications of what the free society is all about: its moral legitimacy, its tremendous efficiency, and its liberating effects in every area of life.

When the FEE began publishing *The Freeman*, there was literally no other source of such popularly written information on the free society. Today, dozens of institutions produce thousands of pages of material every year on the topic.

Despite all the competition (and imitation!), *The Freeman* remains the most effective introduction to the fundamentals of the free society. For newcomers and old-timers, for high school students and Ph.D.'s, *The Freeman* offers new insights of significant value each month.

Since 1956, *The Freeman* has been what today would be called politically incorrect, yet it rarely discusses politics. It was dismissed in 1956 by "people in the know" as a publishing oddity. Well, it was an oddity, and it launched an intellectual revolution in the United States. It was an oasis of liberty in a desert of statism. It has been guided by a constant star: a belief that responsible individuals, not the State, best discern their most personally rewarding opportunities and their most valuable services to others.

Why should you read *The Freeman*? Because the world is still in the midst of a monumental battle of ideas. The collapse of European Communism in 1989 has only changed the terms of the debate. It has not changed the fundamental issues.

What are these issues? Government compulsion vs. private choice, collective responsibility vs. personal responsibility, the wisdom of central planners vs. the forecasting skills of profit-seeking entrepreneurs, compulsory wealth redistribution vs. voluntary charity, Social Security vs. personal thrift.

All over the world, the debate rages. Yet most people don't know where to begin to sort out fact from fiction.

The Freeman is the place to begin. Why? Because its editorial policy is guided by this fundamental premise: the economic issues are at bottom moral. The free society rests on that most crucial of foundations: justice.

The underlying debate between socialists and defenders of the free market is not technical; it is moral. It is a question of what is right, not what is cost-efficient. Freedom works because it is just.

Do you agree? Then you ought to be reading *The Freeman* every month. Find out for yourself. For a free trial subscription, call (914)-591-7230. Or write to FEE, Irvington-on-Hudson, NY 10533. Do it now.